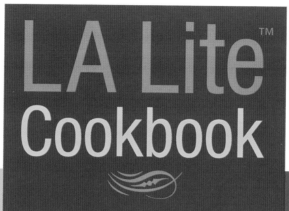

LA Lite™ Cookbook

Simple Recipes

Simply Delicious

The collection of recipes in this book come mainly from clients who have had great success with the L A Weight Loss program. We'd like to send out a special thank you to those clients, who've, over the years, contributed the cherished recipes that helped them to achieve their own weight loss goals. If you have a favorite "lite" recipe you would like to share, for future editions of the cookbook, please submit them to recipes@la-weightloss.com.

LA
WEIGHT LOSS CENTERS

Exclusively distributed by L A Weight Loss Franchise
Company.
All exchanges provided are specific to L A Weight Loss
Program.
6-55958-35002-0

LA LITE™
Cookbook

▶ *Simple
Recipes*

*Simply
Delicious*

The joy of the L A Weight Loss program is the variety of foods available to you while you're losing weight. With the L A Lite Cookbook you now have new and unique ways to prepare the wide array of food choices found in each program. Your entire family will enjoy these light and naturally delicious meals that range from steaming beef vegetable and french onion soup to succulent entrees such as soy-glazed chicken and beef stroganoff, to tantalizing desserts including chocolate truffles and apple crisps. Plus, you'll find hundreds of other recipes for drinks, entrees, vegetable preparations, ethnic meals and sweet delights. Each recipe represents a collection of the best preparations from our centers and clients. You can be certain that all recipes work with your L A Weight Loss program as exchanges are provided for each recipe.

So enjoy and happy eating!

Contents

▶ *Portion sizes may vary according to plan.
Please be certain to check your L A Weight
Loss Menu Plan for the correct portion size.*

Jump
✿ Start

Breakfast is an essential part of your day. It has been shown that eating breakfast each morning may help you to have better concentration throughout the day. Also people who skip breakfast are more likely to eat more at the next meal and therefore may have trouble controlling or losing weight in the long run. It is not essential to sit down to a three course meal at breakfast, but it is important to have a small meal to get you, and your metabolism, running efficiently. The following section will give you some ideas for eating on the run and for a leisurely Sunday breakfast.

◄ Strawberry Cheesecake Crepe recipe can be found on page 11

Basic Methods of Cooking Eggs

- **Poached** — Whole eggs are simmered gently in water; a small amount of vinegar may be added to keep the egg together.
- **Scrambled** — Eggs are whisked until fluffy and cooked over medium heat.
- **Fried** — Whole eggs are fried in butter on a griddle; the yolks may be runny (over-easy) or cooked through (over-hard).
- **Sunny-side up** — Whole eggs are fried in butter on a griddle; the egg is not flipped over in the cooking process, leaving the yolk, and sometimes the white, slightly runny.
- **Hard-boiled** — Whole eggs boiled in water in the shell until cooked through with a firm yolk and white, about 20 minutes.
- **Soft-boiled** — Whole eggs boiled in water in the shell until white is cooked through and yolk is almost set.
- **Coddled** — Similar to a poached egg; a whole egg, without shell, is placed in simmering water in a porcelain or glass dish for 1-2 minutes until soft.

Breakfast Terms

- **Quiche** — A classical breakfast or lunch item; eggs are beat with milk or cream and typically combined with vegetables or meats and cheese; the egg mixture is poured into a savory pie crust and baked.
- **Eggs Benedict** — A restaurant favorite; poached eggs are served atop Canadian bacon and toasted English muffins; it is finished with a rich hollandaise sauce.
- **Strata** — A baked egg and milk mixture with vegetables, cheese and/or meats; the mixture is poured over layers of bread before baking.
- **Frittata** — A baked omelet of eggs and desired fillings; the omelet is cooked on the stovetop and then baked until set; sometimes pasta may be added as well.
- **Omelet** — A classical French menu item; eggs are cooked in a sauté pan and folded over any desired fillings.
- **Crepes** — A very thin pancake-like batter that is cooked in a sauté-like pan and wrapped with either sweet or savory fillings.

Food Safety

Though there is very low risk of food-borne illness with consumption of eggs, you should still make sure eggs are of high quality and fresh, and are cooked thoroughly in order to prevent salmonella. If you are concerned about consuming undercooked egg whites, you may use pasteurized liquid egg whites, or powder or pasteurized liquid egg substitute.

TIP!

Eating breakfast in the morning promotes blood sugar level stability, better concentration, and more energy. Your body depends on breakfast to keep your energy levels high throughout the day.

Jump
❖ Start

Scrambled Egg

1 *serving*

- SERVING SIZE: 1 RECIPE
- COUNTS AS:
  1/2 - 1 PROTEIN

▶ *size according to plan*

☀ Ingredients
egg(s), size according to plan

1 Tbsp (15ml) skim milk

dash of lite salt

freshly ground pepper

nonfat cooking spray

1. In a bowl, whisk eggs, milk, salt and pepper thoroughly until they have reached a uniform yellow color.

2. Coat skillet with nonfat cooking spray. Heat skillet over medium flame.

3. Pour egg mixture into skillet.

4. As mixture begins to set at bottom and sides, gently lift cooked portion with spatula so that the thin, uncooked portion can flow to the bottom.

5. Cook until egg(s) are thickened throughout, but still moist, about 3-5 minutes.

Cheesy Scrambled Egg

1 *serving*

- SERVING SIZE: 1 RECIPE
- COUNTS AS:
  1 PROTEIN
  1/2 DAIRY

▶ *size according to plan*

good source of calcium

☀ Ingredients
1 whole egg

2 or 4 egg whites, size according to plan

1oz (28g) reduced-fat cheddar or swiss cheese

1/4 tsp (1ml) snipped parsley

1/4 tsp (1ml) snipped chives

nonfat cooking spray

1. Break egg into a medium mixing bowl; add egg whites. Mix until well blended.

2. Add cheese, parsley and chives.

3. Coat skillet with nonfat cooking spray and heat over medium flame.

4. Add egg mixture to skillet.

5. As mixture begins to set at bottom and sides, gently lift cooked portion with spatula so that thin, uncooked portion can flow to bottom.

6. Cook until eggs are thickened throughout, but still moist, approximately 3-5 minutes.

Jump
♣ Start

Puffy Omelet

1 *serving*

- SERVING SIZE: 1 OMELET
- COUNTS AS:
  1 PROTEIN

▶ *size according to plan*

☀ Ingredients

2 or 3 eggs, separated

1/4 cup (60ml) water

1/4 tsp (1ml) lite salt

1/8 tsp (.5ml) freshly ground pepper

nonfat cooking spray

1. Preheat oven to 325°F (160°C).

2. With a mixer, beat egg whites, water and salt on high speed until stiff, but not dry.

3. In a separate bowl, beat egg yolks and pepper on high speed until very thick and lemon colored. Fold yolks into egg whites.

4. Coat 10-inch (25cm) ovenproof skillet with nonfat cooking spray. Heat skillet over medium flame.

5. Pour egg mixture into skillet; reduce heat.

6. Cook over low heat until puffy and light brown on bottom, about 5 minutes.

7. Bake, uncovered, in oven, until knife inserted in the center comes out clean, about 10-15 minutes.

8. Fold omelet in half; slip onto a plate.

Broccoli Omelet Bake

1 *serving*

- SERVING SIZE: 1 OMELET
- COUNTS AS:
  1 PROTEIN
  2 VEGETABLES
  1/2 DAIRY

▶ *size according to plan*

good source of fiber

☀ Ingredients

2 or 3 eggs

1/2 cup (125ml / 78g) cooked broccoli, chopped

1 tsp (.5ml) dried onion

1oz (28g) reduced-fat cheddar or swiss cheese

2 Tbsp (30ml) skim milk

1/4 tsp (1ml) lite salt

1/4 tsp (1ml) dried basil

1/2 tsp (2.5ml) garlic powder

1 tomato cut into 6 slices

1. Beat eggs until light and fluffy.

2. Stir in broccoli, onion, half of the cheese, milk, salt, basil and garlic powder.

3. Pour into ungreased baking dish.

4. Arrange tomato slices on top; sprinkle with remaining cheese.

5. Bake, uncovered, in 325°F (160°C) oven for 20-25 minutes.

Jump
❖ Start

Apple Pancake

1 *serving*

- **SERVING SIZE: 1 PANCAKE**
- **COUNTS AS:**
  - 1 PROTEIN
  - 1 STARCH
  - 1 FRUIT

▶ *size according to plan*

✳ Ingredients

1/2 or 3/4 cup (125 or 200ml) of
  egg substitute, size according
  to plan

3 slices Melba toast, crushed

1 small apple, peeled and grated

1/2 tsp (2.5ml) cinnamon

1 packet artificial sweetener

nonfat cooking spray

1 Combine all ingredients in a small bowl; mix well.

2 Coat skillet with nonfat cooking spray. Pour mixture
   into skillet. Heat until lightly brown; flip over and
   brown on other side. Serve.

> "Talk about something new
> and unusual. This is
> definitely it. No more plain
> old pancakes. They are
> absolutely delicious."
>
> *- Michael G.*

French Toast

1 *serving*

- **SERVING SIZE: 1 SLICE**
- **COUNTS AS:**
  - 1/2 PROTEIN
  - 1 STARCH
  - 1 FRUIT

▶ *size according to plan*

meals in minutes

✳ Ingredients

1/4 cup (60ml) egg substitute

1 Tbsp (15ml) skim milk

dash of sugar substitute

dash of cinnamon

dash of nutmeg

1 slice light bread

12 small strawberries, sliced

nonfat cooking spray

1 Combine egg substitute, milk, spices and sugar
   substitute in a shallow bowl; mix well.

2 Add slice of light bread to egg mixture and let stand
   until egg mixture is absorbed.

3 Coat skillet with nonfat cooking spray and heat over
   medium heat. Place bread in skillet and brown both
   sides of light bread.

4 Place on serving dish; top with sliced strawberries.

Jump
❖ Start

serving

- **SERVING SIZE: 1 OMELET**
- **COUNTS AS:**
  1 PROTEIN
  1 FAT
  1 VEGETABLE
  1/2 DAIRY

▶ *size according to plan*

meals in minutes

Greek Omelet

 Ingredients

2 Tbsp (30ml) chopped red onion

1/4 cup (60ml / 14g) fresh spinach

2 Tbsp (30ml) skim milk

1/4 tsp (1ml) garlic powder

1/2 or 3/4 cup (125 or 200ml) egg substitute, size according to plan

1oz (28g) lite feta cheese

9 black olives, diced

nonfat cooking spray

1 Coat medium skillet with nonfat cooking spray; heat over medium flame.

2 Sauté onions and spinach, until onions are tender and spinach has wilted down.

3 Remove vegetables from skillet and place in small mixing bowl; cool for 5 minutes.

4 Add milk, garlic powder and egg substitute to vegetable mixture. Mix well.

5 Coat skillet with nonfat cooking spray and heat over medium heat. Add egg mixture to skillet and cook over low heat until brown.

6 Flip egg mixture over and brown on other side. Turn heat to low and sprinkle with cheese and olives, cover skillet 1-2 minutes or until cheese is softened.

---

2 *servings*

- **SERVING SIZE: 1 MUFFIN**
- **COUNTS AS:**
  1/2 PROTEIN
  1 STARCH

▶ *size according to plan*

good source of fiber

Bran Muffins

Ingredients

1/2 cup (125ml) egg substitute

2 Tbsp (30ml) water

2 Tbsp (30ml) skim milk

1 tsp (5ml) vanilla

1/2 tsp (2.5ml) cinnamon

1 Tbsp (15ml) flour

pinch nutmeg

1/2 cup (125ml / 30g) unprocessed bran

1/2 cup (125ml / 72g) blueberries

3 packets artificial sweetener

nonfat cooking spray

1 In a large bowl, combine egg substitute, water, milk, vanilla, cinnamon, flour, nutmeg, bran and artificial sweetener.

2 Add blueberries to mixture.

3 Coat muffin pan with nonfat cooking spray.

4 Divide batter between 2 muffin cups.

5 Bake in 350°F (180°C) oven for 15 minutes.

 Jump ♣ Start

Crepes

 servings

- **SERVING SIZE: 1 CREPE**
- **COUNTS AS:**
  1 STARCH

▶ *size according to plan*

☼ Ingredients

- 1/2 cup (125ml / 63g) whole wheat flour
- 1/2 cup (125ml / 63g) white flour
- 1/2 cup (125ml) egg substitute
- 1 packet artificial sweetener
- 3/4 cup (200ml) skim milk
- 1/4 cup (60ml) water
- 1/4 tsp (1ml) lite salt
- 2 tsp (10ml) vanilla extract
- 1 Tbsp (15ml) margarine, melted
- nonfat cooking spray

Batter

1 Combine flour, salt and sugar substitute in small bowl. Set aside.

2 In a separate bowl, beat eggs and milk together with an electric mixer.

3 Beat flour mixture slowly into eggs.

4 Once flour is combined into eggs; slowly stir in melted margarine and vanilla extract.

Crepes

1 Coat small skillet, or crepe pan, with nonfat cooking spray and heat over medium-high.

2 Scoop 2 tablespoons (30ml) of batter into skillet.

3 Tip and rotate the skillet to help spread the batter, as thinly as possible, over bottom of pan.

4 Cook 30-60 seconds, or until bottom is lightly browned.

5 Carefully flip over and cook 15-20 more seconds.

6 Remove from pan. Set aside.

7 Continue to cook crepes until all batter is used. Place a piece of wax paper between each cooked crepe to prevent them from sticking together. (Cool skillet for 1-2 minutes periodically during cooking to prevent burning.)

8 Crepes can be frozen in the wax paper for up to a month.

Strawberry Cheesecake Crepe

 serving

- **SERVING SIZE: 1 CREPE**
- **COUNTS AS:**
  1/2 PROTEIN
  1 STARCH
  1 FRUIT

▶ *size according to plan*

☼ Ingredients

- 2oz (56g) reduced-fat ricotta cheese
- 3 small strawberries diced
- 1 packet artificial sweetener
- 1/4 tsp (1ml) vanilla extract
- 1 Tbsp (15ml) fat-free whipped topping
- 1 Crepe (see crepe recipe)
- 3 small strawberries, sliced

1 In small mixing bowl combine cheese, sweetener, diced berries and vanilla extract; mix well.

2 Place filling over one half of the crepe and fold over filling.

3 Top with sliced strawberries and whipped topping.

Jump
✿ Start

Banana Nut Crepe

1 *serving*

- **SERVING SIZE: 1 CREPE**
- **COUNTS AS:**
  - 1 STARCH
  - 1 FRUIT
  - 1 FAT

▸ *size according to plan*

☀ Ingredients

1/2 small banana

4 walnuts

1/2 packet artificial sweetener

1/4 tsp (1ml) cinnamon

1 crepe (see crepe recipe on page 11)

1 Slice banana.

2 Chop walnut into small pieces.

3 Place banana slices over half of the crepe.

4 Sprinkle walnuts, artificial sweetener and cinnamon over bananas.

5 Fold crepe over filling.

6 If desired, heat in microwave 30 seconds to soften banana.

Mushroom & Spinach Crepe

1 *serving*

- **SERVING SIZE: 1 CREPE**
- **COUNTS AS:**
  - 1 STARCH
  - 1 VEGETABLE

▸ *size according to plan*

☀ Ingredients

2 Tbsp (30ml) chopped sweet onions

1/4 tsp (1ml) lite salt

1/4 packet artificial sweetener

1/4 cup (60ml / 18g) chopped white mushrooms

2 tsp (10ml) garlic powder

1/4 cup (60ml / 8g) fresh spinach, chopped

1 crepe (see crepe recipe on page 11)

nonfat cooking spray

1 Defrost crepe if frozen.

2 Coat small skillet with nonfat cooking spray.

3 Place onions in skillet, add salt and sweetener; sauté on high heat for 1-2 minutes until onions begin to soften.

4 Add mushrooms and garlic powder and sauté 3 minutes, or until mushrooms are tender.

5 Add spinach; cook additional 2-3 minutes, until all vegetables are cooked.

6 Reheat crepe for 10-15 seconds in microwave (medium heat).

7 Place vegetable mixture over one half of the crepe. Fold crepe over filling.

8 Serve hot.

Jump
❖ Start

1 *serving*

- SERVING SIZE: 1 OMELET
- COUNTS AS:
  1 PROTEIN
  2 VEGETABLES

▶ *size according to plan*

meals in minutes

Mexican Omelet

☀ Ingredients

1/2 or 3/4 cup (125 or 200ml) egg substitute, size according to plan

2 tsp (10ml) hot sauce

1/4 tsp (1ml) lite salt

1 Tbsp (15ml) skim milk

1 Tbsp (15ml) diced green peppers

1 Tbsp (15ml) diced red peppers

1 Tbsp (15ml) diced white onion

1 tsp (5ml) cilantro

1 Tbsp (15ml) diced tomato

1 Tbsp (15ml) chopped green onion

1 Tbsp (15ml) salsa

1 Tbsp (15ml) fat-free sour cream

nonfat cooking spray

chili powder (optional)

1 Combine egg, hot sauce, salt and milk in mixing bowl. Whisk together vigorously; set aside.

2 Coat medium skillet with nonfat cooking spray. Heat over high flame.

3 Add red and green pepper, white onion and cilantro to skillet. Sauté 2-3 minutes or until vegetables start to soften.

4 Remove veggies from skillet, allow skillet to cool 2-3 minutes.

5 Coat skillet, again, with cooking spray, return to heat over medium flame.

6 Pour egg mixture into skillet, distributing evenly.

7 Continue to cook over medium heat; use a spatula to gently lift the edges of the omelet, allowing uncooked egg to move underneath.

8 Once egg is almost cooked, with only a small amount uncooked, add the pepper mixture and tomatoes. Cover skillet with a lid and cook additional 2-3 minutes over low heat, or until egg fully cooked.

9 Use spatula to remove omelet from pan, flipping in half while transferring to plate.

10 Top with salsa, sour cream and green onion.

11 To spice things up…sprinkle chili powder over your omelet!

1 *serving*

- SERVING SIZE: 1 RECIPE
- COUNTS AS:
  1 PROTEIN
  1 STARCH

▶ *size according to plan*

meals in minutes

Matzo Brie

☀ Ingredients

1 sheet of matzo

1/2 or 3/4 cup (125 or 200ml) egg substitute, size according to plan

1 cup (250ml) warm water

nonfat cooking spray

freshly ground pepper (optional)

cinnamon (optional)

artificial sweetener (optional)

1 Break matzo into pieces. In small bowl, soak the matzo in water for 1-2 minutes, or until soft. Drain matzo well.

2 Add eggs to matzo mixture.

3 Coat medium skillet with nonfat cooking spray. Heat over medium heat.

4 Pour egg mixture into skillet. Cook until lightly brown one side; flip over and brown on other side.

5 Season with pepper, or cinnamon and artificial sweetener.

Jump
❖ Start

Buttermilk Scones

12 *servings*

- SERVING SIZE: 1 SCONE
- COUNTS AS:
  1 STARCH
  1 FRUIT
  1 FAT

▶ *size according to plan*

family fare

☀ Ingredients

1 1/2 cups (375ml / 187g) flour

1 1/2 cups (375ml / 121g) old-fashioned oats

1 Tbsp (15ml) sugar

3 packets artificial sweetener

1 Tbsp (15ml) baking powder

1 tsp (5ml) cream of tartar

1/2 tsp (2.5ml) lite salt

1/3 cup (85ml) unsalted margarine, melted

2/3 cup (170ml) nonfat buttermilk

1/2 cup (125ml) egg substitute

1/2 cup (125ml / 78g) raisins or currants

nonfat cooking spray

1 Preheat oven to 425° (220°C).

2 Combine flour, oats, sugar, artificial sweetener, baking powder, cream of tartar and lite salt in a large bowl.

3 Add margarine, buttermilk and egg.

4 Mix just until batter is moistened.

5 Stir in raisins.

6 With your hands, shape the dough to form a ball.

7 Pat out on a lightly floured surface to form an 8-inch circle.

8 Cut into 12 wedges.

9 Bake on a cookie sheet coated with nonfat cooking spray for 12-15 minutes, or until light brown.

Breakfast Burrito

1 *serving*

- SERVING SIZE: 1 BURRITO
- COUNTS AS:
  1 PROTEIN
  1 STARCH
  1 VEGETABLE
  1/2 DAIRY

▶ *size according to plan*

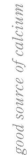

good source of calcium

☀ Ingredients

1 Tbsp (15ml) diced green pepper

1 Tbsp (15ml) chopped green onion

1/2 or 3/4 cup (125 or 200ml) egg substitute, size according to plan

1/4 tsp (1ml) lite salt

1 Tbsp (15ml) diced tomato

1/2 whole wheat tortilla

1oz (28g) reduced-fat pepper jack cheese

1 Tbsp (15ml) fat-free sour cream

nonfat cooking spray

1 Coat medium skillet with nonfat cooking spray. Heat over high heat.

2 Add pepper and onion to skillet. Sauté 2-3 minutes, or until vegetables start to soften.

3 Pour egg substitute into skillet, distributing evenly. Sprinkle with lite salt.

4 Once eggs are cooked through, turn down heat; add tomatoes, cook 1 minute until tomatoes are warm.

5 Place egg in middle of tortilla; top with cheese.

6 Roll up tortilla into a burrito.

7 Top with fat-free sour cream.

Jump
♣ Start

Sausage Patties

12 *servings*

- **SERVING SIZE: 1 PATTY**
- **COUNTS AS:**
  1 PROTEIN

▶ *size according to plan*

family fare

☀ Ingredients

10 green onions, finely chopped

1/2 cup (125ml / 54g) bread crumbs (see recipe on page 154)

1/2 cup (125ml) skim milk

2 pounds (996g) ground lean pork

1 tsp (5ml) white pepper

1/4 tsp (1ml) freshly ground pepper

1/4 tsp (1ml) cayenne

1 tsp (5ml) finely chopped fresh thyme

1 tsp (5ml) finely chopped fresh sage

nonfat cooking spray

1. Coat skillet with nonfat cooking spray and heat over medium heat.

2. Cook onion, stirring occasionally, until softened and beginning to brown. Remove from heat and cool for 10 minutes.

3. While onions are cooling, stir together bread crumbs and milk in a large bowl and let stand until crumbs absorb the milk.

4. Add onions and remaining ingredients to crumb mixture and stir with a fork until blended well.

5. Preheat oven to 250° (120°C).

6. Form sausage patties into 1/2-inch thick patties with dampened hands and arrange on a wax paper lined tray.

7. Make into 12 patties.

8. Spray heavy skillet with nonfat cooking spray; heat over medium-high heat, cook patties, turning once, until browned and just cooked through, 4-6 minutes per batch.

9. Transfer to shallow baking pan and keep warm, covered with foil, in oven while cooking remaining batches.

Turkey Sausage

4 *servings*

- **SERVING SIZE: 1 PATTY**
- **COUNTS AS:**
  1/2 PROTEIN

▶ *size according to plan*

family fare

☀ Ingredients

10 or 14oz (280 or 392g) ground turkey breast, size according to plan

1/2 tsp (2.5ml) dried sage

1/4 tsp (1ml) freshly ground pepper

1/4 tsp (1ml) cayenne pepper

1/4 tsp (1ml) lite salt

nonfat cooking spray

1. In large bowl, combine turkey and seasonings. Mix thoroughly.

2. Shape into 2 1/2 -3 1/2oz (70-98g) patties, size as according to plan.

3. Heat skillet, coated with nonfat cooking spray, over a medium flame.

4. Add patties to skillet and cook thoroughly on each side, or to an internal temperature of 165°F (75°C).

5. Uncooked patties may be frozen.

Jump
✤ Start

Savory Soups & Salads

Many of us think of soups as a type of comfort food; the kind of dish that warms us inside and out. Salad of course is an old meal-starter favorite. There are several varieties of soups and salads such as broth-based or cream-based soups and tossed or Caesar salads. Unfortunately, canned and pre-made soups can be very high in sodium and/or fat. Salad dressing and cheese can also add a lot of extra fat and calories. However, you'll find lots of ways to eliminate fat without sacrificing flavor and all the basic methods of preparing your own soups and salads inside.

Waldorf Salad recipe can be found on page 32

Cooking Methods

Broth or stock is one of the simplest cooking methods. This soup base starts with water and incorporates the meat or bones, as well as vegetables and herbs. The mixture is simmered for a moderately long amount of time to infuse the water with flavor; eventually, the solids are strained out of the broth or stock before use. Broths and stocks are the base of any soup and provides added flavor.

Canned stock and bouillon cubes may be used for ease, but fresh stock will provide optimum flavor. If using canned stock, choose a low-sodium variety! Bouillon cubes can be found also in a "very low-sodium" variety with less than 35mg sodium per serving; this method is quite easy and requires you only to reconstitute the broth by adding warm water.

Cream-based soups have been known to be higher in fat and calories, but there are methods to reduce the fat and calories. Cream-based soups or chowders typically start as a broth-based soup and cream or milk may be added at the end of the recipe, to allow the flavors to meld. Vegetable-cream soups are commonly pureed together for serving to achieve a velvety texture. The cream used in soups may be replaced by fat-free half and half, evaporated skim milk, regular skim or reduced-fat milk, to cut back on calories.

Other Cooking Tips

When making broth-based soups, or other soups that will not be pureed, it is important to cut or chop the vegetables and protein in uniform pieces so that it may cook quickly and in the same amount of time. You may also use leftover proteins and vegetables that are already prepared in order to shorten cooking times even further.

If a thicker soup is desired for texture, you have several options. Eggs provide a rich and creamy texture to soup, but it is easy to make scrambled eggs in the hot broth. The best method is to scramble 1 or 2 eggs in a small bowl and add a small amount of hot soup or broth, whisking together, then gradually incorporate this mixture back into the soup.

Flour may also be used in the early stages of the soup by lightly sprinkling over the vegetables as they sauté or in the final stages by adding a tablespoon of cornstarch (mixed with 1-2 tablespoon of water) into the soup or broth. To thicken pureed soups, you may want to add a half-cup of rice or potatoes or a slice or two of bread before pureeing in a blender or food processor.

TIP!

The cream used in soups may be replaced by fat-free half and half, evaporated skim milk, or regular skim or reduced-fat milk, to reduce the amount of calories.

Greens Dictionary

■ **Endive** — Also known as Belgian endive; a small, cigar-shaped head of pale yellow-green lettuce, with a bitter taste, well paired with nuts and cheese.

■ **Frisee** — Also known as curly endive; a member of the chicory family; thin, curly leaves appear to be frizzy with a slightly bitter taste; commonly found in "spring mix" salads.

■ **Romaine** — Also known as cos lettuce; a common lettuce in the US, with dark green, long leaves that are coarse; inner leaves are paler in color and have a more delicate flavor.

■ **Iceberg** — This lettuce got its name from its original shipping method—growers packed the heads in ice, it was previously known as crisphead lettuce; this particular head of lettuce has one of the highest water content, 90%, of all lettuces.

■ **Looseleaf** — Examples of this variety includes red leaf, green leaf and oak leaf lettuces; the leaves vary in flavor, red lettuces tend to be more sharp or bitter; the oak variety tends to be more coarse than leaf lettuce.

■ **Escarole** — Also a member of the chicory family, though with a milder flavor; leaves are broad and wavy, though smaller than a leaf lettuce; most commonly mixed with other lettuces in salads due to its sharp taste; also used cooked, commonly in Italian cuisine.

■ **Watercress** — A member of the mustard family; has small leaves and thin stems, with a slightly bitter and peppery flavor; also commonly used in soups and sandwiches.

■ **Spring Mix** — Also known as field greens, micro greens, or mesclun; may include a variety of baby lettuces, such as spinach, frisee, oak leaf, radicchio, etc; of growing popularity over the past few years.

■ **Butterhead** — This includes Boston and Bibb lettuces; Bibb lettuce is found to be smaller heads of lettuce with loose, true green leaves with more flavor; Boston lettuce is commonly a larger head of lettuce with leaves lighter in color and flavor.

■ **Spinach** — A dark leafy green, high in fiber, that can be used raw or cooked; approximately 1 pound raw equals 1 cup cooked; choose spinach with smaller leaves and stems, also known as baby spinach, because it will be delicate and tender.

■ **Radicchio** — Also known as red chicory; appears as a red cabbage; coarse, crisp leaves with bitter leaves, commonly mixed with other greens, may be grilled to enhance flavor or used as colorful garnish.

■ **Arugula** — Also known as rocket; peppery flavored delicate green leaves, similar in shape to spinach.

■ **Kale** — A type of cabbage with curly, wrinkled leaves, which are hardy and coarse; most commonly used cooked, but may be used raw as a garnish or mixed into salads with other greens.

■ **Mustard Greens** — A dark leafy green that can be found with red or green leaves; common in the Southern states; known for its sharp, peppery taste.

Savory
Soups&
❖ Salads

Chicken Stock

6 *servings*

- **SERVING SIZE: 1 CUP (250ML)**
- **COUNTS AS:**
  1 FAT

▶ *size according to plan*

☀ Ingredients

1-1/4 pounds (560g) chicken bones

2 Tbsp (30ml) olive oil

1 red onion, sliced

1/2 celery stalk

1 carrot, diced

4 cups (1L) water, or as needed

1/4 tsp (1ml) dried thyme

1/3 tsp (1.5ml) dried basil

2 tsps (10ml) lite salt

1 1/2 tsp (7.5ml) cracked black peppercorns

1 Preheat oven to 450° (230°C). Arrange chicken bones on a baking sheet.

2 Roast 45 minutes until well browned.

3 Heat olive oil in a stock pot over medium heat. Add onion, celery and carrot; cook and stir until browned. If they scorch, add a little water and scrape up bits.

4 Add roasted chicken bones to the pot, fill with water to cover the bones by 2 inches (5cm). Bring to a boil.

5 Add garlic, thyme, parsley, basil, salt and pepper. Reduce heat to low, and simmer uncovered for 2 hours. Add more water if needed.

6 Strain out the solids from the broth, drain the fat, and refrigerate. You can also remove the fat after it has chilled. The stock will be thick. Use full strength for soups and gravies, or dilute with water for a milder flavor. Use freezer bags for longer storage.

Seafood Soup

1 *serving*

- **SERVING SIZE: 1 RECIPE**
- **COUNTS AS:**
  1 PROTEIN
  1 DAIRY
  1 LA LITE

▶ *size according to plan*

good source of fiber

☀ Ingredients

5 or 7oz (150 or 210g) shrimp

1 tsp (5ml) onion, finely minced

1 Tbsp (15ml) red pepper, diced

1 garlic clove, finely minced

1 L A Lite Cream of Mushroom soup mix

8oz (250ml) skim milk

1 Tbsp (15ml) fat-free half & half

hot pepper sauce (optional) to taste

1 In a small saucepan coated with nonfat cooking spray, add shrimp, onion, pepper and garlic. Sauté until seafood is cooked.

2 Add soup mix, milk and half & half; stir until smooth.

3 Heat well.

4 Season with hot pepper sauce (optional).

Savory
Soups&
♣ Salads

Broccoli Soup

 4 *servings*

- **SERVING SIZE:**
  1 CUP (250ML)
- **COUNTS AS:**
  1 STARCH
  1 VEGETABLE
  1 FAT

▶ *size according to plan*

 good source of fiber

✳ Ingredients

2 Tbsp (30ml) olive oil

1 medium onion, sliced

1 garlic clove, smashed

1 potato (russet), peeled and diced

1/4 tsp (1ml) thyme

4 cups (1L) chicken stock
(see recipe on page 20) or very
low-sodium broth

1 pound (448g) frozen broccoli,
thawed

4 Tbsp (60ml) fat-free half & half

freshly ground pepper

1 In a saucepan add olive oil, onion and garlic. Cook over medium heat until translucent, about 5 minutes.

2 Add the potato, thyme and broth and bring to a boil.

3 Adjust the heat to maintain a gentle simmer, and cook uncovered until the potato is fork tender, about 10 minutes.

4 Add the broccoli and simmer for 3 minutes.

5 Puree the soup in batches in a blender.

6 Return the soup to the pot and add the half and half.

7 Bring to a simmer, season with pepper for taste.

Cream of Spinach Soup

 1 *serving*

- **SERVING SIZE: 1 RECIPE**
- **COUNTS AS:**
  1 VEGETABLE
  1 DAIRY
  1 LA LITE

▶ *size according to plan*

meals in minutes

✳ Ingredients

1 L A Lite Cream of Mushroom
soup mix

8oz (250ml) skim milk

1 tsp (5ml) finely minced onion

1/2 cup (125ml / 90g) steamed
fresh spinach

1 tsp (5ml) fresh lemon juice

freshly ground pepper

1 Add milk into a saucepan, warm over medium heat.

2 Empty one envelope of the mushroom soup into saucepan.

3 Add remaining ingredients and stir.

4 Heat until desired temperature, serve.

"There's no extra food. I just made the servings I needed according to my plan."

- Paula R.

Savory
Soups&
✤ Salads

Cream Chicken & Rice Soup

1 *serving*

- **SERVING SIZE: 1 RECIPE**
- **COUNTS AS:**
  1 PROTEIN
  1 STARCH
  1 VEGETABLE
  1 DAIRY
  1 LA LITE

▶ *size according to plan*

good source of fiber

❊ Ingredients

1 L A Lite Cream of Chicken soup mix

8oz (250ml) skim milk

6oz or 8oz (168 or 224g) according to plan, chicken breast, chopped into bite-size pieces

1/4 cup (60ml / 48g) raw brown rice

1 cup (250ml / 70g) fresh broccoli florets

1 tsp (5ml) finely minced onion

freshly ground pepper

nonfat cooking spray

1 In a small sauce pan sprayed with nonfat cooking spray; sauté chicken and onion.

2 Add milk, empty one envelope of the Cream of Chicken soup into saucepan or Dutch oven; stir until blended.

3 Add broccoli and rice; cook until rice is done; serve immediately.

> "No leftovers to go bad."
> *- Paula R.*

New England-Style Clam Chowder

8 *servings*

- **SERVING SIZE: 1 1/2 CUPS**
- **COUNTS AS:**
  1 PROTEIN
  1 STARCH
  1 DAIRY

▶ *size according to plan*

❊ Ingredients

1/4 cup (60ml / 5g) lite margarine

1 1/2 large onions, chopped

3/4 cup (200ml / 94g) all-purpose flour

1 quart (1L) shucked clams, with liquid

48oz (1.5L) clam juice

1 pound (448g) boiling potatoes, peeled and cubed

1 cup (250ml) skim milk

2 cups (500ml) evaporated skim milk

salt and freshly ground pepper

1/2 tsp (2.5ml) chopped fresh dill

1 Melt margarine in a large saucepan or pot over a medium flame. Add onions and sauté until soft and translucent. Add flour, stirring constantly, for 4-5 minutes until lightly brown. Remove from heat and cool to room temperature.

2 In a separate saucepan, add clams with liquid and clam juice. Bring to a boil, reduce heat and simmer for 15-20 minutes.

3 Meanwhile, in a another pot, cover potatoes with cold water by one inch; bring to a boil and cook until fork tender, about 15 minutes.

4 Slowly whisk in warmed clam-broth mixture into flour, stirring constantly. Bring up to a boil, stirring occasionally. Reduce heat, add potatoes, skim milk, evaporated skim milk, salt and pepper and dill. Simmer 5-10 minutes, until heated through.

Savory
Soups&
✦Salads

Minestrone Soup

8 *servings*

- **SERVING SIZE:**
  1 CUP (250ML)
- **COUNTS AS:**
  1 STARCH
  2 VEGETABLES

▶ *size according to plan*

family fare

✳ Ingredients

2 cups (500ml / 320g) chopped onion

2 Tbsp (30ml) low-sodium tomato paste

1/4 cup (60ml / 15g) chopped fresh parsley

4 garlic cloves, chopped

1 tomato, diced

1 carrot, diced

1 celery stalk, diced

1 cup (250ml / 30g) chopped fresh spinach

1 cup (250ml / 20g) lentils, rinsed

2 bay leaves

8 sprigs parsley and 6 sprigs fresh thyme, tied together

9 cups (2.25L) low-sodium vegetable broth

2 cups (500ml / 28g) cooked pasta

freshly ground pepper

1 In a large stock pot sprayed with nonfat cooking spray, sauté onions until brown.

2 Add tomato paste, chopped parsley, garlic, carrots, celery and spinach and cook for 3 minutes.

3 Add lentils, bay leaves, parsley-thyme sprigs and broth and bring to a boil.

4 Lower heat and simmer partially covered for 20 minutes.

5 Add tomato and season with pepper.

6 Simmer for 10 minutes.

7 Remove bay leaves and parsley-thyme sprigs and discard.

8 Add pasta, heat through and serve.

Potato & Leek Soup

1 *serving*

- **SERVING SIZE: 1 RECIPE**
- **COUNTS AS:**
  1 STARCH
  1 VEGETABLE
  1 DAIRY
  1 LA LITE

▶ *size according to plan*

good source of calcium

✳ Ingredients

1 L A Lite Cream of Chicken or Cream of Mushroom soup mix

8oz (250ml) skim milk

1/2 cup (125ml / 45g) chopped fresh leeks

1/2 small potato, chopped

1 garlic clove, finely minced

1 tsp (5ml) onion finely minced

1 Add milk to small sauce pan.

2 Add the soup mix, potato, leeks, onion and garlic.

3 Heat to a boil; lower heat and cook over low heat until potatoes are tender. About 5 minutes.

Savory Soups & ✤ Salads

Cream of Mushroom Pasta Soup

1 serving

good source of fiber

- SERVING SIZE: 1 RECIPE
- COUNTS AS:
  1 STARCH
  1 VEGETABLE
  1 DAIRY
  1 LA LITE

▶ *size according to plan*

☼ Ingredients

1 L A Lite Cream of Mushroom soup mix

8oz (250ml) skim milk

1/3 cup (85ml / 46g) cooked pasta of choice

1 tsp (5ml) onion, finely minced

1 garlic clove, finely minced

1/2 small tomato, chopped

1/4 green pepper, chopped

parsley, oregano, basil to taste

nonfat cooking spray

1. Cook pasta according to directions on the pasta package. Set aside.
2. In a small saucepan coated with nonfat cooking spray, sauté onion, garlic, tomato, pepper and seasonings.
3. Add milk and soup mix blend, heat through.
4. Pour over pasta; stir well and serve immediately.

Chicken Gumbo

6 servings

- SERVING SIZE:
  2 CUPS (500ML)
- COUNTS AS:
  1 PROTEIN
  1 STARCH

▶ *size according to plan*

☼ Ingredients

6 cups (1.5L) low-sodium chicken broth

4-6 cups (1-1.5L) water

3 pounds (1.3kg) chicken breast, boneless and skinless, cut into bite size pieces

1 1/2 pounds (672g) fresh or frozen okra, 1/4-inch (1/2cm) slices

2 Tbsp (30ml) canola oil

1/4 cup (60ml / 32g) all-purpose flour

1 tomato, seeded and chopped

1 large onion, chopped

2 garlic cloves, minced

1/2 tsp (2.5ml) freshly ground pepper

1/4 tsp (1ml) cayenne pepper

2 cups (500ml / 330g) rice, cooked

nonfat cooking spray

1. In large soup pot, over medium heat, combine chicken broth and water.
2. Meanwhile, heat skillet coated with nonfat cooking spray. Sauté chicken pieces until lightly brown, about 10 minutes. Set aside and keep warm.
3. Sauté okra over medium heat until tender, about 10-12 minutes. Remove from skillet and set aside.
4. Add oil to skillet; heat over medium flame for 2-3 minutes. Add flour, stirring constantly. This mixture is called a roux. Reduce heat to medium-low and continue to cook, stirring. Cook roux, stirring, until golden brown, about 15-20 minutes.
5. Add tomatoes, onions, garlic and seasonings to roux mixture, stirring constantly. Stir roux-tomato mixture into heated broth. Bring to a boil; reduce heat to low and add chicken and okra.
6. Cover and cook another 30-40 minutes, before serving. Add more water or broth to reach desired thickness throughout the final cooking process.
7. Add oil to skillet; heat over medium flame for 2-3 minutes. Add flour, stirring constantly.
8. Pour over rice and serve.

Savory
Soups &
❖ Salads

Pasta e Fagioli

4 *servings*

- **SERVING SIZE:**
  1/4 RECIPE
- **COUNTS AS:**
  1 PROTEIN
  2 STARCHES
  2 VEGETABLES

▶ *size according to plan*

family fare

☀ Ingredients

1 tomato, diced

1 celery stalk, diced

1 small onion, diced

2 garlic cloves, minced

2 cans (8oz / 224g each)
low-sodium tomato sauce

2 cups (500ml) low-sodium
chicken broth

freshly ground pepper

1 Tbsp (15ml) dried parsley

2 tsp (10ml) dried basil
leaves

15oz (420g) can cannelloni
beans, drained and rinsed

1 1/3 cups (335ml / 187g)
ditalini pasta

nonfat cooking spray

1 Heat a Dutch oven coated with nonfat cooking spray
over low heat. Sauté celery and onion until soft.

2 Add garlic and sauté briefly.

3 Stir in tomato sauce, chicken broth, pepper, parsley
and basil; simmer for 20 minutes.

4 Cook ditalini pasta in a large pot of boiling water and
cook for 8 minutes or according to directions on the
package; drain.

5 Add beans and tomatoes to the sauce mixture and
simmer for 5 minutes.

6 Stir pasta into sauce and bean mixture.

Bean Soup

4 *servings*

- **SERVING SIZE: 1/4 RECIPE**
- **COUNTS AS:**
  1 PROTEIN
  1 STARCH
  1 VEGETABLE

▶ *size according to plan*

good source of fiber

☀ Ingredients

4 cups (1L / 708g) Great
Northern Beans, cooked

1 small onion, minced

2 small potatoes, quartered and
sliced

28oz (784g) low-sodium canned
tomatoes, diced

6 cups (1.5L) water

freshly ground pepper

nonfat cooking spray

1 In a large stock pot coated with nonfat cooking spray,
sauté onion until brown.

2 Add remaining ingredients and bring to a boil.

3 Reduce heat; simmer for 30 minutes or until potatoes
are tender.

Savory
Soups&
✤ Salads

Creamy Vegetable Soup

1 *serving*

- SERVING SIZE: 1 RECIPE
- COUNTS AS:
  2 VEGETABLES
  1 DAIRY
  1 LA LITE

▶ *size according to plan*

✳ Ingredients

1 L A Lite Cream of Mushroom soup mix

8oz (250ml) skim milk

1 cup (250ml) cooked of any of the following vegetable choices (choose 2 vegetables, 1/2 cup (125ml) cooked each: cauliflower florets, broccoli florets, celery, 1 small tomato, spinach, asparagus, cabbage, carrot, mushrooms

1 tsp (5ml) onion, finely chopped

1 garlic clove, finely minced

2 Tbsp (30ml) fat-free half & half

nonfat cooking spray

1. In a small saucepan coated with nonfat cooking spray, sauté onion and garlic.
2. Add milk, fat-free half & half, soup mix; blend; heat through.
3. Add vegetables. Bring to a simmer and cook 5 minutes.
4. Serve immediately.

Sweet Potato Soup

4 *servings*

- SERVING SIZE: 3/4 CUP (200ML)
- COUNTS AS:
  1 STARCH
  1 VEGETABLE
  1/2 DAIRY

▶ *size according to plan*

✳ Ingredients

2 garlic cloves, crushed

1 small onion, chopped

1 tsp (5ml) curry powder

3 cups (750ml) water

1 1/2 cup (375ml) skim milk

12oz (336g) sweet potato, peeled and chopped

2 low-sodium vegetable broth cubes, crumbled

nonfat cooking spray

1. In a large stock pot, spray with nonfat cooking spray, sauté garlic, onion and curry powder until soft.
2. Add sweet potato, water and broth cubes.
3. Simmer, covered for 15 minutes or until vegetables are cooked. Cool.
4. Blend or process sweet potato mixture until smooth.
5. Gradually add the milk, processing until well combined.
6. Return to stock pot and heat well, do not boil.

Savory Soups & ✿ Salads

Beef Vegetable Soup

1 *serving*

- **SERVING SIZE: 1 RECIPE**
- **COUNTS AS:**
  1 PROTEIN
  3 VEGETABLES

▶ *size according to plan*

☀ Ingredients

4 or 6oz (112 or 168g) chuck roast

2 cups (500ml) very low-sodium beef broth, prepared from bouillon

1/2 medium carrot, thinly sliced

1/2 large celery stalk, sliced

1/2 cup (125ml / 55g) fresh green beans, trimmed and cut into 1/2-inch pieces (1cm)

1 small tomato, seeded and diced

nonfat cooking spray

dash of salt and freshly ground pepper

1 Rinse roast and pat dry; cut into 1 inch (2.5cm) pieces. Season with salt and pepper, to taste.

2 Coat a Dutch oven with nonfat cooking spray. Add beef and cook over a medium flame until lightly browned.

3 Add beef broth; bring to boil.

4 Add remaining ingredients to pot. Return soup to a boil.

5 Reduce heat; cover and simmer until beef and vegetables are tender, approximately 20 minutes.

6 Serve immediately or store in refrigerator up to 24 hours.

Cheddar Cheese Soup

meals in minutes

4 *servings*

- **SERVING SIZE: 1/4 RECIPE**
- **COUNTS AS:**
  1 DAIRY
  1 FAT

▶ *size according to plan*

☀ Ingredients

2 Tbsp (30ml) minced green onion

2 Tbsp (30ml) lite margarine

3 Tbsp (45ml) flour

3 cups (750ml) low-sodium beef broth

2 cups (500ml) skim milk

3/4 cup (200ml) light or reduced-fat cheddar cheese, grated

1/2 tsp (2.5ml) freshly ground pepper

paprika and parsley for garnish

1 Sauté the onion in margarine until softened; add flour and blend.

2 Gradually stir in the broth and add the milk.

3 Bring to a boil and add cheese and pepper.

4 Simmer until cheese is melted.

5 Sprinkle with paprika and chopped parsley.

Savory
Soups&
❖Salads

Split Pea Soup

6 *servings*

- SERVING SIZE: 3/4 CUP (200ML)
- COUNTS AS:
  1 STARCH
  3 VEGETABLES

▸ *size according to plan*

☀ Ingredients

2 cups (500ml) split peas, uncooked

6 cups (1.5L) water

1 bay leaf

2 cups (500ml / 240g) carrots, chopped

1 cup (250ml / 120g) celery, chopped

1 cup (250ml / 160g) onion, chopped

1 tsp (5ml) thyme

1/2 tsp (2.5ml) freshly ground pepper

1 tsp (5ml) garlic powder

1. Rinse and drain split peas.
2. Combine dried split peas, water and bay leaf, in a large stock pot.
3. Bring to a boil and then reduce heat and simmer for 1 hour. Stir occasionally to prevent the split peas from sticking and to make sure there is enough water. Add water if the soup looks like it is becoming dry.
4. Add carrots, celery, onions and seasoning.
5. Continue to simmer for 30 minutes or longer.
6. Add more water if a thinner soup is desired.

French Onion Soup

1 *serving*

- SERVING SIZE: 1 RECIPE
- COUNTS AS:
  1 STARCH
  1 VEGETABLE
  1/2 DAIRY

▸ *size according to plan*

☀ Ingredients

1 packet low-sodium beef bouillon

1 cup (250ml) water

1/2 cup (125ml / 80g) raw white onion slices

3 slices melba toast

1oz (28g) reduced fat or part skim cheese

1 bay leaf

1/4 tsp (1ml) onion powder

1/4 tsp (1ml) lite salt

freshly ground pepper

dash of parsley

nonfat cooking spray

1. Sauté onions in skillet with non-fat cooking spray.
2. Add beef bouillon to onions.
3. Add water, salt, pepper, and bay leaf.
4. Bring to a boil and allow to simmer 10-15 minutes.
5. Remove bay leaf.
6. Place soup in a bowl. Top with melba toast.
7. Sprinkle cheese over melba toast.
8. Microwave soup until cheese is melted.
9. Sprinkle with parsley and serve hot.

Savory
Soups&
♣ Salads

Sweet Red Pepper Soup

4 *servings*

- **SERVING SIZE:**
  1/2 CUP (125ML)
- **COUNTS AS:**
  3 VEGETABLES

▶ *size according to plan*

✳ Ingredients

4 red peppers, halved and deseeded

1 red chili, seeded and finely chopped

3 garlic cloves, chopped

20 green onions, chopped

4 tomatoes, chopped

2 cups (500ml) very low-sodium vegetable stock

freshly ground pepper

1 Tbsp (15ml) freshly chopped parsley or oregano

2 Tbsp (30ml) freshly chopped chives or basil

1 tsp (5ml) olive oil

1. Preheat the grill to high.

2. When very hot, place red pepper, skin-side up, for about 15-20 minutes or until the skin is charred and blistered.

3. Remove and place in a paper bag until cool enough to handle.

4. Heat the oil in a large pot and add the chili, garlic and onions and sauté for 4-5 minutes. Meanwhile, peel and roughly chop the peppers.

5. Add the tomatoes and stock and simmer for 10 minutes, then add the roasted peppers.

6. Cover and cook over a low heat for about 5-10 minutes, then remove from the heat and allow to cool.

7. Puree the soup in a food processor until smooth.

8. Return the soup to a clean pan and gently warm through.

9. Season to taste and serve. Sprinkle with fresh herbs of your choice.

Egg Drop Soup

1 *serving*

- **SERVING SIZE: 1 RECIPE**
- **COUNTS AS:**
  1 PROTEIN
  1 VEGETABLE

▶ *size according to plan*

✳ Ingredients

2 cups (500ml) very low-sodium chicken broth, prepared from bouillon

1/4 tsp (1ml) lite salt

dash of white pepper

5 green onions, sliced

2 or 3 eggs

1. In a medium saucepan, add chicken broth, salt and pepper. Bring to a boil; reduce heat.

2. In a small bowl, lightly beat eggs. Stir in onions.

3. Pour egg mixture slowly into broth, stirring constantly with a fork, until the eggs form strands.

Savory
Soups&
❖ Salads

Garden Vegetable Soup

1 *serving*

- **SERVING SIZE: 1 RECIPE**
- **COUNTS AS:**
  3 VEGETABLES

▶ *size according to plan*

good source of fiber

✳ Ingredients

3 green onions, chopped

1/2 medium carrot, chopped

1/2 celery stalk

2 garlic cloves, minced

1/2 cup (125ml / 35g) green cabbage, shredded

1/2 cup (125ml / 56g) zucchini, sliced

1/2 tsp (2.5ml) dried basil, crushed

1/2 tsp (2.5ml) thyme

freshly ground pepper

1 small tomato, diced

2 cups (500ml) very low-sodium chicken broth

nonfat cooking spray

1 Coat a medium saucepan with nonfat cooking spray. Add onion, carrot, celery and garlic.

2 Cook, stirring occasionally, over medium heat for 15-20 minutes, or until carrots begin to soften.

3 Stir in cabbage, zucchini, basil, thyme and pepper. Cook for 5-10 minutes longer, or until cabbage is tender.

4 Stir in tomato and broth. Bring to a boil. Reduce heat; cover and simmer for another 10 minutes, to allow flavors to meld.

5 Serve immediately.

Chicken Caldo

1 *serving*

- **SERVING SIZE: 1 RECIPE**
- **COUNTS AS:**
  1 PROTEIN
  3 VEGETABLES

▶ *size according to plan*

✳ Ingredients

6 or 8oz (168 or 224g) boneless, skinless chicken breast

freshly ground pepper

3 green onions, chopped

1 garlic clove, minced

2 cups (500ml) water

1/2 large celery stalk, sliced

1/2 medium carrot, sliced

1/2 cup zucchini, sliced

1/2 cup cabbage, chopped

1/4 tsp (1ml) lite salt

1/8 tsp (.5ml) freshly ground pepper

1 Rinse chicken and pat dry. Cut into bite size pieces. Season with pepper, to taste.

2 Place chicken, onion and garlic in a medium saucepan.

3 Cover with water; bring to a boil.

4 Reduce heat; simmer for 30 minutes, or until chicken is tender.

5 Add remaining ingredients; simmer for another 20 minutes, or until vegetables are soft.

6 Serve immediately or refrigerate up to 24 hours.

Savory
Soups &
✤ Salads

Spinach Soup

1 serving

■ SERVING SIZE: 1 RECIPE
■ COUNTS AS:
  2 VEGETABLES

meals in minutes

✳ Ingredients

2 cups (500ml) very low-sodium chicken bouillon

1/4 tsp (1ml) garlic powder

1 1/2 cup (375ml / 45g) fresh spinach, coarsely chopped

1/2 cup (250ml / 3g) fresh mushrooms, chopped

1 Tbsp (15ml) lemon juice

1. In a medium saucepan combine chicken broth and garlic powder. Bring to a boil.

2. Stir in spinach and mushrooms, allowing spinach to wilt; return to boiling.

3. Reduce heat; cover and simmer for 2 minutes, or until vegetables are tender. Stir in lemon juice.

Chicken & Lemongrass Soup

4 servings

■ SERVING SIZE:
  1 CUP (250ML)
■ COUNTS AS:
  1/2 PROTEIN
  1 VEGETABLE
  1 DAIRY
  1 FAT

✳ Ingredients

1 pound (448g) skinless chicken breast filets

4 stalks lemongrass, tender inner part only

2 green onions, finely sliced

finely grated zest and juice of 1 lime

1 Tbsp (15ml) fish sauce

2-3 small fresh red or green chilies, deseeded

3 cups (750ml) low-sodium chicken broth

2 inch (5cm) piece fresh ginger, peeled

1 Tbsp (15ml) fresh coriander

1/2 tsp (2.5ml) fennel seeds, lightly crushed

1 garlic clove

1 Tbsp (15ml) oil

1/2 cup (125ml) light coconut milk

1 cup (250ml) evaporated skim milk

freshly ground pepper

1. Cut the chicken crossways into thin slices. Place in a non-metallic bowl.

2. Very finely slice one of the lemon grass stalks and scatter over the chicken with the onions.

3. Add the zest and fish sauce; mix together. Marinate chicken for 30-60 minutes.

4. Chop the remaining lemongrass and two chilies roughly and put in a pan with the stock, half the ginger, sliced and all the coriander stems (chop leaves and reserve).

5. Bring to the boil, then simmer covered for 30 minutes. Strain, reserving stock.

6. Gently fry the onion, fennel seeds, garlic and remaining ginger, finely chopped, in the oil in a large saucepan until onion is soft.

7. Add the strained stock and simmer for 10 minutes, then add the coconut milk and evaporated milk.

8. When the mixture comes back to a simmer, add the chicken with all its marinade and half the chopped coriander leaves.

9. Simmer gently for 6-7 minutes until chicken is cooked thoroughly.

10. Add the lime juice, seasoning to taste.

11. Sprinkle with the rest of the coriander and the third chili, finely sliced if desired.

Savory
Soups&
✤ Salads

Waldorf Salad

4 *servings*

- **SERVING SIZE:**
  1/4 OF RECIPE
- **COUNTS AS:**
  2 VEGETABLES
  1 FRUIT
  1 FAT

▶ *size according to plan*

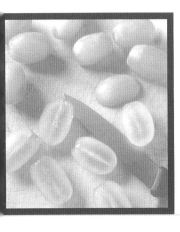

☀ Ingredients

1/4 cup (60ml) lite mayonnaise

1/4 cup (60ml) plain nonfat yogurt

1 Tbsp (15ml) artificial sweetener

3 tart apples, peeled, cored and chopped

1 Tbsp (15ml) lemon juice

1 cup (250ml / 92g) seedless grapes, sliced in half

2 celery stalks, chopped

3 green onions, sliced

1/4 cup (60ml / 29g) chopped walnuts, toasted

1 head of iceberg lettuce, quartered

1 In a small bowl, whisk together mayonnaise, yogurt and artificial sweetener. Set aside.

2 In a large bowl, toss apples with lemon juice. Add grapes, celery, onions and walnuts.

3 Add dressing to apple mixture; toss to coat. Cover and refrigerate for 1 hour.

4 To serve, arrange one quarter of lettuce in a shallow bowl or plate. Divide salad evenly among plates.

Spicy Shrimp Salad

4 *servings*

- **SERVING SIZE:**
  1/4 OF RECIPE
- **COUNTS AS:**
  1 PROTEIN
  2 VEGETABLES

▶ *size according to plan*

meals in minutes

☀ Ingredients

1 1/2 or 1 3/4 pounds (672 or 784g) small shrimp, peeled and deveined

1/4 cup (60ml / 60g) finely chopped celery

1/4 cup (60ml / 24g) finely chopped green onion

1/4 cup (60ml) country-style mustard

1 Tbsp (15ml) fresh chopped parsley

1 Tbsp (15ml) olive oil

1 Tbsp (15ml) cider vinegar

2 tsp (10ml) pepper sauce

8 cups (2L / 240g) salad greens (2 cups (500ml) per salad)

1 Place shrimp and enough water to cover in a 2-quart (2L) saucepan over high heat and bring to boil.

2 Boil 2 minutes until shrimp are tender.

3 Drain well and set aside to cool.

4 Combine celery, green onions, mustard, parsley, olive oil, cider vinegar and pepper sauce in a bowl; toss in shrimp and mix.

5 To serve arrange on salad greens (2 cups) (500ml) of choice.

Savory
Soups&
❖ Salads

Sweet & Sour Cabbage

meals in minutes

serving

SERVING SIZE: 1 RECIPE
COUNTS AS:
1/2 PROTEIN
2 VEGETABLES

▶ *size according to plan*

☼ Ingredients

1 egg

1/2 packet of artificial sweetener

1/4 cup (60ml) rice or red wine vinegar

2 Tbsp (30ml) water

1/4 tsp (1ml) lite salt

1/4 tsp (1ml) dry mustard

1 cup (250ml / 70g) cabbage, shredded

1/2 green pepper, chopped

1 Beat egg until thick and lemon colored.

2 In a saucepan, heat artificial sweetener, vinegar, water, salt and dry mustard to boiling, stirring constantly.

3 Gradually stir at least half of the hot mixture into the egg, this is called tempering. Stir this; then back into the hot vinegar mixture.

4 Cook over low heat, stirring constantly, until slightly thickened.

5 Pour over cabbage and green pepper; toss to coat.

Vegetable Pasta Salad

serving

SERVING SIZE: 1 RECIPE
COUNTS AS:
1 STARCH
3 VEGETABLES

▶ *size according to plan*

☼ Ingredients

1 cup (250ml / 130g) zucchini or yellow summer squash, sliced

1/2 medium green pepper, chopped

1 garlic clove, minced

1/3 cup (85ml / 57g) cooked pasta, such as macaroni

2 Tbsp (30ml) white wine vinegar

1/4 tsp (1ml) dried dill

1/8 tsp (.5ml) lite salt

freshly ground pepper

1 small tomato, chopped

nonfat cooking spray

1 In a large skillet, coated with nonfat cooking spray, sauté squash, green pepper and garlic over medium heat until crisp-tender.

2 Add macaroni, vinegar, dill, salt and pepper to vegetable mixture; toss to combine. Top with chopped tomato.

3 Refrigerate for 1 hour before serving.

Savory
Soups &
❖ Salads

Stir-Fried Chicken Salad

1 *serving*

- **SERVING SIZE: 1 RECIPE**
- **COUNTS AS:**
  1 PROTEIN
  3 VEGETABLES

▸ *size according to plan*

good source of fiber

☀ Ingredients

6 or 8oz (168 or 224g) raw chicken breast, size according to plan

3 Tbsp (45ml) white wine vinegar

2 tsp (10ml) Dijon mustard

1/2 packet artificial sweetener

1/4 tsp (1ml) lite salt

1/8 tsp (.5ml) paprika

1/8 tsp (.5ml) freshly ground pepper

1 1/2 cups (375ml / 84g) fresh spinach

1 small tomato, chopped

1/4 medium carrot, shredded

nonfat cooking spray

1 Place chicken in a large plastic freezer bag.

2 In a small bowl, mix together vinegar, mustard, artificial sweetener, salt, paprika and pepper. Pour over chicken and close bag. Marinate chicken in refrigerator for 2-5 hours, turning bag frequently.

3 In a large bowl, combine spinach, tomato and carrot. Set aside.

4 Coat skillet or wok with nonfat cooking spray. Heat over medium flame.

5 Drain chicken, reserving marinade.

6 Stir-fry chicken for 2-3 minutes or until no longer pink. Add marinade and heat until boiling.

7 Place spinach mixture on dinner plate. Pour hot chicken mixture over salad.

8 Serve immediately

Spaghetti Squash Salad

6 *servings*

- **SERVING SIZE: 1/6 OF RECIPE**
- **COUNTS AS:**
  1 VEGETABLE
  1 STARCH
  1 FAT

▸ *size according to plan*

☀ Ingredients

3 pounds (1.3kg) spaghetti squash

1/4 cup (60ml) parsley, chopped

2 Tbsp (30ml) olive oil

2 garlic cloves, minced

1/2 pound (224g) fresh mushrooms, sliced

1 With a knife, pierce the skin of the squash in several places, to allow steam to escape while cooking.

2 Place whole squash in the microwave and cook on high for 15 minutes, turning twice.

3 Remove from microwave, let stand for 10 minutes.

4 In a small bowl, mix parsley, olive oil and garlic.

5 Sauté mushrooms in a nonstick skillet coated with nonfat cooking spray.

6 Cut squash in half lengthwise and remove seeds with a spoon.

7 With a fork, gently pull spaghetti-like flesh away from the sides of the skin.

8 Combine squash with mushrooms. Toss to combine.

9 Pour oil mixture over; stir and serve.

Savory Soups & Salads

Mediterranean Tuna Salad

1 *serving*

- **SERVING SIZE: 1 RECIPE**
- **COUNTS AS:**
  - 1 PROTEIN
  - 2 VEGETABLES
  - 1 FAT

▶ *size according to plan*

☀ Ingredients

4-6oz (112g or 168g) can of tuna, drained (choose low-sodium as available)

2 tsp (10ml) lite mayonnaise

dash of lite salt

freshly ground pepper

1 Tbsp (15ml) diced white onion

1 Tbsp (15ml) diced red peppers

1 Tbsp (15ml) shredded carrot

1 celery stalk, sliced finely

3 black olives, diced

1 Combine all ingredients; mix well.

2 Cover and refrigerate at least 1 hour. Serve chilled.

---

family fare

Hot & Sour Salad

8 *servings*

- **SERVING SIZE:**
  1/2 CUP (125ML)
- **COUNTS AS:**
  - 1 VEGETABLE

▶ *size according to plan*

☀ Ingredients

3 cups (750ml / 210g) shredded bok choy

1/2 carrot, shredded

1 large red pepper, thinly sliced

5 green onions, sliced

1/4 cup (60ml / 18g) sliced mushrooms

1/2 tsp (2.5ml) red pepper flakes

2 garlic cloves, sliced

1 Tbsp (15ml) ginger, minced

1/2 tsp (2.5ml) lite salt

1 tsp (5ml) olive oil

1 packet artificial sweetener

2/3 cup (170ml) rice wine vinegar

1 tsp (5ml) Dijon mustard

1 Combine bok choy, carrots, mushrooms, pepper and onion in large bowl.

2 Whisk together remaining ingredients in small bowl.

3 Pour vinegar mixture over vegetables.

4 Refrigerate 1-2 hours before serving.

5 Mix well before serving.

Savory
Soups&
❖ Salads

Crab Salad

① *serving*

- ■ SERVING SIZE: 1 RECIPE
- ■ COUNTS AS:
  - 1 PROTEIN
  - 1 VEGETABLE

▶ *size according to plan*

☼ Ingredients

5 or 7oz (140 or 196g) raw crab meat; steamed

1/2 tsp (2.5ml) parsley

1/2 tsp (2.5ml) chives

1 tsp (5ml) fresh lemon juice

1/4 cucumber, peeled and diced

1. Toss together all ingredients in a medium bowl.
2. Cover and refrigerate at least 1 hour. Serve chilled.

Glazed Chicken & Avocado Salad

④ *servings*

- ■ SERVING SIZE: 1/4 OF RECIPE
- ■ COUNTS AS:
  - 1 PROTEIN
  - 3 VEGETABLES
  - 1 FRUIT
  - 1 FAT

▶ *size according to plan*

☼ Ingredients

1 cup (250ml / 48g) artificial sweetener

1/4 cup (60ml) water

1/2 cup (125ml) red wine

1 cup (250ml) fresh squeezed orange juice

1 tsp (5ml) wasabi paste

1 1/2 or 2 pounds (672 or 896g) chicken breast, boneless and skinless, sliced into strips

1 large tomato, diced

1/4 cup (60ml / 40g) red onion, diced

2 Tbsp (30ml) fresh cilantro

juice of 2 limes

1 avocado, peeled, pitted and diced

8 cups (2L / 240g) salad greens

hot sauce, to taste (optional)

nonfat cooking spray

1. Preheat oven to 400°F (200°C).
2. In a large Dutch oven, heat artificial sweetener and water together over medium high heat, stirring occasionally, until it turns to a deep amber color.
3. Remove from heat and slowly add the wine.
4. Return to heat and stir until all particles dissolve.
5. Add orange juice and wasabi paste; cook, stirring occasionally, until well combined.
6. Brush chicken strips with the glaze. Place on a baking sheet coated with nonfat cooking spray.
7. Bake until thoroughly cooked, about 20 minutes.
8. While the chicken is cooking, toss together the tomatoes, red onion, cilantro, lime juice, avocados and hot sauce (optional).
9. Arrange 2 cups (500ml) salad greens on 4 salad plates.
10. Top with 1/4 of the vegetable mixture and chicken strips; serve.

Savory
Soups&
❖ Salads

Rainbow Salad

- **SERVING SIZE:**
  1 CUP (250ML)
- **COUNTS AS:**
  1 VEGETABLE

▶ *size according to plan*

good source of fiber

☀ Ingredients

1 pound (448g) fresh spinach

1/2 green pepper, diced

1/2 red pepper, diced

1/2 cup (125ml / 40g) fresh
broccoli florets

1/2 red onion, diced

1 yellow summer squash, diced

10 cherry tomatoes

1 carrot, shredded

1/2 cup (125ml / 35g) fresh
mushrooms, sliced

1 Place spinach in a large bowl.

2 Top with peppers, broccoli, onion, yellow summer
squash, tomatoes, carrots and mushrooms.

3 Serve chilled with your choice of fat-free dressings.

Cheesy Taco Salad

1 *serving*

- **SERVING SIZE: 1 RECIPE**
- **COUNTS AS:**
  1 PROTEIN
  2 VEGETABLES
  1 STARCH
  1/2 DAIRY

▶ *size according to plan*

good source of calcium

☀ Ingredients

5 or 7oz (140 or 196g) fresh
ground turkey breast

1/4 tsp (1ml) garlic powder

1/4 tsp (1ml) chili powder

1/4 tsp (1ml) lite salt

1 cup (250ml / 30g) lettuce

1 small tomato

1oz (28g) reduced-fat
cheddar cheese

1 bag L A Cheese Curls

2 Tbsp (30ml) salsa

1 Cook turkey in medium sauté pan; add garlic powder,
chili and salt to flavor.

2 Drain any excess oil or fat from turkey.

3 Assemble lettuce on plate.

4 Top lettuce with meat, tomatoes and cheese.

5 Top with L A Cheese Curls.

6 Garnish with salsa.

Savory
Soups&
❖ Salads

Garlic Tomato **Salad**

1 *serving*

- **SERVING SIZE: 1 RECIPE**
- **COUNTS AS:**
  1 VEGETABLE

▶ *size according to plan*

☀ Ingredients

1 medium tomato, cut into 1-inch slices

2 Tbsp (30ml) fat-free Italian salad dressing

2 Tbsp (30ml) red wine vinegar

1/8 tsp (.5ml) lite salt

dash red pepper sauce

2 large garlic cloves, finely chopped

1 cup (250ml / 56g) salad greens, torn into bite size pieces

1 Place tomato slices in glass dish.

2 Combine dressing, vinegar, salt, pepper sauce and garlic in covered container or jar and shake, vigorously, to mix.

3 Pour mixture over tomato slices.

4 Refrigerate for 1 hour before serving.

5 Serve on a bed of salad greens.

Cucumber & **Shrimp Salad**

1 *serving*

- **SERVING SIZE: 1 RECIPE**
- **COUNTS AS:**
  1 PROTEIN
  2 VEGETABLES

▶ *size according to plan*

☀ Ingredients

1/4 cup (60ml) vinegar

1/2 packet artificial sweetener

1 tsp (5ml) low-sodium soy sauce

1/4 tsp (1ml) lite salt

4 or 6oz (112 or 168g) cooked shrimp

1/4 medium cucumber, thinly sliced

1 cup (250ml / 56g) lettuce or salad greens torn in bite-size pieces

1/2 Tbsp (7.5ml) sesame seeds

1 Mix vinegar, artificial sweetener, soy sauce and salt in a medium bowl.

2 Add shrimp and cucumbers; toss. Cover and refrigerate at least 1 hour.

3 Line salad plate with lettuce or salad greens.

4 Remove shrimp with slotted spoon; place on top of salad greens. Sprinkle with sesame seeds.

Savory
Soups&
✿ Salads

Fruited Chicken Salad

1 *serving*

- SERVING SIZE: 1 RECIPE
- COUNTS AS:
  1 PROTEIN
  1 VEGETABLE
  1 FRUIT
  1 FAT

▶ *size according to plan*

☀ Ingredients

5 or 7oz (140 or 196g) chicken, cooked and cut into bite-size pieces

1 Tbsp (15ml) lite mayonnaise

1/2 Tbsp (7.5ml) lemon juice

1 celery stalk, thinly sliced

15 green grapes, cut in half

dash lite salt

freshly ground pepper

1/8 tsp (.5ml) dried onion flakes

1 Combine all ingredients in a large bowl; toss to mix well.

2 Cover and refrigerate at least 1 hour. Serve chilled.

Oriental-Style Shrimp Salad

4 *servings*

family fare

- SERVING SIZE:
  1/4 OF RECIPE
- COUNTS AS:
  1 PROTEIN
  1 STARCH
  3 VEGETABLES

▶ *size according to plan*

☀ Ingredients

1-1 1/2 pounds (448 - 559g) large shrimp, peeled and deveined

1 garlic clove, minced

1 inch (2.5cm) piece of ginger, peeled and minced

1/4 cup (60ml) low-sodium soy sauce, divided

6oz (168g) uncooked capellini/angel hair pasta

10oz (28g) baby spinach

1 cup (25ml / 200g) mung beans, cooked and drained

1/4 cup (60ml) mint leaves, firmly packed

5 medium scallions, chopped

2 baby carrots, shredded

juice from 1 lime

1 Toss shrimp with garlic, ginger and 2 Tbsp (30ml) low-sodium soy sauce.

2 Cover; refrigerate and marinate for at least 30 minutes.

3 Meanwhile, cook pasta according to package directions.

4 Toss pasta with spinach, mung beans, mint, scallions and carrots.

5 Mix together lime juice and 2 Tbsp (30ml) of low-sodium soy sauce and pour over the salad.

6 Allow to sit for 15 minutes while the shrimp is cooking.

7 Grill shrimp, or sauté, in a nonstick pan.

8 Allow shrimp to cool, and then toss with the salad.

Savory
Soups &
✤ Salads

Grilled Chicken Cobb Salad

4 *servings*

- **SERVING SIZE:**
  1/4 OF RECIPE
- **COUNTS AS:**
  1 PROTEIN
  2 VEGETABLES
  1 FAT

▶ *size according to plan*

☀ Ingredients

3 Tbsp (45ml) lemon seasoning (see recipe on page 218)

12 or 16oz (336 or 448g) chicken breast, boneless and skinless

6 cups (1.5L / 180g) salad greens, of your choice, torn

2oz (56g) light cheese, shredded

2 large, hard-boiled eggs, sliced

1 large tomato, chopped

2 pieces low-sodium turkey bacon, cooked and drained, chopped

1 Preheat grill to medium high.

2 Put lemon seasoning on a plate. Coat chicken thoroughly in seasoning.

3 Cook on grill 5 minutes; turn and cook for another 5 minutes, or until juices run clear when a fork is inserted.

4 Remove from grill; cool and cut into chunks or strips. Set aside.

5 Onto each of four salad plates, arrange salad greens. Top greens with chicken, cheese, egg, chopped tomato and crumbled bacon. Drizzle with your favorite fat-free salad dressing.

Grape & Cabbage Salad

3 *servings*

- **SERVING SIZE:**
  1/3 OF RECIPE
- **COUNTS AS:**
  1 VEGETABLE
  1 FRUIT
  1 FAT

▶ *size according to plan*

☀ Ingredients

1 cup (250ml / 160g) green grapes

3 cups (750ml / 210g) cabbage, shredded

freshly ground pepper

1 Tbsp (15ml) lemon juice, freshly squeeze

1/4 cup (60ml) lite mayonnaise

1 Combine grapes, cabbage, black pepper, lemon juice and mayonnaise in a bowl.

2 Mix well, tossing to coat.

3 Refrigerate, at least 30 minutes, or until ready to serve.

> "The recipes from the L A Lite Cookbook take food items right from my menu plan!"
>
> *- Lynn K.*

Savory
Soups &
❀ Salads

1 *serving*

- SERVING SIZE: 1 RECIPE
- COUNTS AS:
  1 PROTEIN
  2 VEGETABLES

▶ *size according to plan*

meals in minutes

Steak Caesar **Salad**

☀ Ingredients

4 or 6oz (112 or 168g) sirloin steak

1 cup (25ml / 30g) romaine lettuce

2 Tbsp (30ml) fat-free Caesar salad dressing, divided

1 tsp (5ml) parmesan cheese

2 green onions, chopped

nonfat cooking spray

1 Combine 1 Tbsp (15ml) Caesar dressing, parmesan cheese and onions in medium bowl.

2 Cut beef into strips and place in bowl with marinade; toss to coat.

3 Coat skillet with nonfat cooking spray and heat over medium flame. Remove beef from marinade and place in skillet; discard marinade.

4 Sauté 5-6 minutes, or until beef is cooked to your liking.

5 Place lettuce on a serving plate. Top with beef and remaining dressing.

---

4 *servings*

- SERVING SIZE:
  1/4 OF RECIPE
- COUNTS AS:
  3 VEGETABLES

▶ *size according to plan*

family fare

Blackened Portabella **Salad**

☀ Ingredients

1/4 cup (60ml) red wine vinegar

1/4 cup (60ml) balsamic vinegar

1/4 cup (60ml) low-sodium tomato juice

2 tsp (10ml) Dijon mustard

2 tsp (10ml) stone ground mustard

1/4 tsp (1ml) freshly ground pepper

4 whole portabella mushrooms

1 Tbsp (15ml) Cajun seasoning (see recipe on page 215)

8 cups (2L / 240g) romaine lettuce

1 tomato

1/2 cup (125ml / 60g) red onion, thinly sliced

1 Combine the first 6 ingredients in a large zip-top plastic bag.

2 Add mushrooms to bag; seal. Marinate 10 minutes, turning occasionally.

3 Remove mushrooms from bag, reserving marinade.

4 Season mushrooms with Cajun spice.

5 Over medium-high heat, grill mushrooms for 2 minutes on each side, or until tender and browned.

6 Cool; cut diagonally into thin slices.

7 Arrange 2 cups (500ml) romaine on each of 4 salad plates. Top with mushroom slices, 2 tomato wedges and onions.

8 Drizzle with the reserved marinade or use fat-free dressing of your choice.

Savory
Soups&
✤ Salads

Carrot Salad

1 *serving*

- SERVING SIZE: 1 RECIPE
- COUNTS AS:
  2 VEGETABLES
  1 FRUIT

▶ *size according to plan*

good source of fiber

☀ Ingredients

1/2 medium carrot, shredded

1 celery stalk, thinly sliced

1 tsp (5ml) lemon zest

1 tsp (5ml) lemon juice

1/2 tsp (2.5ml) brown sugar
artificial sweetener

2 Tbsp (30ml) raisins

dash of ground ginger

1 Mix all ingredients together in small bowl.

2 Cover and chill for at least 1 hour before serving.

"So many recipes in the cookbook I can choose something new every day."
- Amanda P.

Chicken Broccoli Pasta Salad

6 *servings*

- SERVING SIZE:
  1/6 OF RECIPE
- COUNTS AS:
  1 PROTEIN
  2 VEGETABLES
  1 STARCH
  1 FAT

▶ *size according to plan*

☀ Ingredients

1/4 cup (60ml) lemon
seasoning (see recipe on
page 218), divided

8oz (224g) dry penne pasta (or
pasta of choice)

2 1/4 or 3 pounds (1 or 1.3 kg)
boneless chicken breast, cut
into bite size pieces

2 Tbsp (30ml) olive oil

2 cups (500ml / 160g) broccoli
florets

3 Tbsp (45ml) parmesan cheese

1/4 cup (60ml) very low-sodium
chicken broth

1 cup (250ml / 150g) cherry
tomatoes, halved

5 green onions, chopped

1 Add half of lemon seasoning to a large pot of boiling water; add pasta and cook according to package directions. Drain; set aside.

2 While pasta is cooking, heat 1 Tbsp (15ml) olive oil in a large skillet. Sauté the chicken, about 6-8 minutes per side, over medium heat.

3 Add broth, broccoli, and lemon seasoning to the chicken; cover and cook for 3-5 minutes.

4 Toss pasta in a large bowl with remaining 1 Tbsp (15ml) olive oil and parmesan cheese. Add chicken and broccoli and toss again.

5 Chill at least 1 hour.

6 Divide among 6 plates. Garnish with cherry tomatoes.

Savory
Soups &
�֍ Salads

Sweet Potato **Salad**

■ SERVING SIZE:
  1/2 CUP (125ML)
■ COUNTS AS:
  1 STARCH
  1 VEGETABLE

▶ *size according to plan*

☀ Ingredients

6 sweet potatoes, boiled, peeled and cubed

1/2 cup (125ml / 75g) chopped red pepper

1/4 cup (60ml / 40g) chopped onion

1/2 tsp (2.5ml) lite salt

1/4 tsp (1ml) freshly ground pepper

1/3 cup (85ml) lite mayonnaise

1/4 tsp (1ml) hot pepper sauce

1/2 tsp (2.5ml) paprika

1 In large bowl, combine onion, pepper and potatoes.

2 Gently fold in remaining ingredients.

3 Chill 1-2 hours before serving.

"This cookbook is fantastic. It puts variety into my meals, and at the same time helps me stick to my meal plan."

- Karen D.

Asparagus **Salad**

1 *serving*

■ SERVING SIZE: 1 RECIPE
■ COUNTS AS:
  1/2 PROTEIN
  2 VEGETABLES
  1/2 DAIRY

▶ *size according to plan*

☀ Ingredients

4oz (125ml) nonfat plain yogurt

2 Tbsp (30ml) fat-free French dressing

1/2 cup (125ml / 90g) cooked asparagus spears

1 hard cooked egg, sliced

1 cup (250ml / 56g) salad greens, torn in bite-size pieces

1 Mix nonfat yogurt and French dressing in a small bowl.

2 Cover and refrigerate at least 1 hour.

3 Arrange chilled asparagus on salad greens; top with egg slices.

4 Spoon dressing over top.

Savory
Soups**&**
❖ Salads

Strawberry & Melon Salad

6 *servings*

- **SERVING SIZE: 1 CUP (250ML)**
- **COUNTS AS:**
  - 1 VEGETABLE
  - 1 FRUIT
  - 1 FAT

▶ *size according to plan*

☀ Ingredients

1/4 cup (60ml) freshly squeezed orange juice

1 Tbsp (15ml) olive oil

2 Tbsp (30ml) water

10oz (280g) salad greens, of your choice

1 cup (250ml / 170g) honeydew, cubed

1 cup (250ml / 160g) cantaloupe, cubed

1 cup (250ml / 152g) watermelon, cubed

1 cup (250ml / 144g) strawberries, sliced

3 Tbsp (45ml) sunflower seeds, unsalted

1. Mix juice, oil and water until blended.

2. Place salad greens, melon cubes and strawberry slices in a large bowl; toss.

3. Pour dressing over salad and sprinkle with sunflower seeds.

> "The L A Lite Cookbook recipes are so easy to follow, my boyfriend has meals made and ready to eat when I get home from work."
>
> *- Rachel P.*

Tomato Basil & Mozzarella Salad

1 *serving*

meals in minutes

- **SERVING SIZE: 1 RECIPE**
- **COUNTS AS:**
  - 1 VEGETABLE
  - 1 FAT
  - 1 DAIRY

▶ *size according to plan*

☀ Ingredients

1 very ripe, small tomato

2oz (56g) light or reduced-fat mozzarella cheese, shredded or sliced

4 basil leaves, fresh

1 tsp (5ml) olive oil

1 tsp (5ml) balsamic vinegar

freshly ground pepper

1. Cut tomato into 4 thick slices.

2. Arrange slices on a salad plate. Top tomato slices with mozzarella.

3. Thinly slice basil; sprinkle over tomato and cheese.

4. Drizzle with oil and vinegar and a dash of freshly ground pepper.

Savory
Soups&
❖ Salads

7 Layer **Salad**

 servings

4

- **SERVING SIZE:**
  1/4 CUP (250ML)
- **COUNTS AS:**
  2 VEGETABLES
  1 FAT
  1/2 DAIRY

▶ *size according to plan*

good source of calcium

❊ Ingredients

1/2 head iceberg lettuce, chopped

1/2 cup (125ml / 60g) celery, chopped

1/4 cup (60ml / 24g) green onions, chopped

1/4 cup (60ml / 37g) green peppers, chopped

1/2 small (10oz / 280g) package frozen peas, thawed and drained

1/4 cup (60ml / 57g) lite mayonnaise

4 packets of artificial sweetener

4oz (112g) low-fat shredded cheddar cheese

1 In large salad bowl layer the lettuce, celery, onion, pepper and peas.

2 Spread mayo on top.

3 Sprinkle with artificial sweetener; then cheese.

4 Cover tightly and refrigerate at least 4 hours and up to 24 hours.

Citrus **Salad**

servings

6

- **SERVING SIZE:**
  1-1/2 CUPS (375ML)
- **COUNTS AS:**
  1 VEGETABLE
  1 FRUIT
  1 FAT

▶ *size according to plan*

❊ Ingredients

1/4 cup (60ml) red wine vinegar

1 tsp (5ml) Dijon mustard

1 tsp (5ml) fennel seeds, crushed, toasted

1/3 cup (85ml) olive oil

freshly ground pepper

1 ruby red grapefruit, segmented

1 blood orange, segmented

1/2 head radicchio, torn into bite-size pieces

6 cups (1.5L / 180g) baby spinach leaves

3 leaves of endive, shredded

1 Combine vinegar, mustard and fennel seeds in a medium bowl.

2 Gradually whisk in oil.

3 Season with pepper.

4 Add in grapefruit segments and orange segments into the dressing and toss. Let stand about 15 minutes.

5 Toss radicchio, spinach and endive in a bowl.

6 Add fruit and dressing. Toss before serving.

Savory
Soups&
❖ Salads

Dilled Pasta Salad

1 *serving*

- SERVING SIZE: 1 RECIPE
- COUNTS AS:
  - 1 STARCH
  - 1 FAT
  - 2 VEGETABLES

▶ *size according to plan*

☀ Ingredients

1/2 Tbsp (7.5ml) snipped fresh dill or 1/4 tsp (1ml) dried dill

1/4 tsp (1ml) lite salt

1/4 tsp (1ml) dry mustard

freshly ground pepper

1 Tbsp (15ml) lite mayonnaise

1/3 cup (85ml / 57g) cooked rotini pasta

1/4 cucumber, diced

1/4 medium carrot, shredded

2 green onions, diced

1. Mix together all ingredients in a large bowl.
2. Cover and refrigerate at least 2 hours before serving.

"The L A Lite Cookbook recipes are so simple to make and so good to eat."

- Lynn K.

Cucumber & Tomato Salad

1 *serving*

- SERVING SIZE: 1 RECIPE
- COUNTS AS:
  - 3 VEGETABLES
  - 1/2 DAIRY

▶ *size according to plan*

☀ Ingredients

1/4 medium cucumber

5 green onions, thinly sliced

1 tomato, chopped

1/4 tsp (1ml) lite salt

1/2 Tbsp (7.5ml) snipped parsley

1/8 tsp (.5ml) ground cumin

freshly ground pepper

1 garlic clove, finely chopped

1/2 cup (125ml) nonfat plain yogurt

1. Cut cucumbers in half, lengthwise. Scoop seeds from cucumber with a spoon, then chop into bite-size pieces.
2. Mix cucumber, green onion and salt. Let stand 10 minutes.
3. Add tomatoes, parsley, cumin, pepper and garlic to cucumbers.
4. Cover and refrigerate 1 hour.
5. Just before serving, drain vegetables thoroughly in a colander or sieve. Add yogurt; mix well to combine.

Savory
Soups&
❖Salads

Oriental Chicken Salad

1 *serving*

■ SERVING SIZE: 1 RECIPE
■ COUNTS AS:
  1 PROTEIN
  3 VEGETABLES
  1 FRUIT

▶ *size according to plan*

✳ Ingredients

1 cup (250ml / 56g) lettuce, shredded

5 or 7oz (140 or 196g) chicken, cooked and cut into bite-size pieces

1/2 medium carrot, shredded

1/2 cup (125ml / 125g) mandarin oranges, drained

5 green onion with tops, sliced

1 Tbsp (15ml) toasted sesame seeds

Ginger Dressing:
1/4 cup (60ml) white wine vinegar
1/2 to 1 packet artificial sweetener
2 tsp (10ml) low-sodium soy sauce
1/4 tsp (1ml) lite salt
freshly ground pepper
1/4 tsp (1ml) ground ginger

1 Prepare dressing first. Combine vinegar, artificial sweetener, soy sauce, salt, pepper and ginger. Shake all ingredients in covered container or jar. Refrigerate.

2 Toss together lettuce, chicken, carrot, green onion and ginger dressing.

3 Place mixture on plate and top with oranges. Sprinkle with sesame seeds.

4 May also be served over brown rice for additional starch serving.

Tomato Pasta Salad

1 *serving*

■ SERVING SIZE: 1 RECIPE
■ COUNTS AS:
  1 STARCH
  1 VEGETABLE

▶ *size according to plan*

✳ Ingredients

1 small tomato, chopped

1 garlic clove, finely chopped

1 Tbsp (15ml) snipped parsley

2 Tbsp (30ml) fat-free Italian dressing

1/4 tsp (1ml) dried basil leaves

1/3 cup (85ml / 57g) cooked pasta shells

1 Mix tomato, garlic, parsley, Italian dressing and basil.

2 Toss pasta shells with tomato mixture.

3 Cover and refrigerate at least 2 hours.

Savory Soups & Salads

Cantaloupe with Chicken Salad

1 serving

- **SERVING SIZE: 1 RECIPE**
- **COUNTS AS:**
  - 1 PROTEIN
  - 1 VEGETABLE
  - 2 FRUIT
  - 1 FAT

▶ *size according to plan*

☀ Ingredients

5 or 7oz (140 or 196g) cooked chicken breast, cubed

1/4 cup (60ml / 36g) blueberries

10 grapes

1 celery stalk, sliced

1/8 cantaloupe, cubed

Dressing

1 Tbsp (15ml) low-fat mayonnaise

1 Tbsp (15ml) fat-free sour cream

1/4 tsp (1ml) grated lemon peel

1 packet of sugar substitute

1. In a medium bowl, combine chicken, blueberries, celery, and grapes.
2. In a small bowl, mix dressing ingredients whisking vigorously.
3. Pour dressing over chicken mixture and toss to coat.
4. Arrange cantaloupe on a serving plate or shallow bowl; top with chicken salad.

Spinach Tossed Salad

1 serving

- **SERVING SIZE: 1 RECIPE**
- **COUNTS AS:**
  - 1 STARCH
  - 3 VEGETABLES

▶ *size according to plan*

good source of fiber

☀ Ingredients

1 cup (250ml / 56g) spinach leaves

1/2 cup (125ml / 35g) mushrooms, sliced

1 cup (250ml / 45g) bean sprouts

3 melba toast, crumbled

2 green onions, thinly sliced

1. Tear spinach into small pieces. Toss all ingredients together.
2. Serve with freshly ground pepper and fat-free dressing of choice.

Savory
Soups&
� Salads

Coleslaw

1 *serving*

SERVING SIZE: 1 RECIPE
COUNTS AS:
2 VEGETABLES
1 FAT
1/2 DAIRY

size according to plan

☀ Ingredients

4oz (125ml) nonfat plain yogurt

1 Tbsp (15ml) lite mayonnaise

1/2 packet artificial sweetener

1/4 tsp (1ml) dry mustard

1/4 tsp (1ml) lite salt

freshly ground pepper

1 cup (250ml / 70g) cabbage, shredded

1/2 medium carrot, finely shredded

dash of paprika or dried dill

1 Mix yogurt, mayonnaise, artificial sweetener, dry mustard, salt and pepper.

2 Toss with cabbage and carrot.

3 Sprinkle with paprika or dried dill.

4 Cover and refrigerate for 1-2 hours.

Grilled Chicken Caesar **Salad**

4 *servings*

SERVING SIZE: 1/4 OF RECIPE
COUNTS AS:
1 PROTEIN
2 VEGETABLES
1 FAT

size according to plan

☀ Ingredients

Chicken

6 or 8oz (168 or 224g) chicken breasts, boneless and skinless

2 Tbsp (30ml) citrus rub (see recipe on page 224)

1 Tbsp (15ml) olive oil

Dressing

2 Tbsp (30ml) fresh lemon juice

1/2 tsp (2.5ml) freshly ground pepper

1/4 cup (60ml) lite mayonnaise

1 Tbsp (15ml) lemon seasoning (see recipe on page 218)

Salad

8 cups (2L / 240g) romaine lettuce, torn

1/4 cup (60ml) lite parmesan cheese, grated

1/2 cup (125ml) unseasoned fat-free croutons

1 Preheat grill or broiler to medium high.

2 Brush chicken on both sides with olive oil.

3 Season chicken with citrus rub, until well coated.

4 Grill for 5 minutes then turn and grill for 5 additional minutes or until juices run clear when pierced with a fork.

5 Remove from grill; cool and cut into strips; set aside.

6 For dressing, combine the lemon juice, mayonnaise, pepper and lemon seasoning; prepare while chicken is cooking.

7 For the salad, place 2 cups (500ml) romaine on each of four salad plates. Divide chicken strips, evenly, among romaine; top with cheese, croutons and 2 Tbsp (30ml) of dressing.

❖ Shrimp or steak may be substituted for the chicken in this recipe.

Savory
Soups**&**
❖Salads

Grilled Asparagus, Tomato & Carrot Salad

family fare

6 *servings*

- **SERVING SIZE: 1 CUP**
- **COUNTS AS:**
  3 VEGETABLES
  1 FAT

▶ *size according to plan*

✺ Ingredients

2 bunches asparagus

5 green onions

3 carrots, chopped into matchstick pieces

12 cherry tomatoes, halved

Marinade

1/4 cup (60ml) olive oil

1/4 cup (60ml) balsamic vinegar

freshly ground pepper

Vinaigrette

1/4 cup (60ml) olive oil

1/4 cup (60ml) vinegar

3 Tbsp (45ml) fat-free sour cream

1 Tbsp (15ml) chopped garlic

2 Tbsp (30ml) finely chopped savory

1/2 tsp (2.5ml) cumin

dash of low-sodium Worcestershire sauce

1 tsp (5ml) lime juice

freshly ground pepper

1 Snap the bottom section off asparagus stalks at their natural break point.

2 Chop the remaining asparagus into thirds.

3 Remove bottoms from green onions and place in a large mixing bowl with the asparagus pieces.

4 Add the marinade ingredients to mixing bowl and toss well.

5 Grill vegetable mixture lightly over medium high heat for 2-3 minutes, so they still have crunch.

6 Remove from the grill to cool and chop green onions into small pieces.

7 In a separate salad bowl, mix all ingredients of vinaigrette and whisk vigorously.

8 Add grilled asparagus and green onions.

9 Add carrot pieces and cherry tomatoes.

10 Mix gently by hand, tossing to coat, cover and refrigerate until serving.

Shrimp Salad

1 *serving*

- **SERVING SIZE: 1 RECIPE**
- **COUNTS AS:**
  1 PROTEIN
  1 VEGETABLE
  1 FAT

▶ *size according to plan*

✺ Ingredients

4 or 6oz (112 or 168g) cooked shrimp

1 Tbsp (15ml) lite mayonnaise

1/2 Tbsp (7.5ml) lemon juice

dash of lite salt

freshly ground pepper

1 celery stalk, finely sliced

1/2 tsp (2.5ml) dried onion flakes

1 Combine all ingredients; mix well.

2 Cover and refrigerate at least 1 hour.

3 Serve chilled.

Savory
Soups &
✿ Salads

Oriental Bean Salad

serving

good source of fiber

SERVING SIZE: 1 RECIPE
COUNTS AS:
3 VEGETABLES

▶ *size according to plan*

☀ Ingredients
1 Tbsp (15ml) lime or lemon juice

1/2 Tbsp (7.5ml) light soy sauce

1/2 Tbsp (7.5ml) parsley

1/2 packet artificial sweetener

dash of garlic powder

dash of crushed red pepper

1/2 cup (125ml / 62g) cooked wax beans

1/2 cup (125ml / 62g) cooked green beans

1/2 cup (125ml / 42g) fresh bean sprouts

1/4 medium green pepper, cut into 1/2-inch (1.3cm) pieces

1 tsp (5ml) toasted sesame seeds

1. In a mixing bowl, stir together lime or lemon juice, soy sauce, parsley, artificial sweetener, garlic powder and crushed red pepper.

2. Add wax and green beans, bean sprouts and green pepper; toss to coat. Cover and refrigerate 1 hour.

3. Before serving, sprinkle with toasted sesame seeds.

Chicken Salad

serving

SERVING SIZE: 1 RECIPE
COUNTS AS:
1 PROTEIN
1 VEGETABLE
1 FAT

▶ *size according to plan*

☀ Ingredients
5 or 7oz (140 or 196g) chicken, cooked and cut into bite-size pieces

1 Tbsp (15ml) lite mayonnaise

1 tsp (5ml) mustard

1 celery stalk, thinly sliced

freshly ground pepper

1/2 tsp (2.5ml) parsley

1/2 tsp (2.5ml) dried minced onion (optional)

1. Combine all ingredients. Cover and refrigerate, at least 1 hour.

2. Serve chilled.

Savory
Soups&
❖Salads

Tuna Pasta Salad

1 *serving*

- **SERVING SIZE: 1 RECIPE**
- **COUNTS AS:**
  - 1 PROTEIN
  - 1 STARCH
  - 2 VEGETABLES

▶ *size according to plan*

☼ Ingredients

4-6oz (112g / 168g) can of tuna, drained (choose low-sodium if available)

1 tomato, chopped

1/2 celery stalk, chopped

1 Tbsp (15ml) white onion, chopped

1/4 medium carrot, diced

1 garlic clove, crushed

1/4 tsp (1ml) dried onion flakes

1 Tbsp (15ml) snipped parsley

1/4 tsp (1ml) lite salt

1/4 tsp (1ml) dried basil leaves

1/8 tsp (.5ml) dried oregano leaves

freshly ground pepper

2 Tbsp (30ml) fat-free Italian dressing

1/3 cup (85ml / 57g) cooked pasta bows

1 Mix all ingredients, except pasta bows, in a large bowl.

2 Cover and refrigerate at least 1-2 hours.

3 Toss pasta with tuna mixture just before serving.

> "I love leftovers, so I double up the recipe."
>
> *- Kirsten D.*

Strawberry Spinach Salad

4 *servings*

- **SERVING SIZE: 1/4 OF RECIPE**
- **COUNTS AS:**
  - 1 VEGETABLE
  - 1 FRUIT
  - 1 FAT

▶ *size according to plan*

good source of fiber

☼ Ingredients

8oz (224g) spinach leaves

1 cup (250ml / 144g) fresh strawberries, sliced

1 kiwi, sliced

1 Tbsp (15ml) slivered almonds

Dressing

2 Tbsp (30ml) sugar-free raspberry preserves

1 Tbsp (15ml) olive oil

1 Tbsp (15ml) rice vinegar

1 Place salad ingredients in a large bowl.

2 For dressing, combine remaining ingredients in a small bowl; whisk vigorously.

3 Toss dressing with salad.

Savory Soups & Salads

Fresh Vegetable Salad

6 *servings*

- SERVING SIZE: 1 CUP (250ML)
- COUNTS AS:
  2 VEGETABLES

▶ *size according to plan*

✳ Ingredients

1 red bell pepper, sliced

1 yellow pepper, sliced

1 green pepper, sliced

1 medium red onion, thinly sliced

1 head of broccoli, cut into bite-size pieces

1 head of cauliflower, cut into bite-size pieces

1 small zucchini, thinly sliced

1 medium carrot, shredded

Dressing

2 Tbsp (30ml) red wine vinegar

2 Tbsp (30ml) fresh lemon juice

dash of white pepper

1/4 tsp (1ml) dry mustard

1 Tbsp (15ml) olive oil

fresh herbs, such as tarragon, basil, chives, dill, oregano, basil or mint (optional)

1. Combine all vegetable ingredients in a large salad bowl.

2. For dressing, whisk together vinegar, lemon juice, pepper and dry mustard.

3. Slowly stream olive oil into bowl, whisking continuously, to emulsify the dressing.

4. Stir in the herbs just before adding to the salad (optional).

> "I still use this cookbook weekly even after completing and exceeding my goal. Thanks L A Weight Loss!"
>
> *- Michele G.*

Sweet & Sour Dressing

6 *servings*

- SERVING SIZE: 1 TBSP (15ml)
- COUNTS AS:
  1 CONDIMENT

▶ *size according to plan*

✳ Ingredients

1 Tbsp (15ml) lemon juice

1 Tbsp (15ml) apple cider vinegar

1/3 cup (85ml) water

1 garlic clove, minced

1/4 tsp (1ml) lite salt

freshly ground pepper

1/2 packet artificial sweetener

1. Combine all ingredients in a jar and shake to mix.

2. Store in the refrigerator for up to 1 week.

Savory Soups & Salads

Lite Vinaigrette

8 *servings*

- **SERVING SIZE: 1 TBSP (15ml)**
- **COUNTS AS:**
  - 1 CONDIMENT

▸ *size according to plan*

☀ Ingredients

1 packet artificial sweetener

1/4 tsp (1ml) lite salt

2 garlic cloves, minced

1/8 tsp (.5ml) dry mustard

freshly ground pepper

1/4 cup (60ml) water

3 Tbsp (45ml) wine vinegar or lemon juice

1. In a screw-top jar, combine artificial sweetener, salt, garlic, dry mustard and pepper.

2. Add water and vinegar.

3. Cover tightly with lid and shake until well blended. Let stand 3-4 minutes. Shake again.

4. Store in the refrigerator for up to 1 week.

Chicken Salad with Orange Vinaigrette

1 *serving*

- **SERVING SIZE: 1 RECIPE**
- **COUNTS AS:**
  - 1 PROTEIN
  - 2 VEGETABLES
  - 1 FRUIT

▸ *size according to plan*

☀ Ingredients

3 Tbsp (45ml) fat-free red wine vinaigrette salad dressing

1 Tbsp (15ml) lemon pepper seasoning blend

6 or 8oz (168 or 224g) chicken breast, boneless and skinless

1 cup (250ml / 30g) romaine lettuce, torn

1/2 cup (125ml / 112g) mandarin oranges

1 cup (250ml / 70g) fresh mushroom slices

1 Tbsp (15ml) chopped onion

1. Mix together dressing and lemon pepper seasoning blend, set aside.

2. Brush chicken with 1 Tbsp (15ml) of dressing mixture.

3. Grill chicken until done.

4. Cool slightly and then cut chicken into strips.

5. Place romaine lettuce on a large dinner plate, top with mandarin oranges, mushrooms, onion and chicken. Drizzle dressing over the salad.

Savory
Soups&
❖ Salads

Poppy Seed Vinaigrette

16 *servings*

- SERVING SIZE: 1 TBSP (15ml)
- COUNTS AS:
  1 CONDIMENT

size according to plan

☀ Ingredients

1/2 cup (125ml) cold water

1/2 cup (125ml) cider vinegar

1 tsp (5ml) lemon juice

1/2 tsp (2.5ml) lite salt

1/2 tsp (2.5ml) freshly ground pepper

2 Tbsp (30ml) poppy seeds

1 packet artificial sweetener

1. Combine all ingredients in a jar or container and shake well.

2. Store in the refrigerator for up to 1 week. Shake well before each use.

Yogurt-Dill Dressing

16 *servings*

- SERVING SIZE: 1 TBSP (15ml)
- COUNTS AS:
  1 CONDIMENT

size according to plan

☀ Ingredients

8oz (250ml) plain, nonfat yogurt

3 green onions, chopped fine

1 tsp (5ml) lemon juice

1/4 tsp (1ml) dry mustard

1/4 tsp (1ml) garlic powder

1/2 tsp (2.5ml) dried dill weed

1. Mix all ingredients in a bowl; whisk thoroughly.

2. Store in the refrigerator for up to 1 week. Mix well before each use.

Savory
Soups&
❖ Salads

Appetite
❖ Delights

Appetizers are a family favorite! Appetizers can be a great combination with any soup or salad for a light meal, or be a perfect choice for entertaining. We have lightened up some old favorites to use for any eating occasion. We have also provided a number of dips that can be a great compliment to any vegetable snack. Enjoy!

◀ Tortilla Roll-Up recipe can be found on page 60

Let's get the party started!

Appetizers are the main ingredients to any get together or special occasion. Keep in mind you don't want to fill up before the main course, so appetizers should be simple, tasty…and of course, light. Here are some tips to remember when preparing and serving appetizers for your own gathering, or bringing a special dish to a special occasion.

- Be sure not to offer excessive servings of appetizers. Appetizers are meant to tease the pallet, not to replace a full course meal.

- Using colorful garnish such as a sprig of parsley or a lemon and lime wedge give that extra added festive touch on any tray of appetizers.

- Try serving a medley of appetizers. Be sure that there is a little something for everyone – it doesn't need to be extravagant, perhaps roasted peppers for the veggie lovers and deviled eggs for those who are looking for a heartier snack.

- When preparing a veggie platter, try and incorporate some unusual and interesting vegetables such as fresh brussels sprouts and sugar snap peas. The platter will look more interesting and appealing.

- Spice up the dip by placing it in a brightly colored bowl. Get creative by hollowing out bread loaves, heads of cabbage or winter squash.

- Guests should be able to eat appetizers without utensils. Most partygoers are busy mingling and would rather not think about cutting their food.

- Keep the appetizer simple. Some guests may avoid food that looks messy to prevent the embarrassment of getting it all over their hands and faces.

♣ TIP!

If an appetizer needs to be cooled before serving, use shallow containers and leave air space around the containers to promote rapid cooling of the food.

♣ TIP!

When deciding how many appetizers to serve, estimate each guest will eat 5-6 pieces. If it's closer to mealtime, then assume they will eat 10-12 pieces. Younger guests tend to eat more and the older company will usually have less of an appetite.

Appetite
♣ Delight

Deviled Eggs

3 servings

SERVING SIZE: 2 OR 3 EGGS
COUNTS AS:
1 PROTEIN
1 FAT

▸ *size according to plan*

☀ Ingredients

6 eggs

2 Tbsp (30ml) lite mayonnaise

dash onion powder

1 tsp (5ml) Dijon mustard

1/2 tsp (2.5ml) paprika

1 Prepare hard cooked eggs.

2 Drain eggs and allow to cool. Cut eggs in half, lengthwise.

3 Remove egg yolks and mash them with a fork in a small mixing bowl.

4 Add mayonnaise, onion powder and dry mustard to egg yolks.

5 Spoon mixture into egg whites. Sprinkle with paprika. Chill before serving.

Creamed Crab & Veggie Dip

2 servings

SERVING SIZE:
1/2 OF RECIPE
COUNTS AS:
1 PROTEIN
1/2 DAIRY
2 VEGETABLES
1 FAT

▸ *size according to plan*

good source of calcium

☀ Ingredients

2oz (56g) part-skim ricotta cheese

4oz (125ml) skim milk

1 cup (125ml / 30g) fresh raw spinach

2 cups (500ml / 168g) fresh chopped artichoke hearts

3 green onions, chopped

1/4 red pepper, chopped

1/4 tsp (1ml) garlic powder

2 garlic cloves, minced

1oz (28g) shredded reduced-fat cheese (recommend Monterey Jack or Mozzarella)

1 Tbsp (15ml) low-fat mayonnaise

4 or 6oz (112g) fresh crabmeat

1/4 tsp (1ml) hot sauce

nonfat cooking spray

1 Spray casserole dish with nonfat cooking spray.

2 In small casserole dish, combine ricotta, mayonnaise and skim milk. Stir well and set aside.

3 Spray medium skillet with nonfat cooking spray. Add artichokes, onion, pepper, garlic powder and garlic. Sauté 2 minutes. Remove from heat.

4 Add spinach, hot sauce, vegetable mixture and crabmeat to cheese mixture.

5 Stir in 3/4 oz (21g) shredded cheese. Place in 350°F (180°C) preheated oven.

6 Bake 15 minutes, stir mixture well and then top with remaining 1/4oz (7g) of cheese.

7 Bake 10-15 minutes, or until all cheese is melted and casserole is bubbly.

8 Serve over roasted veggies or as a dip for crackers and fresh veggies.

Appetite
❖ Delights

Tortilla Roll-Up Appetizer

10 *servings*

- SERVING SIZE: 4 PIECES
- COUNTS AS:
  - 1 VEGETABLE
  - 1 STARCH
  - 1 CONDIMENT

▶ *size according to plan*

☀ Ingredients

2oz (56g) fat-free cream cheese, softened

2oz (56g) lite cream cheese, softened

5 green onions, sliced

1/4 cup (60ml) salsa

2oz (56g) lite or reduced-fat cheddar cheese, shredded

5- 8 inch (20cm) whole wheat or spinach tortillas

1/4 cup (60ml) chopped black olives

1/2 cup (125ml / 36g) iceberg lettuce, shredded

1. In a medium bowl, with a hand-mixer, blend cream cheeses, until soft.

2. Add onion, salsa and cheese. Stir until well combined.

3. Divide cream cheese mixture among tortillas. Spread a thin layer on each.

4. Sprinkle each tortilla with black olives and lettuce.

5. Roll each tortilla and refrigerate about 4-6 hours before slicing.

6. Just before serving, slice each tortilla roll into 1-inch (2.5cm) pieces.

5 Layer Dip

1 *servings*

- SERVING SIZE: 1 RECIPE
- COUNTS AS:
  - 1/2 PROTEIN
  - 1 VEGETABLE
  - 1 FAT
  - 1/2 DAIRY

▶ *size according to plan*

good source of fiber

☀ Ingredients

2 green onions, chopped

1 tsp (5ml) oil

1/2 cup (125ml / 88g) cooked kidney beans

1/2 tomato, chopped

1oz (28g) reduced-fat cheddar cheese

2 Tbsp (30ml) salsa

1 Tbsp (15ml) fat-free sour cream

1. In medium bowl, combine 1 chopped green onion, oil and cooked beans.

2. With a fork, mash beans to form a paste.

3. Place bean paste in bottom of small bowl.

4. Top with chopped tomato.

5. Top tomato with cheese, and then follow with salsa.

6. Spread sour cream over cheese layer.

7. Sprinkle with remaining green onion.

Appetite
❖ Delight

Eggplant Caponata

18 *servings*

☀ Ingredients

1 Tbsp (15ml) olive oil

1 medium eggplant, peeled and diced

2 garlic cloves

1/2 cup (125ml / 80g) red onion, chopped

1/2 cup (125ml / 74g) green bell pepper, chopped

1/4 cup (60ml) water

1/4 cup (60ml / 15g) fresh parsley, chopped

3-4 Tbsp (45-60ml) black olives, pitted and chopped

2 Roma tomatoes, seeded and chopped

2 Tbsp (30ml) red wine vinegar

1/4 tsp (1ml) lite salt

1/8 tsp (.5ml) freshly ground pepper

1. Preheat oven to 350°F (180°C).

2. In a baking dish, combine olive oil, eggplant, garlic, onion and green pepper. Cover and bake in oven for 15 minutes.

3. Remove from oven; add water, parsley, black olives, tomatoes, vinegar, salt and pepper to baking dish. Stir to combine.

4. Return to oven and continue to bake 30 minutes, or until eggplant is soft.

5. Remove from oven and transfer to a bowl; cover and refrigerate at least 8 hours or overnight before serving.

Guacamole

4 *servings*

☀ Ingredients

2 avocados, diced

1/2 small onion, diced

1-2 garlic cloves, minced

1 Roma tomato, seeded and diced

juice of 1 lime

1/2 tsp (2.5ml) lite salt

1 jalapeño, diced (optional)

1. In a large bowl, lightly mash avocado with a fork.

2. Next add remaining ingredients; toss to combine.

3. Chill 30 minutes before servings.

Appetite
❖ Delights

Roasted Garlic Spread

6 *servings*

- ▦ SERVING SIZE: 2-3 CLOVES
- ▦ COUNTS AS:
  - 1 CONDIMENT

▶ *size according to plan*

☀ Ingredients

1 head of garlic

1 tsp (5ml) olive oil

1. Preheat oven to 450°F (230°C).
2. Trim 1/4-inch of top off the head of garlic. Place in the middle of a square piece of aluminum foil.
3. Drizzle with olive oil. Tightly form foil over the garlic bulb.
4. Roast in oven for approximately 1 hour.
5. Allow to cool at least 15 minutes before serving.
6. To use, squeeze cloves from bulb by applying pressure to the bottom, as if a tube of toothpaste.
7. With its creamy texture and sweet aroma, roasted garlic is great to use in place of butter on bread or bruschetta, as well as in dishes, such as pastas, vegetables, beef or poultry.

Balsamic Grilled Bruschetta

12 *servings*

- ▦ SERVING SIZE: 1 SLICE
- ▦ COUNTS AS:
  - 1 VEGETABLE
  - 1 STARCH

▶ *size according to plan*

☀ Ingredients

10 Roma tomatoes, seeded and diced

2-3 Tbsp (30-45ml) fresh basil, chopped

2-3 garlic cloves, minced

2 Tbsp (30ml) parmesan cheese, shredded

1 Tbsp (15ml) olive oil

1 Tbsp (15ml) balsamic vinegar

1/4 tsp (1ml) lite salt

1/8 tsp (.5ml) freshly ground pepper

1 loaf French bread, cut into 12 slices

1. In a bowl, toss together tomatoes, basil, garlic, cheese, oil, vinegar, and salt and pepper.
2. Cover and refrigerate for 1-2 hours, to allow flavors to meld.
3. Meanwhile, grill bread until lightly browned.
4. Divide tomato mixture evenly among sliced bread before serving. If desired, garnish with extra basil and an extra drizzle of balsamic vinegar.

Appetite
❖ Deligh

Tzatziki

8 *servings*

- **SERVING SIZE: 1/2 CUP (125ML)**
- **COUNTS AS:**
  1/2 DAIRY

▶ *size according to plan*

☀ Ingredients

2 cups (500ml) plain nonfat
  yogurt

2 medium cucumbers, peeled
  and shredded

2-3 garlic cloves, minced

1-2 Tbsp (15-30ml) lemon juice

1 Tbsp (15ml) olive oil

2 Tbsp (30ml) fresh mint,
  chopped

1/2 tsp (2.5ml) lite salt

1/4 tsp (1ml) freshly ground
  pepper

1. In a colander, squeeze any excess liquid out from
   cucumber; discard liquid.

2. In a bowl, combine all ingredients. Mix well.

3. Refrigerate, allowing flavors to combine, at least 2
   hours, before serving.

4. Great with fresh vegetables or pitas as a dip, or as a
   dressing for lamb or chicken.

Romaine Roll-up

1 *serving*

- **SERVING SIZE: 1 LETTUCE ROLL**
- **COUNTS AS:**
  1 PROTEIN
  1 VEGETABLE
  1 FAT

▶ *size according to plan*

☀ Ingredients

1 leaf romaine lettuce

filling of your choice
  - tuna
  - ground beef
  - fresh sliced chicken or turkey

1 Tbsp (15ml) lite mayonnaise
  (optional)

1. Place lettuce sideways on a plate, gently press down to
   flatten lettuce. Spread with mayonnaise.

2. Place filling in center of lettuce leaf and roll up.

3. Use toothpick to hold in place.

4. Cut in half and serve.

Appetite
❖ Delights

Veggies with Tarragon Dip

7 *servings*

- **SERVING SIZE:**
  1 CUP (250ML) WITH 1 TBSP DIP
- **COUNTS AS:**
  2 VEGETABLES
  1 FAT

▶ *size according to plan*

☀ Ingredients

1 pound (448g) asparagus, trimmed

1 pound (448g) fresh green beans, trimmed

1/2 cup (125ml) lite mayonnaise

zest and juice of 1 lemon

1 small green onion, finely chopped

2 Tbsp (30ml) chopped fresh tarragon

2 Tbsp (30ml) chopped parsley leaves

1 Cook asparagus spears and green beans in 1-inch of boiling water, covered, for 3 or 4 minutes.

2 Drain and cool the vegetables and arrange them on a serving plate.

3 Combine remaining ingredients in a small bowl.

4 Place dip on side of serving plate.

Roasted Peppers

8 *servings*

- **SERVING SIZE: 1/2 PEPPER**
- **COUNTS AS:**
  1 VEGETABLE
  [IF USING OLIVE OIL TO STORE, COUNTS AS 1 VEGETABLE, 1 FAT]

▶ *size according to plan*

☀ Ingredients

4 large red or yellow bell peppers, halved

olive oil (optional)

Balsamic vinegar (optional)

crushed garlic (optional)

1 Preheat oven to 500°F (260°C).

2 Place clean peppers onto a baking sheet. Roast until skin begins to blister and turn black, approximately 30-45 minutes.

3 Remove peppers from oven and place in a paper or plastic bag for about 15-20 minutes, this will allow the skin to separate from the flesh using steam.

4 Once cool enough to touch, gently peel the skin from the flesh.

5 Store peppers in an air-tight container in the refrigerator; sprinkle with olive oil, balsamic vinegar and crushed garlic, if desired.

Appetite
♣ Delight

Spinach & Artichoke Dip

family fare

9 servings

SERVING SIZE:
1/3 CUP (85ML)
COUNTS AS:
1 VEGETABLE
1 FAT

size according to plan

✸ Ingredients

1 cup (250ml /156g) frozen spinach, drained and thawed

1 cup (240ml / 180g) cooked sliced artichoke hearts

1/4 cup (60ml /4g) chopped white onions

1 tsp (5ml) fat-free Italian salad dressing

1/2 tsp (2.5ml) lite salt

freshly ground pepper

1 cup (250ml) lite sour cream

2 Tbsp (30ml) dried onion

1 tsp (5ml) garlic powder

1 Tbsp (15ml) capers

3 Tbsp (45ml) grated parmesan cheese

1 In large mixing bowl combine spinach, artichokes, onion and salad dressing. Sprinkle with salt and pepper.

2 Fold in sour cream and blend well. Add dried onion, garlic and capers. Mix in parmesan cheese. Chill for at least 1 hour.

Creamy Fruit Dip

2 servings

SERVING SIZE:
1/2 CUP (125ML)
COUNTS AS:
1/2 DAIRY

size according to plan

✸ Ingredients

8oz (250ml) lite fruited yogurt, any flavor (such as strawberry or raspberry)

2 Tbsp (30ml) fat-free whipped topping

1 Combine ingredients in a medium bowl and blend until smooth.

2 Cut up your fruit in bite sizes and dip.

"So many recipes to choose from, choose something new every day."

- Sharon T.

Appetite
❖ Delights

In House Steak House

Are you a meat and potatoes lover? Then you'll love our variety-packed In House Steak House recipes. From easy to elaborate, our savory beef dishes are hardy and satisfying. Whether you prefer to cozy up by the fire with a delicious cup of beef stew, or throw some marinated filets on the grill, we've got the recipes that will add that extra bit of zest to each mouthwatering bite. Plus you'll learn more ways to cook, prepare and store beef than you ever thought possible.

Stuffed Pepper recipe can be found on page 74

In House Steak House

- Beef Kabobs
- Beef Roast
- Beef Dijon
- Beef Teriyaki
- London Broil
- Italian-Style Beef
- Beef & Broccoli
- Sesame Beef
- Meatloaf
- Stuffed Pepper
- Stuffed Cabbage
- Salisbury Steak
- Steak Fajitas
- Herb-Crusted Steak
- Beef Burgundy
- Steak & Onions
- Open-Faced Beef Sandwich
- Italian-Style Burger
- Meatball Sandwich
- Mushroom & Swiss Burger
- Beef Tenderloin with
  Mushroom Wine Sauce
- Open-Face Burger with
  Mustard Sauce
- Beef Stroganoff
- Steak Burger
- Savory Beef Stew
- Cheesy Beef & Broccoli
- Hot Beef Sandwich
- Beef and Mushroom Kabobs
- Hamburger
- Philly Cheesesteak
- BBQ Cheddar Burger

Cuts of Beef

Loin Cuts

- Porterhouse steak
- T-bone steak
- Strip steak
- Sirloin roast
- Tenderloin roast
- Tenderloin steak
- Sirloin steak

Round Cuts (Leg)

- Top round steak
- Eye round steak
- Round cube steak
- Top round roast
- Eye round roast

Rib Cuts

- Boneless rib roast
- Boneless rib eye steak

Chuck/Shoulder Cuts

- Brisket
- Chuck eye steak
- Chuck roast
- Chuck steak
- Shoulder roast
- Shoulder steak
- Stew beef chunks

Flank

- Flank steak

Plate

- Short ribs
- Skirt steak

Basic cooking methods

- **Braising** — Cooking with a moist heat, which is great for less tender cuts of beef. Meat may be browned first to seal in juices and flavor, a small amount of liquid such as broth is then added to pan. Beef is then cooked at a low heat for a lengthy period of time. This works well for round, flank, plate and chuck cuts.

- **Oven Roasting** — Dry heat method. Best used for larger quantities of meat such as a loin or round roast. Meat cooked in the oven in an uncovered pan.

- **Grilling** — Preparing food on a grill over hot coals or other direct heat source. This method is great for cooking loin cuts and steaks.

- **Stir-Frying** — Quickly cooking food in a large pan or wok over very high heat. Food needs to be constantly stirred to prevent sticking. Good cooking method for sirloin steak strips.

- **Pan Searing** — Uses high heat to create a crust and seal in meat juices. Cooking is usually finished in the oven. Use this for loin, rib and round cuts.

TIP!

Beef is a great source of zinc, which helps keep your immune system working well.

Know what's best to buy

Sometimes it gets confusing to understand the labels of meat in the supermarket. Grades on the packages are determined mostly by marbling and age of the animal. There are three USDA grades that you should keep in mind when buying beef:

- **Prime** — Usually found in restaurants or specialty meat stores. Even though it holds one of the highest grades of meat, it's often the most marbling of the three grades and the most flavorful steak you can find.

- **Choice** — It is the most common grade in the supermarket. It's your next best choice under prime cut for flavor because it has less marbling.

- **Select** — This grade has the least fat of the three grades. It's leaner and often more tender.

Look for "loin" or "round" in any grade of meat for the leanest cuts, such as "sirloin" or "top round steak." When you want the freshest, most flavorful steak in the supermarket, look for meat that is bright red and any marbling should be creamy white.

TIP!

Beef is packed with protein that is essential for your body's tissues, muscles and organs. So for your active lifestyle, remember beef is a good source to keep your body strong.

Food Safety

- Keep raw beef away from cooked and ready to eat foods.

- Use a separate cutting board for beef.

- Never defrost beef at room temperature. Thaw overnight in the refrigerator; under cold running water; or in the microwave.

- Cook ground beef to an internal temperature of 160°F (70°C).

- Cook whole cuts of beef such as roasts and steaks to an internal temperature of 145°F (60°C) (medium) to 160°F (70°C) (well done).

Beef Roasting

- Preheat oven to 450°F (230°C).

- Season meat and place on roasting rack in roasting pan.

- Roast for 15 minutes at 450° (230°C).

- Reduce heat to 350°F (180°C).and cook:
  - Tenderloin: 8-11 minutes per pound (.5kg).
  - Sirloin, top rounds, rib roasts: 20-25 minutes per pound (.5kg).

- Check internal temperature to be sure meat is at desired doneness.

- Allow meat to rest 10-15 minutes before carving.

In House
❖ Steak
House

Beef Kabobs

1 *serving*

- **SERVING SIZE: 2-3 KABOBS**
- **COUNTS AS:**
  - 1 PROTEIN
  - 2 VEGETABLES
  - 1 FRUIT

▶ *size according to plan*

☀ Ingredients

juice from 1 orange

1 Tbsp (30ml) brown sugar artificial sweetener

1/4 tsp (1ml) ground ginger

4 or 6oz (112 or 168g) sirloin steak, cut into 1 inch (2.5cm)

1/4 medium green pepper, cut into 1 inch (2.5cm) squares

1 cup (250ml /113g) zucchini or yellow squash, cut into 1-inch (2.5cm) pieces

1/4 medium red onion, cut into 1-inch (2.5cm) squares

1 Mix orange juice, brown sugar and ginger. Add beef and pepper; stir to coat meat. Cover and marinate for 1 hour in refrigerator. Drain reserve marinade.

2 On a skewer, alternate beef, pepper, zucchini or yellow squash and onion, leaving 1/4 inch (1/2cm) between pieces. Place kabobs on broiler pan. Brush with marinade.

3 Broil 4 inches from heat about 8 minutes, or until desired doneness, turning and brushing kabobs with marinade while cooking.

Beef Roast

4 *servings*

family fare

- **SERVING SIZE: 3 OR 5OZ COOKED (84 OR140G)**
- **COUNTS AS:**
  - 1 PROTEIN
  - 2 VEGETABLES

▶ *size according to plan*

☀ Ingredients

1 pound (448g) eye round roast

1/2 cup (125ml) red wine

2 cups (500ml / 140g) fresh mushrooms, finely chopped

1/2 tsp (2.5ml) dried dill weed

1/4 tsp (1ml) lite salt

1/4 cup (60ml / 24g) green onions, thinly sliced

4oz (125ml) plain nonfat yogurt

dash white pepper

1 cup (250ml) low-sodium beef broth

2 Tbsp (30ml) flour

1/2 cup (125ml) water

1 Trim any excess, visible fat from roast. Cut 2 pockets into sides of roast, making a 3-inch (8cm) deep cut. Place roast in large, zip-top plastic bag set in bowl or baking pan. Pour wine over roast. Close the bag. Marinate for 3-6 hours.

2 Combine mushrooms, water, dill weed and salt. Cook, uncovered, over medium heat until the liquid is evaporated. Stir in onion.

3 Remove roast from marinade. Place filling into pockets.

4 Bake in 325°F (160°C) oven for 1-1 1/2 hours, or until meat temperature of 150°F (65°C) .

5 For sauce, mix together yogurt, flour and pepper in a small saucepan. Stir in broth. Cook, until sauce thickened, over medium heat.

6 Slice roast between the 2 filled pockets. Place on dinner plate top with sauce.

In House
❖ Steak
House

Beef Dijon

1 *serving*

- SERVING SIZE: 1 RECIPE
- COUNTS AS:
  - 1 PROTEIN
  - 3 VEGETABLES
  - 1/2 DAIRY

▸ *size according to plan*

☀ Ingredients

4 or 6oz (112 or 168g) beef flank steak

1 tsp (5ml) freshly ground pepper

1 cup (250ml / 70g) fresh mushrooms, sliced

5 green onions, thinly sliced

1/4 cup (60ml) water

1/2 packet low-sodium beef bouillon

1/2 cup (125ml) nonfat plain yogurt

1 Tbsp (15ml) flour

2 tsp (10ml) Dijon mustard

1 cup (250ml / 134g) fresh asparagus spears

nonfat cooking spray

1. Rub pepper on both sides of the steak.

2. Broil steak, 3 inches (8cm) from heat, for 6 minutes. Turn steak over and brown for 6-8 minutes more. Keep warm, allowing to rest 5-10 minutes before slicing.

3. Coat skillet with nonfat cooking spray. Combine mushrooms, green onion, water and beef bouillon; cook until mushrooms are tender.

4. Mix together yogurt, flour, and mustard. Stir into mushroom mixture. Cool and stir until thickened.

5. Cook asparagus by microwaving or steaming.

6. Slice steak, thinly, against the grain. Arrange steak slices and asparagus on dinner plate. Serve with sauce.

Beef Teriyaki

1 *serving*

- SERVING SIZE: 1 RECIPE
- COUNTS AS:
  - 1 PROTEIN

▸ *size according to plan*

☀ Ingredients

4 or 6oz (112 or 168g) sirloin steak, cubed

2 Tbsp (30ml) low-sodium soy sauce

2 Tbsp (30ml) white wine

1/4 tsp (1ml) ground ginger

1 packet artificial sweetener

1/2 tsp (2.5ml) garlic powder

1. Place beef in a bowl.

2. Combine all other ingredients in a measuring cup or small bowl; pour over beef. Cover and refrigerate, at least 1 hour.

3. Remove beef from marinade; save marinade.

4. Brush meat with marinade and broil 4 inches (10cm) from heat, about 5 minutes. Turn meat over; brush with marinade and broil another 5-6 minutes longer.

5. Another option is to serve the beef over brown rice; this would count as an additional 1 starch serving.

In House
❖ Steak
House

London Broil

1 *serving*

- **SERVING SIZE: I RECIPE**
- **COUNTS AS:**
  1 PROTEIN
  1 VEGETABLE
  1 FAT

▶ *size according to plan*

☀ Ingredients

4 or 6oz (112 or 168g) flank steak

5 green onions, thinly sliced

1/4 tsp (1ml) lite salt

1 tsp (5ml) canola oil

1 tsp (5ml) lemon juice

1/8 tsp (.5ml) freshly ground pepper

1 garlic clove, crushed

nonfat cooking spray

1 Score flank steak with a knife, diagonally, in a diamond pattern, about 1/8-inch (.3cm) deep.

2 Coat skillet with nonfat cooking spray. Sauté onion; set aside.

3 Combine salt, oil, lemon juice, pepper and garlic. Brush half of the mixture on one side of beef.

4 Broil 2-3 inches (5-8cm) from heat until brown, about 5 minutes; turn meat over. Brush with remaining mixture and broil another 5-7 minutes.

5 Cut beef, against the grain, on a bias (an angle).

6 Serve with sautéed onions.

Italian-Style Beef

1 *serving*

- **SERVING SIZE: I RECIPE**
- **COUNTS AS:**
  1 PROTEIN
  3 VEGETABLES

▶ *size according to plan*

☀ Ingredients

4 or 6oz (112 or 168g) beef round steak

1/2 cup (125ml / 35g) fresh mushrooms, sliced

1/4 cup (60ml / 40g) white onion, diced

1/2 green pepper, chopped

1/2 celery stalk, chopped

1 garlic clove, minced

1/2 tomato, diced

1/4 tsp (1ml) dried basil, crushed

1/4 tsp (1ml) dried oregano, crushed

1/8 tsp (.5ml) cayenne pepper

1 Tbsp (30ml) grated parmesan cheese

nonfat cooking spray

1 Cut meat into 2-3 pieces. Coat skillet with nonfat cooking spray. Brown meat on all sides. Remove from skillet.

2 Combine mushrooms, onion, green pepper, celery and garlic in skillet; cook until vegetables are tender. Add tomatoes, basil, oregano and cayenne pepper.

3 Place meat back in skillet, top with vegetable mixture. Cover and simmer about 45-60 minutes, or until meat is tender, stirring occasionally.

4 Place meat on dinner plate, spoon vegetables over meat.

5 Top with grated parmesan cheese.

72

In House
✿ Steak
House

Beef & Broccoli

1 *serving*

■ **SERVING SIZE: 1 RECIPE**
■ **COUNTS AS:**
   1 PROTEIN
   2 VEGETABLES

▶ *size according to plan*

※ Ingredients

4 or 6oz (112 or 168g) beef
   round steak

1 Tbsp (15ml) low-sodium soy
   sauce

1 Tbsp (15ml) vinegar

1 Tbsp (15ml) brown sugar
   artificial sweetener

1 garlic clove, minced

1/8 tsp (.5ml) cayenne pepper

1/2 medium carrot, thinly sliced

1 cup (250ml / 70g) fresh broccoli
   florets

1 tsp (5ml) cornstarch

1 Tbsp (15ml) water

nonfat cooking spray

1 Partially freeze meat. Thinly slice meat across the grain
   into bite-size strips. Set aside.

2 In a bowl, stir together soy sauce, vinegar, artificial
   sweetener, garlic and cayenne pepper. Stir in meat.
   Cover and refrigerate for 10 minutes.

3 Coat skillet with nonfat cooking spray and heat over
   medium-high flame; add sauce mixture and meat.
   Cook until meat is no longer pink.

4 Add vegetables and cook until vegetables are tender.

5 Stir while cooking until thickened.

6 Stir together cornstarch and water; stir into skillet and
   cook until thickened.

7 May be served over brown rice for an additional starch
   exchange.

Sesame Beef

1 *serving*

■ **SERVING SIZE: 1 RECIPE**
■ **COUNTS AS:**
   1 PROTEIN
   1 FAT
   1 VEGETABLE

▶ *size according to plan*

※ Ingredients

4 or 6oz (112 or 168g) sirloin
   steak

1 packet artificial sweetener

1 tsp (5ml) canola oil

1 Tbsp (15ml) low-sodium soy
   sauce

1 Tbsp (15ml) chopped green
   pepper

1/8 tsp (.5ml) freshly ground pepper

2 green onions, finely chopped

1 garlic clove, crushed

1 Tbsp (15ml) sesame seeds

nonfat cooking spray

1 Cut beef into strips.

2 Mix artificial sweetener, oil, soy sauce, green pepper,
   freshly ground pepper, onions and garlic in non-metal
   bowl; stir in beef until well coated. Marinate for at least
   30 minutes.

3 Drain beef from marinade. Coat skillet with nonfat
   cooking spray and stir in sesame seeds; cook until light
   brown. Remove from skillet.

4 Add beef to skillet and cook until browned. Sprinkle
   with sesame seeds and serve.

5 May be served over salad greens for additional
   vegetable exchanges.

In House
❀ Steak
House

4 *servings*

- SERVING SIZE: 1/4 OF LOAF
- COUNTS AS:
  1 PROTEIN
  1 STARCH

▶ *size according to plan*

family fare

Meatloaf

✲ Ingredients

1 pound (448g) lean ground sirloin

1/2 cup (125ml / 54g) breadcrumbs

1/4 cup (125ml) egg substitute

2 Tbsp (30ml) dried onion

1 tsp (5ml) low-sodium Worcestershire sauce

1/4 tsp (1ml) lite salt

1/4 tsp (1ml) freshly ground pepper

1 tsp (5ml) garlic powder

3 Tbsp (45ml) ketchup, divided

nonfat cooking spray

1 Mix together all ingredients, reserving 2 Tbsp of ketchup. Form into loaf.

2 Coat loaf pan with nonfat cooking spray. Place meatloaf in pan. Spoon remaining ketchup on top of loaf and spread evenly.

3 Bake at 350°F (180°C) until desired doneness, or about 45 minutes. To be sure meat is fully cooked, insert thermometer and bake until internal temperature reaches 160°F.

---

2 *servings*

- SERVING SIZE: 2 PEPPERS HALVES
- COUNTS AS:
  1 PROTEIN
  1 STARCH
  3 VEGETABLES
  1/2 DAIRY

▶ *size according to plan*

good source of calcium

Stuffed Pepper

✲ Ingredients

2 whole green peppers

8 or 12oz (224 or 336g) lean ground sirloin

1/4 cup (60ml / 40g) chopped white onion

2/3 cup (170ml / 106g) cooked brown rice

1/4 tsp (1ml) lite salt

1 tsp (5ml) garlic powder

1 small tomato, chopped

1/3 cup (85ml) lite tomato sauce

2oz (56g) reduced-fat mozzarella cheese, shredded

1/4 cup (60ml) water

nonfat cooking spray

1 Cut pepper in half and remove seeds. Cook peppers in boiling water for approximately 5 minutes, until just tender; drain and set aside.

2 Brown beef and onion in skillet that has been coated with nonfat cooking spray. Add rice, salt and garlic powder to skillet and heat through.

3 Stuff each pepper half with beef mixture. Coat baking pan with nonfat cooking spray. Place peppers in baking pan. Top with chopped tomato and tomato sauce. Add water to bottom of baking pan.

4 Cover and bake at 350°F (180°C) for 30-45 minutes, or until peppers and tomatoes are tender.

5 Uncover; sprinkle with cheese. Place back in oven and bake until cheese is melted.

In House
❖ Steak
House

Stuffed Cabbage

(1) serving

- **SERVING SIZE: 3-4 ROLLS**
- **COUNTS AS:**
  1 PROTEIN
  1 STARCH
  2 VEGETABLES

▶ *size according to plan*

good source of fiber

☀ Ingredients

3-4 cabbage leaves

4 or 6oz (112 or 168g) lean ground sirloin

1/3 cup (85ml / 53g) cooked brown rice

1/4 cup (60ml) low-sodium beef broth

1/4 tsp (1ml) lite salt

1/8 tsp (.5ml) freshly ground pepper

1 tsp (5ml) garlic powder

1 Tbsp (15ml) dried onion

1/2 tomato, chopped

2 Tbsp (30ml) lite tomato sauce

1 Tbsp (15ml) water

nonfat cooking spray

1. Steam cabbage leaves until tender.

2. Mix together beef, rice, broth, salt, pepper, garlic powder and onion. Divide meat mixture between the cabbage leaves. Roll and tuck in ends. Secure with a toothpick, if necessary.

3. Coat baking pan with nonfat cooking spray. Place cabbage rolls in baking pan.

4. In small bowl, combine chopped tomato, tomato sauce and water. Top rolls with tomato mixture.

5. Bake in 350°F (180°C) oven for about 1 hour, or until beef has reached an internal temperature of 160°F (70°C) .

Salisbury Steak

(1) serving

- **SERVING SIZE: 1 RECIPE**
  COUNTS AS:
  1 PROTEIN
  1 STARCH
  1 VEGETABLE

▶ *size according to plan*

☀ Ingredients

4 or 6oz (112 or 168g) lean ground sirloin

1/4 cup (60ml / 27g) breadcrumbs

1/4 tsp (1ml) lite salt

1/8 tsp (.5ml) freshly ground pepper

1 Tbsp (15ml) dried onion

1 cup (250ml) low-sodium beef broth

1 cup (250ml / 70g) fresh mushrooms, sliced

1 Tbsp (15ml) water

1 tsp (5ml) cornstarch

nonfat cooking spray

1. Mix ground beef, breadcrumbs, salt, pepper and 1/4 cup (60ml) broth in a bowl; combine well. Form meat into oval patty.

2. Coat skillet with nonfat cooking spray. Heat skillet over medium flame. Cook patty in a skillet over medium heat, until brown on both sides.

3. Add onion, remaining broth and mushrooms. Heat to boiling; reduce heat and cover. Simmer until desired doneness.

4. Remove patty; keep warm. Again, heat mixture to boiling; mix in water and cornstarch and cook until thickened. Serve sauce over patty.

In House
☘ Steak
House

Steak Fajitas

1 *serving*

- **SERVING SIZE: 1 RECIPE**
- **COUNTS AS:**
  1 PROTEIN
  3 VEGETABLES
  1/2 DAIRY

▸ *size according to plan*

good source of calcium

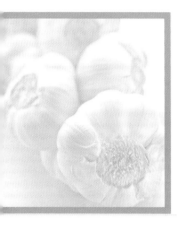

☀ Ingredients

4 or 6oz (112 or 168g) sirloin steak

1/4 cup (60ml) red wine vinegar

1 packet artificial sweetener

1/2 tsp (2.5ml) oregano

1/2 tsp (2.5ml) chili powder

1/4 tsp (1ml) garlic powder

dash of freshly ground pepper

1/4 tsp (1ml) lite salt

1/2 cup (125ml / 80g) raw white onions, sliced

1/2 green pepper, sliced

1oz (28g) reduced-fat cheddar or monterey jack cheese

3-4 large leaves of iceberg lettuce

1 Tbsp (15ml) salsa

nonfat cooking spray

1 To make marinade, combine vinegar, artificial sweetener, oregano, chili powder, garlic powder, pepper and salt.

2 Cut beef in to strips and place into bowl with marinade. Refrigerate 30 minutes.

3 Coat large skillet with nonfat cooking spray and heat over high flame. Sauté green peppers and onions about 3-5 minutes, until they begin to soften.

4 Remove steak from marinade and place in skillet with vegetables. Cook 5-10 minutes, or until beef in cooked through.

5 Remove fajita mixture from skillet and place on plate. Use lettuce leaves as fajita wraps; top with cheese and salsa.

Herb-Crusted Steak

1 *serving*

- **SERVING SIZE: 1 RECIPE**
- **COUNTS AS:**
  1 PROTEIN
  1 STARCH

▸ *size according to plan*

☀ Ingredients

4 or 6oz (112 or 168g) sirloin steak

small handful of mixed herbs to taste (such as thyme, rosemary, basil, sage, parsley)

2 garlic cloves, peeled

1 Tbsp (15ml) green onion, finely chopped

1 slice (1oz / 28g) white country-loaf style bread

freshly ground pepper

nonfat cooking spray

1 Place the herbs, garlic, onion, bread and seasoning in a food processor and blend.

2 Coat skillet with nonfat cooking spray.

3 Sear the steak in a hot pan; top with herbed breadcrumb mixture.

4 Finish the steak in a preheated 375°F (190°C) oven.

5 Cook for 8-10 minutes.

In House
❧ Steak
House

Beef Burgundy

1 *serving*

- **SERVING SIZE: 1 RECIPE**
- **COUNTS AS:**
  1 PROTEIN
  2 VEGETABLES

▶ *size according to plan*

☀ Ingredients

4 or 6oz (112 or 168g) sirloin steak

1/4 cup (60ml) burgundy wine

1/4 cup (60ml) low-sodium beef broth

1/4 tsp (1ml) garlic powder

1/4 tsp (1ml) freshly ground pepper

1/4 tsp (1ml) thyme

1/4 tsp (1ml) lite salt

1/8 tsp (.5ml) oregano

1/4 tsp (1ml) dried onion

1 cup (250ml / 70g) fresh mushroom slices

1/2 celery stalk, chopped

nonfat cooking spray

1. In a small bowl, combine garlic powder, pepper, salt, thyme, oregano and onion.
2. Rub seasoning blend into steak.
3. Coat medium skillet with nonfat cooking spray and heat over high flame.
4. Place beef on skillet, sear on each side, approximately 3 minutes, or until browned.
5. While beef is cooking, combine wine and broth in small bowl.
6. Once beef has been browned on all sides, pour wine mixture over beef. Add mushrooms and celery. Continue to cook until all liquid has evaporated. Serve hot.

Steak & Onions

4 *servings*

family fare

- **SERVING SIZE: 3 OR 5OZ (84-140G) COOKED; AND 1/4 CUP (60ML) SAUCE**
- **COUNTS AS:**
  1 PROTEIN
  1 VEGETABLE

▶ *size according to plan*

☀ Ingredients

2 pounds (900g) beef top round, cut into thin slices

1/3 cup (85ml) white vinegar

freshly ground pepper, to taste

10 large olives, sliced

3 garlic cloves, peeled and chopped

1 cup (250ml) low-sodium beef broth, divided

1 cup (250ml / 148g) green pepper, cut into strips

2 cups (500ml / 230g) Spanish yellow onion slices

nonfat cooking spray

1. Pound meat to tenderize. Season with freshly ground pepper.
2. Combine vinegar, 3/4 cup (200ml) of the broth. Add the olives and garlic; set aside.
3. Coat skillet with nonfat cooking spray, heat the remaining broth. Add green peppers and onions and sauté.
4. Remove peppers and onions with a slotted spoon and set aside.
5. Reheat skillet and sear beef on all sides.
6. Return peppers and onions to the skillet with the meat.
7. Pour the broth and vinegar mixture over the meat.
8. Cook, partially covered for 20 minutes, or until tender.

In House
❖ Steak House

Open-Faced Beef Sandwich

 4 *servings*

- **SERVING SIZE: 1/4 RECIPE**
- **COUNTS AS:**
  1 PROTEIN
  1 STARCH
  2 VEGETABLES

▶ *size according to plan*

family fare

☀ Ingredients

4 slices lite whole-wheat bread

1-1 1/2 pound (448 - 680g) round steak

2 tomato, diced

4 garlic cloves, minced

2 cups (500ml) low-sodium beef broth

1 tsp (5ml) lite salt

1 Tbsp (15ml) hot sauce

1 green pepper, diced

5 green onions, diced

water

nonfat cooking spray

1. Coat large saucepan with nonfat cooking spray. Heat over high heat.

2. Add onion, pepper, and garlic to skillet. Sauté 2 minutes.

3. Cut beef into cubes and add to skillet. Sprinkle with salt.

4. Sauté beef until brown.

5. Add tomato and hot sauce to beef mixture and cook 1-2 minutes.

6. Add beef broth the beef mixture and bring to a boil.

7. Reduce heat and cook 1-2 hours, stirring occasionally. More water may be added to cover meat while cooking; add 1/4 cup (60ml) of warm water at a time.

8. Meat is done when it can be shredded with a fork. Once beef is done, drain any remaining liquid. Place beef on plate and shred.

9. Serve shredded beef over bread.

Italian-Style Burger

 1 *serving*

- **SERVING SIZE: 1 BURGER**
- **COUNTS AS:**
  1 PROTEIN
  1 STARCH
  1/2 DAIRY

▶ *size according to plan*

good source of calcium

☀ Ingredients

4 or 6oz (112 or 168g) lean ground sirloin

1/3 cup (85ml / 36g) breadcrumbs

1/4 cup (60ml) low-sodium beef broth

1 Tbsp (15ml) dried onion

1 Tbsp (15ml) fresh parsley, snipped

1/8 tsp (.5ml) garlic powder

1/8 tsp (.5ml) freshly ground pepper

1 slice of tomato

1/8 tsp (.5ml) dried oregano, crushed

1oz (28g) reduced-fat mozzarella cheese, shredded

1. Mix together breadcrumbs, broth, onion, parsley, garlic powder and pepper. Add meat; mix well. Shape into patty.

2. Broil 3 inches (8cm) from heat for 6 minutes. Turn and broil 6-8 minutes longer, or until meat is no longer pink.

3. Top patty with tomato slices. Sprinkle with oregano, then mozzarella cheese. Broil another 1-2 minutes more, or until cheese is melted.

In House
☘ Steak
House

Meatball Sandwich

 4 *servings*

family fare

■ SERVING SIZE: 3 OR 5OZ
 (84 OR 140G) COOKED WITH
 1/2 CUP (125ML) SAUCE

■ COUNTS AS:
 1 PROTEIN
 1 VEGETABLE
 1 STARCH
 1/2 DAIRY

▶ *size according to plan*

※ Ingredients

1 pound (448g) ground sirloin

1 tsp (5ml) oregano

1 tsp (5ml) basil

1 tsp (5ml) lite salt

1 tsp (5ml) freshly ground pepper

3 Tbsp (45ml) chopped onion

5 garlic cloves, minced, divided

1 cup (250ml / 30g) chopped
 fresh spinach

1 cup (250ml) lite tomato sauce

1/2 cup (125ml) hot water

1 tomato, seeded and diced

four 4-inch (10cm) whole wheat
 pitas

4oz (112g) reduced-fat
 mozzarella cheese

nonfat cooking spray

1 In medium bowl combine meat, oregano, basil, salt, pepper, onion and half of the minced garlic. Mix well.

2 Form small balls with meat mixture.

3 Spray medium sauce pan with cooking spray. Sauté remaining minced garlic. Gently add meatballs to saucepan and sauté until brown.

4 Add spinach and sauté 1 minute.

5 Add tomato sauce, water, and tomato to pan. Continue to simmer, until meatballs are cooked and sauce reduces.

6 Use slotted spoon to remove meatballs and from sauce. Place in pita and top with cheese.

Mushroom & Swiss Burger

 1 *serving*

good source of calcium

■ SERVING SIZE: 1 BURGER
■ COUNTS AS:
 1 PROTEIN
 1 DAIRY
 1 VEGETABLE

▶ *size according to plan*

※ Ingredients

Hamburger Patty (see recipe on
 page 84)

2oz (56g) reduced-fat Swiss cheese

1/4 cup (60ml / 18g) sliced
 mushrooms

1/4 tsp (1ml) garlic powder

1 green onion, sliced

nonfat cooking spray

1 Coat small skillet with nonfat cooking spray.

2 Place mushrooms, garlic powder and onion in skillet and sauté until mushrooms are fully cooked.

3 Place mushrooms on top of burger.

4 Place cheese on burger and place on grill or under broiler to melt cheese.

In House
❧ Steak
House

7 *servings*

- SERVING SIZE: 3 OR 5OZ (84-140G) COOKED AND 1/4 CUP (60ML) SAUCE
- COUNTS AS:
  1 PROTEIN
  1 STARCH
  1 VEGETABLE
  1 FAT

▶ *size according to plan*

family fare

Beef Tenderloin with Mushroom Wine Sauce

☀ Ingredients

1 1/2 pounds (672g) beef tenderloin

1/2 cup (125ml / 63g) flour

2 Tbsp (30ml) olive oil

1 cup (250ml / 96g) chopped green onion

2 garlic cloves, chopped

2 celery stalks, chopped

2 cups (500ml / 140g) shitake mushrooms, chopped

2 Tbsp (30ml) fresh thyme, chopped

1 bay leaf

1/2 tsp (2.5ml) freshly ground pepper

1 1/2 cups (375ml) red wine

1 Tbsp (15ml) low-sodium Worcestershire sauce

1 Tbsp (15ml) balsamic vinegar

1. Preheat oven to 350°F (180°C) .

2. Roll tenderloin, lightly, in flour. Sear all sides in a hot grill pan, and then remove to an ovenproof dish.

3. Place in oven for 15-20 minutes. Allow to rest 10-15 minutes; slice tenderloin thinly. Cover loosely with foil to keep warm.

4. In a pan, sauté the onion, garlic and celery in oil for about 2 minutes.

5. Add the mushrooms and continue to sauté for about 4-5 minutes.

6. Add all remaining ingredients and bring to a boil.

7. Reduce heat, cover and simmer about 20 minutes.

8. Remove bay leaf and serve over sliced beef tenderloin.

---

1 *serving*

- SERVING SIZE: 1 BURGER
- COUNTS AS:
  1 PROTEIN
  1 STARCH
  1 FAT

▶ *size according to plan*

Open-Face Burger with Mustard Sauce

☀ Ingredients

4 or 6oz (112 or 168g) lean ground sirloin

1/3 cup (85ml / 36g) breadcrumbs

1/4 cup (60ml) low-sodium beef broth

1 Tbsp (15ml) dried onion

1 Tbsp (15ml) fresh parsley, snipped

1/8 tsp (.5ml) lite salt

2 Tbsp (30ml) fat-free sour cream

1 Tbsp (15ml) lite mayonnaise

1 tsp (5ml) Dijon mustard

1/8 tsp (.5ml) dried dill

1. Mix breadcrumbs, broth, onion, parsley and salt. Add meat and mix well. Shape into patty.

2. Broil patty 3 inches (8cm) for 5 minutes. Turn and broil 5-7 minutes more, or until meat is no longer pink.

3. Stir together sour cream, mayonnaise, mustard and dill weed. Spoon sauce over burger.

4. Arrange on 1 leaf of lettuce.

In House
❖ Steak
House

Beef Stroganoff

servings

- **SERVING SIZE: 1 1/2 CUPS (375ML)**
- **COUNTS AS:**
  1 PROTEIN
  1 STARCH
  2 VEGETABLES
  1 FAT

▶ *size according to plan*

family fare

☀ Ingredients

2 1/2 pounds (1.2kg) beef tenderloin, thinly sliced

1 Tbsp (15ml) olive oil

1 tsp (5ml) freshly ground pepper

1 Tbsp (15ml) butter

1 cup (250ml / 70g) mushrooms, sliced

1/2 cup (125ml / 48g) chopped green onion

1/4 cup (60ml) white wine

2 Tbsp (30ml) tomato paste, no salt added

2 tsp (10ml) Dijon mustard

3 cups (750ml) low-sodium beef broth

1 1/4 cups (310ml) fat-free sour cream

1. In a large pot, heat oil over high heat.

2. Season beef with the pepper and sauté until browned.

3. Remove the beef from the pot and set aside, pour off any excess fat from the pot.

4. Melt the butter in the pot and sauté the mushrooms and onions.

5. Add the white wine and simmer until liquid is reduced by half.

6. Stir in the tomato paste and mustard; cook for 2 minutes.

7. Add the broth and beef, bring to a boil.

8. Reduce the heat and simmer for 5 minutes.

9. Stir in the sour cream and adjust the seasoning to taste.

Steak Burger

serving

- **SERVING SIZE: 1 BURGER**
- **COUNTS AS:**
  1 PROTEIN
  1 VEGETABLE

▶ *size according to plan*

☀ Ingredients

Hamburger Patty (see recipe on page 84)

1/4 cup (60ml / 18g) sliced mushrooms

1/4 tsp (1ml) garlic powder

1 green onion, sliced

2 tsp (10ml) steak sauce

1/4 tsp black pepper

nonfat cooking spray

1. Coat small skillet with nonfat cooking spray.

2. Place mushrooms, garlic powder, pepper and onion in skillet; sauté until vegetables are fully cooked.

3. Place vegetables on top of burger.

4. Drizzle steak sauce over burger and vegetables.

In House
❖ Steak
House

servings 4

- **SERVING SIZE: 1 CUP (250ML)**
- **COUNTS AS:**
  - 1 PROTEIN
  - 1 STARCH
  - 1 VEGETABLE
  - 1 FAT

▶ *size according to plan*

family fare

Savory Beef Stew

☀ Ingredients

24oz (672g) beef top round, cut into 1-inch (2.5cm) cubes

1 green pepper, seeded and chopped

4 sweet chili peppers, seeded and chopped

1 small onion, chopped

4 garlic cloves, chopped

6 fresh cilantro leaves, chopped

2 Tbsp (30ml) vinegar

2 cups (500ml) low-sodium beef broth, divided

1 cup (250ml) hot water

1/2 tsp (2.5ml) dried oregano, crushed

1/2 cup (125ml) lite tomato sauce

2 bay leaves

1/2 pound (224g) carrots, peeled and chopped

1/2 pound (224g) potatoes, peeled and cubed

1/4 pound (112g) green peas

12 olives, stuffed with pimientos

1 Tbsp (15ml) capers

1. In a Dutch oven, heat 1 Tbsp (15ml) of broth.

2. Add the beef and stir constantly, until meat begins to brown.

3. Add the next 11 ingredients (through bay leaves); mix and bring to a boil. Reduce heat to low, cover and cook for 1 hour.

4. Add carrots, to Dutch oven and stir.

5. Bring back to a boil, reduce heat to low, cover and cook until the meat is fork tender.

6. Add potatoes, peas, olives and capers.

7. Mix well, bring to a boil, then reduce heat to low. Cover and cook until vegetables are tender.

In House
❖ Steak
House

4 servings

SERVING SIZE: 1/4 RECIPE

COUNTS AS:
- 1 PROTEIN
- 1 VEGETABLE
- 1/2 DAIRY

size according to plan

good source of calcium

Cheesy Beef & Broccoli

✳ Ingredients

- 1-1 1/2 pound (448 - 680g) ground lean sirloin
- 1/2 cup (125ml / 80g) raw white onions
- 4 garlic cloves, minced
- 2 cup (500ml /140g) raw broccoli florets
- 2 Tbsp (30ml) white flour
- 2 cups (500ml) skim milk
- 2 tsp (10ml) Worcestershire sauce
- 4oz (112g) reduced-fat sharp cheddar cheese
- nonfat cooking spray

1. Coat large skillet with nonfat cooking spray and heat over high flame.
2. Sauté onions and garlic 1-2 minutes, or until onions begin to soften.
3. Add beef and sauté until beef begins to brown.
4. Add broccoli and reduce heat to medium. Continue to cook until broccoli begins to soften.
5. While broccoli and beef are cooking, whisk together flour, milk and Worcestershire sauce in small bowl.
6. Once broccoli is cooked, pour flour mixture over beef and bring to a simmer.
7. Slowly sprinkle cheese over beef mixture and mix well. Once cheese is melted, turn off heat and allow to sit for 3 minutes before serving. Serve hot.

---

4 servings

SERVING SIZE: 3 OR 5OZ COOKED BEEF (84 OR 140G), AND 1 SLICE OF LITE BREAD

COUNTS AS:
- 1 PROTEIN
- 1 STARCH
- 1 VEGETABLE

size according to plan

family fare

Hot Beef Sandwich

✳ Ingredients

- 1 pound (448g) beef round steak
- 1/4 tsp (1ml) garlic powder
- 1/4 tsp (1ml) freshly ground pepper
- 1/4 tsp (1ml) lite salt
- 1 tomato, diced
- 3 Tbsp (45ml) dried onion
- 1/2 medium carrot, chopped
- 2 Tbsp (30ml) low-sodium Worcestershire sauce
- 2 Tbsp (30ml) vinegar
- 2 Tbsp (30ml) brown sugar artificial sweetener
- 2 tsp (10ml) chili powder
- 1 tsp (5ml) dried oregano, crushed
- 2 garlic cloves, minced
- 1 bay leaf
- 4 slices lite bread
- nonfat cooking spray

1. Cut meat into 5-6 pieces. Sprinkle beef with garlic powder, pepper and salt.
2. Coat Dutch oven with nonfat cooking spray. Add beef and brown on both sides.
3. Add tomato, onion, carrot, Worcestershire sauce, vinegar, brown sugar, chili powder, oregano, garlic and bay leaf. Bring to boil; reduce heat.
4. Cover; simmer for 1 hour, or until meat is very tender.
5. Remove meat and shred with a fork. Remove bay leaf from sauce.
6. Return meat to sauce and heat through. Serve hot over bread.

In House
❖ Steak
House

Beef & Mushroom Kabobs

1 *serving*

- **SERVING SIZE: 1 RECIPE**
- **COUNTS AS:**
  1 PROTEIN
  2 VEGETABLES

▶ *size according to plan*

☀ Ingredients
4 or 6oz (112 or 168g) beef round steak

2 large slices white onion

1/2 green pepper

1 cup (250ml / 70g) fresh mushrooms

2 Tbsp (30ml) balsamic vinegar

1/4 tsp (1ml) lite salt

1/4 tsp (1ml) freshly ground pepper

1/2 tsp (2.5ml) onion powder

1/2 tsp (2.5ml) garlic powder

1/4 tsp (1ml) paprika

1/4 tsp (1ml) thyme

kabob skewers

1 If using wooden skewers, soak in warm water.

2 Cut steak into cubes.

3 Slice onions and peppers into 1-inch (2.5cm) chunks.

4 Place beef, onion, pepper and mushrooms on skewers, alternating meat and vegetables.

5 Brush the kabobs with balsamic vinegar, set remaining vinegar aside.

6 In a small bowl, combine salt, pepper, onion powder, garlic powder, paprika and thyme.

7 Sprinkle spice mixture over kabobs.

8 Place kabobs and grill over medium heat. Cook approximately 4-5 minutes and then turn them over and cook additional 4-5 minutes. Baste with remaining vinegar halfway through cooking.

9 Serve immediately.

Hamburger

4 *servings*

- **SERVING SIZE: 4 OR 6OZ (112 OR 168G) RAW HAMBURGER PATTY**
- **COUNTS AS:**
  1 PROTEIN

▶ *size according to plan*

☀ Ingredients
1 pound (448g) lean ground sirloin

3 Tbsp (45ml) dried onion

1/4 tsp (1ml) garlic powder

1 Tbsp (15ml) water

1/2 tsp (2.5ml) lite salt

1/2 tsp (2.5ml) freshly ground pepper

1 Mix all ingredients together. Form into patties.

2 Broil 3 inches (8cm) from heat until desired doneness.

3 Place any uncooked burgers in freezer bags, seal well and freeze up to 3 months.

In House
❖ Steak
House

Philly Cheesesteak

 4 *servings*

SERVING SIZE: 1 SANDWICH

COUNTS AS:
1 PROTEIN
2 STARCHES
1/2 DAIRY
1 FAT

size according to plan

☀ Ingredients

1-1 1/2 pound (448 - 680g) beef sirloin

nonfat cooking spray

1/2 tsp (2.5ml) salt

1/2 tsp (2.5ml) freshly ground pepper

1/2 tsp (2.5ml) onion powder

1/2 tsp (2.5ml) garlic powder

1/2 tsp (2.5ml) dried basil

1 onion, sliced

1 green bell pepper, sliced

four 6-inch (15cm) hoagie rolls, split

4oz (112g) lite mozzarella cheese, sliced

1 Combine seasonings in a small bowl; rub mixture into sirloin.

2 Wrap in plastic or wax paper. Partially freeze beef sirloin for about 30-60 minutes.

3 Remove from freezer and thinly slice sirloin.

4 Coat large skillet with nonfat cooking spray. Heat skillet over medium flame. Add onion and green pepper; sauté until soft and lightly browned. Remove from pan.

5 Coat skillet again with spray. Increase flame to high; add beef and cook about 5 minutes, or until desired level of doneness.

6 Divide meat and vegetables evenly among the 4 rolls; top with cheese. If desired, place in a warm oven or under a broiler to melt the cheese before serving.

BBQ Cheddar Burger

 1 *serving*

SERVING SIZE: 1 BURGER

COUNTS AS:
1 PROTEIN
1/2 DAIRY
1 VEGETABLE

size according to plan

☀ Ingredients

Hamburger Patty (see recipe on page 84)

1 Tbsp (15ml) barbeque sauce

2 slices red onion

1 leaf lettuce

1 slice tomato

1oz (28g) reduced-fat cheddar cheese

1 Spread barbeque sauce over burger.

2 Top burger with cheese and place on grill or under broiler to melt cheese.

3 Once cheese is melted, top with onion, lettuce and tomato; serve immediately.

In House
Steak
House

Sultry ✤
Poultry

If chicken and turkey are on the tip of your taste buds than you'll be delighted with all the sultry poultry recipes inside. Hot dishes, wraps, chili, whatever suits your mood. You'll find a simple recipe for simply delicious dishes like Baked Chicken Parmesan, Garlic Chicken, Lemon Herb Roasted Turkey and Rolled Turkey Divan. Plus you'll learn all of the latest trends and healthiest methods for preparing, storing and cooking poultry.

◀ Marinated Chicken Kabobs recipe can be found on page 94

Chicken Cooking Techniques

Cuts of chicken

- **Whole Fryer** — Whole chicken with skin and bones. Recommended cooking methods include oven roasting and braising.

- **Cut up Fryer** — Whole chicken that has been separated into parts. Still contains skin and bones. Recommended cooking methods include oven roasting, braising, and grilling.

- **Wings** — Usually still contain both skin and bones. They can be grilled, oven roasted or braised.

- **Thighs** — Dark meat cut from the leg. Can be found with bone-in or boneless. May still have skin attached. Tastes great grilled, oven roasted or braised.

- **Drumstick** — Dark meat cut from the leg. Usually contains both skin and bones. Recommended cooking methods include oven roasting, braising and grilling.

- **Leg Quarters** — Contains dark meat from both thigh and drumstick. Tastes great grilled, oven roasted or braised.

- **Split Breast** — White meat cut. Usually contains skin and bones. Recommended cooking methods include oven roasting, braising and grilling.

- **Boneless Skinless Breast** — White meat cut. Easy to use in recipes. They can be pan seared, oven roasted or stir-fried.

- **Tenders** — White meat slices of boneless breast meat. Convenient to use. Great in stir fries. Can also be pan seared.

- **Chicken Cutlet** — A thin cut of meat. Often pounded to increase tenderness. Best preparation method is pan searing.

TIP!

Rubbing fresh herbs such as basil, oregano or parsley on chicken before cooking is great way to add a burst of flavor, without adding any extra calories.

Basic cooking methods

- **Braising** — Cooking with a moist heat. Great for less tender cuts of chicken. Meat may be browned first to seal in juices and flavor, a small amount of liquid such as chicken broth is then added to pan. Chicken is then cooked at a low heat for a lengthy period of time. This method produces a very tender chicken.

- **Oven Roasting** — Dry heat method. Chicken will have a well-browned exterior and a moist interior. Best used for larger quantities of meat such as a whole chicken. Chicken is cooked in the oven in an uncovered pan.

- **Grilling** — Preparing food on a grill over hot coals or other direct heat source.

- **Stir-Frying** — Quickly cooking food in a large pan or wok over very high heat. Food needs to be constantly stirred to prevent sticking.

- **Pan-Searing** — Uses high heat to create a crust and seal in meat juices. Cooking is usually finished in the oven.

TIP!

When preparing chicken, be sure to cook or freeze chicken by the "use-by" date. However, chicken should remain fresh for 2-3 days after the "sell-by" date.

Food Safety

It's important to know the food safety rules when preparing dishes for yourself and your family. In today's busy world we often find ourselves throwing meals together without truly preparing in a way that is healthy and safe. Here is a quick "at a glance" safe cooking guide, when cooking poultry.

- Keep raw chicken away from cooked and ready to eat foods.

- Use a separate cutting board for raw chicken. Use plastic cutting boards for raw meats and poultry.

- Never defrost chicken at room temperature. Thaw overnight in the refrigerator; under cold running water; or in the microwave.

- Cook chicken to an internal temperature of 165° (75°C).

Roasting Times

To roast chicken, use 375°F (190°C) oven. Cook breast side up uncovered.

- *1/2 to 2 pounds (672 - 896g): 45-60 minutes*

- *2 to 2-1/2 pounds (896 - 1.1kg): 60-90 minutes*

- *2-1/2 to 3 pounds (1.1 - 1.3kg): 1-1/2 ₂ hour – 1-1/2 hours*

- *3 to 4 pounds (1.3 - 1.8kg): 1-1/2 – 2-1/4 hours*

- *4+ pounds (0.8kg): at least 3 hours*

Chicken is done cooking when it reaches an internal temperature of 165°F (75°C).

Sultry
Poultry

Cuts of Turkey

▶

Whole Turkey

Whole or Half Bone-In Breast

Medallions/Tenderloins

Turkey Breast Steaks

Turkey Breast Cutlets

Turkey Beast Chops

Ground Turkey

Ground Turkey Breast

Thighs — Boneless or Bone-In

Legs/Drumsticks

Wings

Basic Cooking Methods

- **Grilling** — This method is to cook on a rack directly over hot coals or other direct heat source. Grilling works well for turkey breast, tenderloins, ground turkey, turkey burgers, thighs, legs and wings.

- **Broil** — To cook directly under heat source, usually in the oven under the top broiling element. This works well for turkey breast, tenderloins, ground turkey and turkey burgers.

- **Braising** — Cooking with a moist heat. Meat may be browned first to seal in juices and flavor, then a small amount of liquid such as broth is added to the pan. The meat is then cooked at a low heat for a lengthy period of time. This works well for turkey breast, legs and wings.

- **Oven Roasting** — This is the process of cooking meat, uncovered, on a rack in a shallow pan in the oven without adding liquids. This works well for whole turkeys, turkey breast, tenderloins, thighs, legs and wings.

- **Stir-Frying** — Quickly cooking food in a large pan or wok over high heat. Food needs to be moved constantly to prevent sticking and promote even cooking. This is a great method for cooking turkey breast and tenderloins.

- **Pan-Searing** — This method uses high heat to create a crust and seal in meat juices; cooking is usually then finished in the oven. Use this method for cooking turkey breast, tenderloins, ground turkey or thighs.

TIP!

Cranberry sauce, made with fresh cranberries, as opposed to pre-made sauce, is a great light side for turkey. You can go as light on the sugar as you'd like and keep the sauce tart and lo-cal.

Roasting Turkey
Pre-heat oven to 325°F

■ Unstuffed

Weight	Roasting Time
8 to 12 pounds (3.5 to 5.4kg)	2-3/4 hours to 3 hours
12 to 14 pounds (5.4 to 6.3kg)	3 hours to 3-3/4 hours
14 to 18 pounds (6.3 to 8kg)	3-3/4 hours to 4-1/4 hours
18 to 20 pounds (8 to 9kg)	4-1/4 to 4-1/2 hours
20 to 24 pounds (9 to 11kg)	4-1/2 hours to 5 hours
24 to 30 pounds (11 to 13.5kg)	5 hours to 5-1/4 hours

■ Stuffed

8 to 12 pounds (3.5 to 5.4kg)	3 hours to 3-1/2 hours
12 to 14 pounds (5.4 to 6.3kg)	3-1/2 hours to 4 hours
14 to 18 pounds (6.3 to 8kg)	4 hours to 4-1/4 hours
18 to 20 pounds (8 to 9kg)	4-1/4 hours to 4-3/4 hours
20 to 24 pounds (9 to 11kg)	4-3/4 hours to 5-1/4 hours
24 to 30 pounds (11 to 13.5kg)	5-1/4 hours to 6-1/4 hours

❧TIP!

Sweet potatoes are a tasty compliment to any turkey dish. When preparing sweet potatoes be sure to substitute whole milk with nonfat or low-fat milk, and try using maple syrup in place of melted butter. Your taste buds will never know the difference, but your waistline will!

Food Safety
Keep raw turkey away from cooked and ready to eat foods. Never defrost turkey at room temperature. Thaw overnight in the refrigerator, allowing approximately 24 hours for each 5 pounds (2.3kg); under cold running water allowing 30 minutes for each pound; or in the microwave. Cook whole turkeys to an internal temperature of 180°F (85°C) in the thigh or 170°F (80°C) in the breast.

Easy Steps for Carving
As friends and guests look on in anticipation, you can carve that picture-perfect turkey like a pro! Just follow these simple steps and you'll be have a perfect plate of turkey in no time.

1. Cut band of skin holding drumsticks. Grasp end of drumstick. Place knife between drumstick/thigh and body of the turkey and cut through skin to joint. Remove entire leg by pulling out and back, using the point of the knife to disjoin it. Separate the thigh and drumstick at the joint.

2. Insert fork in upper wing to steady turkey. Make a long horizontal cut above wing joint through to body frame. Wing may be disjointed from body, if desired.

3. Slice straight down with an even stroke, beginning halfway up the breast. When knife reaches the cut above the wing joint, slice will fall free.

4. Continue to slice breast meat, starting the cut at a higher point each time.

Poof! You'll have a perfectly carved turkey that everyone will enjoy. Don't forget to save the wishbone!

Sultry ✤ Poultry

Adobo Chicken

1 *serving*

- **SERVING SIZE: 1 RECIPE**
- **COUNTS AS:**
  1 PROTEIN

▶ *size according to plan*

☀ Ingredients

6 or 8oz (168 or 224g) boneless-skinless, chicken breast,

1-2 garlic cloves, crushed

2 Tbsp (30ml) low-sodium soy sauce

3/4 cup (200ml) water

1/4 cup (60ml) distilled vinegar

1/8 tsp (.5ml) freshly ground pepper

1 bay leaf

nonfat cooking spray

1. Rinse chicken; pat dry. Set aside.

2. In a medium pot, mix garlic, soy sauce, water, vinegar, freshly ground pepper and bay leaf.

3. In a skillet coated with nonfat cooking spray, sear chicken over medium high heat, approximately 3-4 minutes.

4. Add chicken to marinade.

5. Simmer over low heat for 20-25 minutes, or until chicken is cooked through.

6. Remove chicken from pot. Continue to cook sauce until slightly thick or desired consistency.

Roast Chicken

4 *servings*

- **SERVING SIZE: 1 RECIPE COOKED CHICKEN BREAST**
- **COUNTS AS:**
  1 PROTEIN

▶ *size according to plan*

family fare

☀ Ingredients

whole chicken, skin removed

lite salt

freshly ground pepper, to taste

1 tsp (5ml) dried thyme

1 tsp (5ml) dried rosemary, crushed

nonfat cooking spray

1. Preheat oven to 350°F (180°C)

2. Rinse chicken, inside and out; pat dry.

3. Combine salt, freshly ground pepper, thyme and rosemary.

4. Rub chicken with herb mixture.

5. Place chicken in a roasting pan, with rack, coated with nonfat cooking spray. Place chicken on rack, breast side up.

6. Cook in 350°F (180°C) oven and cook until done, or approximately 180°F (85°C), as measured by a meat thermometer when placed in the thigh.

7. Use the following roasting times:
   - 3-4 pound (1.3-1.8kg) whole chicken for 1 1/4-1 1/2 hours.
   - 5-7 pound (2.2-3.1kg) whole chicken for 2-2 1/4 hours.

Sultry ✿
Poultry

Chicken Marsala

1 *serving*

meals in minutes

- SERVING SIZE: 1 RECIPE
- COUNTS AS:
  - 1 PROTEIN
  - 2 VEGETABLES

▸ *size according to plan*

☀ Ingredients

6 or 8oz (168 or 224g) boneless-skinless, chicken breast

1 cup (250ml / 70g) fresh mushrooms

5 green onions, sliced

2 Tbsp (30ml) water

1/8 tsp (.5ml) lite salt

1/4 cup (60ml) dry Marsala or cooking sherry

nonfat cooking spray

1. With meat mallet, pound chicken to 1/4-inch thickness.

2. Coat skillet with nonfat cooking spray. Preheat over medium heat. Add chicken to pan and cook until tender and no longer pink.

3. Remove chicken from pan and keep warm.

4. Add mushrooms, green onions, water and salt to skillet. Cook mushrooms until tender and most of the liquid has evaporated. Add Marsala or cooking sherry to skillet. Heat through.

5. Top chicken with vegetables before serving.

Curried Stuffed Chicken Breast

1 *serving*

- SERVING SIZE: 1 RECIPE
- COUNTS AS:
  - 1 PROTEIN
  - 1 STARCH
  - 2 VEGETABLES
  - 1 FRUIT

▸ *size according to plan*

☀ Ingredients

6 or 8oz (168 or 224g) boneless-skinless, chicken breast

1 Tbsp (15ml) water

1/2 medium carrot, shredded

5 green onions, sliced

1/2 tsp (2.5ml) curry powder

1 slice lite bread, toasted and cubed

2 Tbsp (30ml) raisins

1/8 tsp (.5ml) lite salt

1/8 tsp (.5ml) paprika

1. In a small saucepan combine, 1 Tbsp (15ml) water, carrot, green onion and curry powder. Cook until vegetables are tender.

2. Remove pan from heat; add bread cubes and raisins. Toss ingredients together to combine.

3. With meat mallet, pound chicken to 1/4-inch (1/2cm) thickness. Sprinkle chicken with salt. Place chicken in a baking dish.

4. Place stuffing on one half of chicken breast; fold breast in half. Sprinkle with paprika. If needed, secure with a toothpick.

5. Bake in a 350°F (180°C) oven for 20 minutes, or until chicken is no longer pink and juices run clear.

Sultry ❧ Poultry

Marinated Chicken Kabobs

1 *serving*

- SERVING SIZE: 2-3 KABOBS
- COUNTS AS:
  1 PROTEIN
  2 VEGETABLES

▶ *size according to plan*

✷ Ingredients

6 or 8oz (168 or 224g) boneless-skinless, chicken breast, cut into 1-inch (2.5ml) cubes

2 Tbsp (30ml) lemon juice

2 Tbsp (30ml) water

1/2 tsp (2.5ml) dried tarragon, crushed

1/8 tsp (.5ml) lite salt

1 clove garlic, minced

1 cup (250ml / 120g) zucchini, cut into 1-inch (2.5cm) pieces

1/2 medium green pepper, cut into 1-inch (2.5cm) pieces

1 For the marinade, combine lemon juice, water, tarragon, salt and garlic in a non-metal bowl. Add chicken cubes and toss to combine.

2 Place bowl in refrigerator and marinate for approximately 20 minutes.

3 Drain chicken; reserve marinade.

4 On skewers alternate chicken, zucchini and green pepper. Place on broiler pan.

5 Broil 4-5 inches (10 - 13cm) from heat about 8-10 minutes or until chicken is tender and no longer pink. Brush chicken with marinade throughout cooking.

Italian-Style Chicken Tenders

2 *servings*

- SERVING SIZE: 5 OR 7OZ (140 OR 196G) COOKED
- COUNTS AS:
  1 PROTEIN
  1 STARCH

▶ *size according to plan*

✷ Ingredients

1 pound (448g) boneless chicken tenders

1 cup (250ml / 108g) breadcrumbs (see recipe on pg 154)

1/2 cup (125ml) egg substitute

1/2 tsp (2.5ml) hot sauce (optional)

1 Tbsp (15ml) water

nonfat cooking spray

1 In a small bowl, combine egg substitute, water and hot sauce.

2 Coat cooking sheet with nonfat cooking spray; preheat oven to 350° (190°C).

3 Sprinkle 1/2 of the breadcrumbs on to a plate.

4 Drip each chicken tender in the egg mixture and then into breadcrumbs. Place on baking sheet.

5 Once all tenders have been breaded, coat them with nonfat cooking spray.

6 Bake at 375°F (190°C) for approximately 10 minutes.

7 Remove from oven and turn over, coat again with cooking spray.

8 Place back in the oven and bake additional 10 minutes, or until crispy.

9 Serve over salad or with your favorite dipping sauce.

Sultry ✿ Poultry

Caraway Chicken

1 *serving*

SERVING SIZE: 1 CHICKEN BREAST WITH SAUCE

COUNTS AS:
1 PROTEIN
2 VEGETABLES
1/2 DAIRY

size according to plan

☀ Ingredients

6 or 8oz (168 or 224g) boneless-skinless, chicken breast

1/2 cup (125ml) low-sodium chicken broth

1 green onion, thinly sliced

1/2 tsp (2.5ml) caraway seed, slightly crushed

freshly ground pepper

1/2 cup (125ml) skim milk

1 1/2 (7.5ml) tsp cornstarch

nonfat cooking spray

1 Coat skillet with nonfat cooking spray. Add chicken and cook 10 minutes, turning to brown evenly.

2 Add broth, green onion, caraway seed and pepper. Bring to a boil; reduce heat.

3 Cover and simmer for 20-30 minutes or till chicken is no longer pink. Remove chicken from skillet; keep warm.

4 Stir milk and cornstarch together; add to skillet.

5 Stir while cooking until thickened.

6 Top chicken with sauce before serving.

7 Serving suggestion: serve over 1/3 cup (85ml / 12.5g) cooked noodles or 1/3 cup (85ml / 65g) cooked rice, count as 1 Starch.

Oven Fried Chicken

1 *serving*

SERVING SIZE: 1 CHICKEN BREAST

COUNTS AS:
1 PROTEIN
1 STARCH
1/2 DAIRY

size according to plan

☀ Ingredients

6 or 8oz (168 or 224g) boneless-skinless, chicken breast

1/2 cup (125ml / 54g) breadcrumbs (see recipe on page 154)

1 Tbsp (15ml) snipped fresh parsley

1/2 cup (125ml) nonfat plain yogurt

1 garlic clove, minced

2 tsp (10ml) white wine or water

dash cayenne pepper

1 Combine breadcrumbs and parsley in a shallow bowl; set aside.

2 In a separate shallow bowl, combine yogurt, garlic, wine and red pepper.

3 Dip chicken into yogurt mixture, then coat with breadcrumbs.

4 Bake at 350°F (180°C) in oven for 30-45 minutes, or until chicken is no longer pink and juices run clear.

95

Sultry ❖ Poultry

Indian-Style Chicken

1 *serving*

- **SERVING SIZE: 1 CHICKEN BREAST WITH RICE AND VEGETABLES**
- **COUNTS AS:**
  1 PROTEIN
  2 STARCHES
  2 VEGETABLES
  1 DAIRY

▶ *size according to plan*

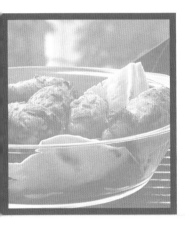

☀ Ingredients

6 or 8oz (168 or 224g) boneless-skinless, chicken breast

2 garlic cloves, minced

1/3 cup (85ml / 65g) cooked brown rice

1 cup (250ml) plain nonfat yogurt

2 Tbsp (30ml) flour

1 tsp (5ml) ground cumin

1/4 tsp (1ml) ground ginger

1 medium green pepper, chopped

1 small tomato, seeded and chopped

1/2 onion, chopped

nonfat cooking spray

1. Coat skillet with nonfat cooking spray. Sauté onion and garlic. Stir in cooked rice.

2. Coat casserole dish with nonfat cooking spray. Spread rice mixture on bottom of casserole. Place chicken on top of rice.

3. In a bowl, mix together yogurt, flour, cumin and ginger. Stir in chopped green pepper. Spoon over chicken.

4. Cover and bake in a 350°F (180°C) oven for 30-40 minutes, or until chicken is cooked through and no longer pink.

5. Add tomatoes before serving.

Orange Chicken with Carrots

1 *serving*

- **SERVING SIZE: 1 CHICKEN BREAST WITH VEGETABLES AND SAUCE**
- **COUNTS AS:**
  1 PROTEIN
  2 VEGETABLES
  1 FRUIT

▶ *size according to plan*

☀ Ingredients

6 or 8oz (168 or 224g) boneless-skinless, chicken breast

juice from 1 orange

1/4 tsp (1ml) ground ginger

1/4 medium carrot, shredded

3 green onions, thinly sliced

2 Tbsp (30ml) sherry

2 tsp (10ml) cornstarch

1/2 cup (125ml) low-sodium chicken broth

1. In a bowl, mix together orange juice, sherry, cornstarch, broth and ginger. Set aside.

2. In a casserole, combine carrot and green onion. Arrange chicken on top of vegetables.

3. Pour orange juice mixture over chicken and vegetables.

4. Cover and bake in a 350°F (180°C) oven for 30-40 minutes, or until chicken is cooked through.

Sultry ❖ Poultry

Vegetable Chicken Bake

1 *serving*

- SERVING SIZE: 1 CHICKEN BREAST WITH VEGETABLES WITH SAUCE.
- COUNTS AS:
  1 PROTEIN
  1 STARCH
  3 VEGETABLES
  1/2 DAIRY

size according to plan

☀ Ingredients

6 or 8oz (168 or 224g) boneless-skinless, chicken breast, cut into cubes

1/2 cup (125ml) low-sodium chicken broth

1/2 cup (125ml / 55g) fresh green beans, cut into bite-size pieces

1/4 medium carrot, thinly sliced

1 large celery stalk, thinly sliced

1/4 tsp (1ml) poultry seasoning

1/8 tsp (.5ml) lite salt

freshly ground pepper

2 Tbsp (30ml) cornstarch

1/2 cup (125ml) skim milk

2 Tbsp (30ml) white wine

1/3 cup (85ml / 36g) breadcrumbs (see recipe on page 154)

nonfat cooking spray

1. Coat skillet with nonfat cooking spray and sauté chicken until cooked through. Set aside.

2. In a saucepan, combine broth, green beans, carrot, celery, poultry seasoning, salt and pepper.

3. Bring to a boil; reduce heat. Cover and simmer for 5 minutes.

4. In a small bowl, mix cornstarch and milk.

5. Add milk to vegetable mixture. Cook until thickened.

6. Stir cooked chicken and wine into vegetable mixture.

7. Pour into a casserole dish. Sprinkle with breadcrumbs.

8. Bake, uncovered, in a 350°F (180°C) oven for 15-20 minutes, or until heated through and bubbling.

Soy-Glazed Chicken

1 *serving*

- SERVING SIZE: 1 CHICKEN BREAST
- COUNTS AS:
  1 PROTEIN

size according to plan

☀ Ingredients

6 or 8oz (168 or 224g) boneless-skinless, chicken breast,

1/4 cup (60ml) white vinegar

2 Tbsp (30ml) brown sugar artificial sweetener

2 Tbsp (30ml) low-sodium soy sauce

2 garlic cloves, minced

1/4 tsp (1ml) ground ginger

1/4 tsp (1ml) -onion powder

1. For marinade, mix together vinegar, brown sugar, soy sauce, garlic, ginger and onion powder. Add chicken and marinate in refrigerator for at least 20 minutes, but no longer than 24 hours.

2. Remove chicken and save marinade. Arrange chicken in baking dish and pour marinade over the chicken.

3. Bake, uncovered, at 350°F (180°C) for 20 minutes, or until chicken is cooked through.

Sultry ❖ Poultry

Lemon Chicken

1 *serving*

- **SERVING SIZE: 1 SERVING**
- **COUNTS AS:**
  1 PROTEIN
  2 FRUITS

▶ *size according to plan*

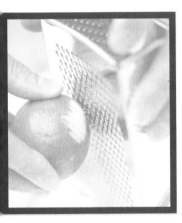

※ Ingredients

6 or 8oz (168 or 224g) boneless-skinless chicken breast

2 lemons

1/4 cup (60ml) low-sodium broth

2 tsp (10ml) flour

1 packet artificial sweetener

1/4 tsp (1ml) lite salt

1/4 tsp (1ml) freshly ground pepper

1/4 tsp (1ml) dried oregano

2 Tbsp (30ml) dry white wine

1 garlic clove, minced

nonfat cooking spray

1 Slice lemons in half. Juice 3 of the lemon halves, set aside.

2 Zest the 3 lemon halves (that have been juiced already). You will need 1-2 tsp (5-10ml) lemon zest, depending on taste.

3 Use a meat mallet to pound out chicken until approximately 1/4-inch (1/2cm) thick.

4 Sprinkle chicken with salt, pepper, oregano and flour.

5 Coat large skillet with nonfat cooking spray.

6 Place chicken in pan, cook 1-2 minutes on each side on high heat.

7 Turn down heat to medium; add white wine, sweetener, lemon juice, garlic and broth.

8 Cook approx 5-10 minutes or until liquid reduces and forms thin syrup.

9 Add lemon zest and serve over rice or roasted vegetables.

10 Slice remaining lemon half and use as garnish. You may squeeze juice over chicken for additional lemon flavor.

Chicken Nuggets

1 *serving*

- **SERVING SIZE: 1 CHICKEN BREAST, OR APPROXIMATELY 8 CHICKEN NUGGETS**
- **COUNTS AS:**
  1 PROTEIN
  1 STARCH
  1/2 DAIRY

▶ *size according to plan*

※ Ingredients

6 or 8oz (168 or 224g) boneless-skinless, chicken breast, cut into bite-size pieces

1/2 cup (125ml) nonfat buttermilk

1/2 cup (125ml / 54g) breadcrumbs (see recipe on page 154)

dash of lite salt

freshly ground pepper

1 Place chicken and buttermilk in a bowl and refrigerate for 20-30 minutes, allowing to marinade. Drain chicken and set aside.

2 Combine breadcrumbs and seasonings in a plastic, zip-top bag.

3 Add chicken to breadcrumbs and shake bag to coat chicken.

4 Bake in a 350°F (180°C) oven for 20-30 minutes, or until cooked through.

Sultry ❖ Poultry

1 *serving*

■ SERVING SIZE: RECIPE
■ COUNTS AS:
  1 PROTEIN
  2 VEGETABLES
  1 FRUIT

• *size according to plan*

meals in minutes

Sweet & Sour Chicken

☀ Ingredients

6 or 8oz (168 or 224g) boneless-skinless, chicken breast

3 green onions, thinly sliced

1/4 medium green pepper, cut into 1-inch (2.5cm) pieces

2 Tbsp (30ml) red wine vinegar

1 Tbsp (15ml) cornstarch

3/4 cup (200ml / 147g) fresh pineapple, cut into 1-inch (2.5cm) pieces

2 Tbsp (30ml) brown sugar artificial sweetener

2 Tbsp (30ml) ketchup

1/2 tomato, seeded and diced

1/2 cup (125ml) low-sodium chicken broth

nonfat cooking spray

1. Cut chicken into strips or 1-inch (2.5cm) pieces.

2. Coat skillet or wok with nonfat cooking spray. Add onion and green pepper; stir-fry over medium heat until vegetables are crisp-tender. Remove and set aside.

3. Coat skillet or wok, again, with nonfat cooking spray. Add chicken pieces and stir-fry over medium heat until chicken is cooked through.

4. Mix vinegar, cornstarch, chicken broth, brown sugar and ketchup together.

5. Add sauce to skillet, or wok, with chicken. Cook, stirring constantly, until sauce thickens.

6. Return onion and green pepper to skillet or wok. Stir in pineapple chunks. Cover and cook 2 minutes, or until heated through. Stir in tomato just before serving.

---

1 *serving*

■ SERVING SIZE: 1 CHICKEN BREAST
■ COUNTS AS:
  1 PROTEIN

• *size according to plan*

meals in minutes

Herbed Chicken Breast

☀ Ingredients

6 or 8oz (168 or 224g) boneless-skinless, chicken breast

1 Tbsp (15ml) dried minced onion

1 clove garlic, crushed

1 Tbsp (15ml) water

1/2 tsp (2.5ml) dried thyme

1/4 tsp (1ml) lite salt

freshly ground pepper

1/4 tsp (1ml) dried rosemary

1/8 tsp (.5ml) rubbed sage

1/8 tsp (.5ml) dried marjoram

dash of hot sauce (optional)

nonfat cooking spray

1. In a bowl, combine minced onion, garlic, water, thyme, salt, pepper, rosemary, sage, marjoram and hot sauce.

2. Dip chicken in sauce, coating all sides.

3. Coat baking pan with nonfat cooking spray. Place chicken in pan.

4. Bake at 350°F (180°C) oven for 20 minutes, or until chicken is cooked through.

Sultry ✢
Poultry

Greek Chicken Pita

serving

- **SERVING SIZE: 1 SERVING**
- **COUNTS AS:**
  1/2 PROTEIN
  1 STARCH
  1 VEGETABLE
  1/2 DAIRY

▶ *size according to plan*

meals in minutes

☀ Ingredients

3 or 4oz (84 or 112g) raw boneless-skinless chicken breast

4 inch (10cm) whole wheat pita

1oz (28g) reduced-fat or lite feta cheese

2 tsp (10ml) lemon juice

dash of oregano

1/4 tsp (1ml) salt

freshly ground pepper

1 tsp (5ml) fat-free Italian dressing

1/8 cucumber, sliced

1/2 tomato, diced

nonfat cooking spray

1. Cut chicken into cubes. With a fork, pierce each piece of chicken to tenderize.

2. In a medium bowl, combine lemon juice, dressing, salt, pepper and oregano. Add chicken to marinade and coat well.

3. Coat skillet with nonfat cooking spray and heat over medium heat. Add chicken and cook approximately 5 minutes, or until chicken is no longer pink when cut.

4. Place chicken in pita and top with cheese, tomato and cucumber.

Creamy Chicken Casserole

serving

- **SERVING SIZE: 1 SERVING**
- **COUNTS AS:**
  1 PROTEIN
  1 STARCH
  1 VEGETABLE
  1 LA LITE

▶ *size according to plan*

☀ Ingredients

6 or 8oz (168 or 224g) boneless-skinless chicken breast

1 packet L A Lite Cream of Chicken soup mix

1 cup (250ml / 70g) raw white mushrooms, sliced

8oz (250ml) boiling water

2 green onions, sliced

1 garlic clove, minced

1/3 cup (85ml / 55g) cooked brown rice

nonfat cooking spray

1. Dice chicken breasts.

2. Coat medium skillet with nonfat cooking spray. Sauté mushrooms, onion and garlic 2-3 minutes over high heat. Set aside.

3. In a small casserole or baking dish, combine boiling water and L A Lite soup mix. Whisk together until smooth.

4. Add chicken, mushroom mixture and rice and mix well.

5. Cover casserole and place in 375°F (190°C) preheated oven. Bake 15 minutes. Remove cover and bake additional 5-10 minutes, or until chicken is cooked through. Serve hot.

Sultry ✤
Poultry

Almond Chicken

4 *servings*

family fare

- SERVING SIZE: 1/4 OF RECIPE
- COUNTS AS:
  - 1 PROTEIN
  - 3 VEGETABLES
  - 1 FAT

➤ *size according to plan*

☀ Ingredients

2 Tbsp (30ml) almonds, chopped

24 or 32oz (670 or 900g) boneless-skinless chicken breast

3 celery stalks, diced

1 carrot, diced

1 cup (250ml / 120g) raw white onion, diced

2 cups (500ml / 68g) raw bean sprouts

2 cups (500ml) low-sodium broth

1 tsp (5ml) ground ginger

1 Tbsp (15ml) low-sodium soy sauce

4 garlic cloves, minced

nonfat cooking spray

1. Dice chicken into small cubes, set aside.
2. Spray large skillet with cooking spray. Add onion and cook 1-2 minutes; add carrots and celery and sauté over high heat 1-2 minutes.
3. Add chicken, garlic and ginger to pan and sauté over medium high heat, until chicken is no longer pink.
4. Add broth, bean sprouts and soy sauce and bring to boil.
5. Reduce heat and simmer.
6. Once liquid has evaporated and chicken is cooked through, add chopped almonds.
7. Serve immediately.

BBQ Chicken Skewers

4 *servings*

family fare

- SERVING SIZE: 1/4 OF RECIPE
- COUNTS AS:
  - 1 PROTEIN
  - 1 VEGETABLE

size according to plan

☀ Ingredients

24 or 32oz (670 or 900g) boneless-skinless chicken breast

1/4 cup (60ml) BBQ sauce

1-2 Tbsp (15-30ml) hot sauce

2 Tbsp (30ml) water

2 green peppers

4 packets brown sugar artificial sweetener

kabob skewers

1. Cut chicken into cubes.
2. In a small bowl, combine hot sauce, water, sugar substitute and half of the BBQ sauce.
3. Toss chicken in marinade to coat.
4. Cut green pepper in to 1-inch (2.5cm) squares.
5. Alternate chicken and pepper on skewers; grill or cook in 400°F (200°C) preheated oven.
6. While cooking, brush remaining BBQ sauce over skewers.
7. Cook approx 10-15 minutes, or until chicken is no longer pink.

Sultry ✤ Poultry

Cheese & Apple-Stuffed Chicken

1 *serving*

- **SERVING SIZE: 1 ROLLED CHICKEN BREAST AND SLICED APPLES**
- **COUNTS AS:**
  1 PROTEIN
  1 VEGETABLE
  1 FRUIT
  1/2 DAIRY

▶ *size according to plan*

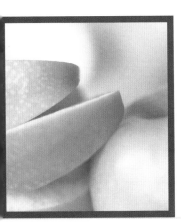

☀ Ingredients

6 or 8oz (168 or 224g) boneless-skinless, chicken breast

1 small apple, divided

1oz (28g) reduced-fat mozzarella or cheddar cheese, shredded

5 green onions, sliced

1/4 cup (60ml) low-sodium chicken broth

1 tsp (5ml) cornstarch

1 tsp (5ml) water

1 With meat mallet pound chicken to 1/4-inch thickness.

2 Chop one half of the apple and set aside. Slice the other half.

3 Top chicken with chopped apple and cheese.

4 Roll-up chicken, folding in sides. Secure with toothpicks or string.

5 Arrange apple slices and green onion in a baking dish. Top with chicken.

6 Mix 1 teaspoon cold water and cornstarch. Add to chicken broth and pour over rolled chicken breast and sliced apple.

7 Bake at 350°F (180°C) for 20 minutes or until chicken is cooked through.

Chicken Caesar Wrap

1 *serving*

- **SERVING SIZE: 1 WRAP**
- **COUNTS AS:**
  1 PROTEIN
  2 STARCHES
  1 VEGETABLE

▶ *size according to plan*

☀ Ingredients

6 or 8oz (168 or 224g) boneless-skinless chicken breast

6-inch (15cm) whole wheat flour tortilla

2 Tbsp (30ml) fat-free Caesar dressing

1 tsp (5ml) lemon juice

1/2 cup (125ml) romaine lettuce

1/4 small tomato, diced

2 green onions, diced

1/4 tsp (1ml) freshly ground pepper

nonfat cooking spray

1 In a small bowl, combine 1 Tbsp Caesar dressing, pepper and lemon juice.

2 Cut chicken in to 1-inch (2.5cm) cubes and place in dressing marinade. Allow to marinade 1 hour to overnight.

3 Remove chicken from marinade and place on baking sheet that has been coated with nonfat cooking spray.

4 Bake in 350°F (180°C) preheated oven for 15 minutes, or until chicken is cooked through.

5 Cool chicken 5 minutes.

6 To make wrap, place chicken, lettuce, tomato and onion in middle of tortilla. Drizzle with remaining dressing. Roll up all ingredients.

Sultry ✿
Poultry

Chicken & Greenbean Casserole

1 *serving*

SERVING SIZE: 1 CASSEROLE
COUNTS AS:
1 PROTEIN
2 VEGETABLES
1/2 DAIRY
1 LA LITE

▶ *size according to plan*

☀ Ingredients

6 or 8oz (168 or 224g) boneless-skinless chicken breast

1 cup (250ml / 110g) fresh cut green beans

1/2 cup (125ml / 35g) fresh chopped mushrooms

3 green onions

1/4 tsp (1ml) freshly ground pepper

1/4 tsp (1ml) garlic powder

1 packet L A Lite Cream of Mushroom soup

3/4 cup (200ml) boiling water

1/2 cup (125ml) skim milk

nonfat cooking spray

1. Coat small casserole dish with nonfat cooking spray.
2. Use meat mallet to pound out chicken until approximately 1/4 inch (1/2cm) thick.
3. Sprinkle chicken with pepper and garlic powder.
4. Combine boiling water and soup mix in casserole dish; mix well.
5. Add chopped mushrooms, cut green beans, chicken and milk to casserole dish.
6. Cover and place in preheated 375°F (190°C) oven for 20 minutes.
7. Uncover and bake additional 10-15 minutes, or until chicken is no longer pink. Serve hot.

Chicken Cheesesteak

1 *serving*

meals in minutes

SERVING SIZE: 1 SERVING
COUNTS AS:
1 PROTEIN
1 STARCH
1 VEGETABLE
1/2 DAIRY

▶ *size according to plan*

☀ Ingredients

6 or 8oz (168 or 224g) ground white meat chicken breast

1oz (28g) reduced-fat provolone or mozzarella cheese

1/4 cup (125ml / 40g) raw white onions

1 Tbsp (15ml) green pepper, chopped

1/4 tsp (1ml) lite salt

1/4 tsp (1ml) onion powder

4 inch (10cm) whole wheat pita

nonfat cooking spray

1. Coat medium skillet with nonfat cooking spray.
2. Place onion and pepper in skillet and sauté over high heat 1 minute.
3. Add chicken, sprinkle with salt and onion powder.
4. Stir-fry the chicken and vegetables until chicken is fully cooked.
5. Turn off heat, push all of the chicken to one side of skillet.
6. Place cheese over chicken meat and cover loosely with foil to melt.
7. Place chicken and cheese in pita. Serve hot.

Sultry ❖ Poultry

3 *servings*

■ SERVING SIZE: 5 OR 7OZ
(140 OR 196G) COOKED
■ COUNTS AS:
  1 PROTEIN
  1 FAT

▶ *size according to plan*

family fare

Buffalo Chicken Tenders

☀ Ingredients

1-1 1/2 pound (448 - 680g)
  boneless chicken tenders

3 Tbsp (45ml) lite margarine

1-2 Tbsp (15-30ml) hot sauce

1/4 tsp (1ml) garlic powder

1/8 tsp (.5ml) lemon juice

nonfat cooking spray

1 Melt margarine in small sauce pan.

2 Whisk in hot sauce, lemon juice and garlic powder.

3 Place chicken tenders on baking sheet that has been coated with nonfat cooking spray.

4 Drizzle hot sauce mixture over chicken. Toss chicken to coat well.

5 Bake at 375°F (190°C) approx 15-20 minutes, or until chicken is cooked through.

6 Serve warm over salad with celery sticks and fat-free blue cheese dressing, if desired.

---

1 *serving*

■ SERVING SIZE: 1 SERVING
■ COUNTS AS:
  1 PROTEIN
  1/2 DAIRY

▶ *size according to plan*

good source of calcium

Spinach & Feta Stuffed Chicken

☀ Ingredients

6 or 8oz (168 or 224g) boneless-
  skinless chicken breast

1/4 cup (60ml / 7.5g) frozen
  chopped spinach, thawed and
  drained well

2 garlic cloves, minced

1oz (28g) reduced-fat feta cheese

1/4 tsp (1ml) freshly ground pepper

nonfat cooking spray

1 Use meat mallet to pound chicken breast until 1/4-inch (1/2cm) thick.

2 In small bowl combine spinach, feta and half of the garlic; mix well.

3 Place chicken on piece of aluminum foil that has been coated with cooking spray. Sprinkle chicken with pepper.

4 Place spinach mixture in middle of chicken and roll up chicken.

5 Top chicken with remaining minced garlic.

6 Roll chicken in foil to help keep it together, place in refrigerator for 1 hour to set.

7 Preheat oven to 375°F (190°C).

8 Place chicken in the foil on baking sheet and bake 20 minutes.

9 Cut open top of foil and place back in oven for 5 minutes, to brown top of chicken and garlic.

10 Serve hot with your favorite roasted veggies.

Sultry ❊
Poultry

Broccoli & Cheddar **Stuffed Chicken**

1 *serving*

SERVING SIZE: 1 SERVING

COUNTS AS:
1 PROTEIN
1 VEGETABLE
1/2 DAIRY

▶ *size according to plan*

☀ Ingredients

6 or 8oz (168 or 224g) boneless-skinless chicken breast

1/4 cup (60ml / 46g) frozen chopped broccoli, thawed and drained well

1 Tbsp (15ml) chopped red pepper

2 garlic cloves, minced

1oz (28g) reduced-fat cheddar cheese

1/4 tsp (1ml) freshly ground pepper

nonfat cooking spray

1. Use meat mallet to pound chicken breast until 1/4-inch (1/2cm) thick.

2. In a small bowl, combine broccoli, red pepper, cheddar and half of the garlic. Mix well.

3. Place chicken on piece of aluminum foil that has been coated with cooking spray.

4. Sprinkle chicken with pepper.

5. Place broccoli mixture in middle of chicken and roll up chicken.

6. Top chicken with remaining clove of minced garlic.

7. Roll chicken in foil to help keep it together, place in fridge for 1 hour to set.

8. Pre-heat oven to 375°F (190°C).

9. Place chicken inside the foil on baking sheet and bake 20 minutes.

10. Cut a slit in the top of foil packet and place back in oven for 5 minutes, to brown top of chicken and garlic.

11. Serve hot with your favorite roasted veggies.

Garlic **Chicken**

1 *serving*

SERVING SIZE: 1 SERVING

COUNTS AS:
1 PROTEIN
1 VEGETABLE

▶ *size according to plan*

meals in minutes

☀ Ingredients

6 or 8oz (168 or 224g) boneless chicken tenders

1/2 tsp (2.5ml) Italian herb blend (see recipe on pg 224)

4 garlic cloves, slices

1/2 cup (125ml / 35g) fresh mushrooms, sliced

2 green onions, sliced

1/4 tsp (1ml) garlic powder

1/4 tsp (1ml) lemon juice

1 Tbsp (15ml) dry white wine

nonfat cooking spray

1. With a fork, pierce each chicken tender to tenderize.

2. Sprinkle chicken with Italian herb blend.

3. Coat large skillet with nonfat cooking spray.

4. Place chicken, garlic, mushrooms, and onions in skillet; sauté 5 minutes or until chicken is cooked through.

5. Add lemon juice, garlic powder, and wine.

6. Continue to sauté chicken additional 5-10 minutes, or until chicken is no longer white inside.

7. Serve hot over rice or roasted veggies.

Sultry ✤ Poultry

4 *servings*

- SERVING SIZE: 1 SLICE
- COUNTS AS:
  - 1 PROTEIN
  - 1 STARCH
  - 1 VEGETABLE

▸ *size according to plan*

family fare

Vegetable Chicken Loaf

※ Ingredients

1-1 1/2 pound (448 - 680g) ground white meat chicken breast

1/4 cup (60ml / 30g) zucchini, finely chopped

1/4 cup (60ml / 18g) mushrooms, finely chopped

1/4 cup (60ml / 40g) chopped white onions

1/4 cup (60ml / 37g) green peppers, chopped

1/4 cup (60ml / 30g) chopped carrot

1/4 cup (60ml / 15g) parsley, chopped

1 Tbsp (15ml) fresh basil, chopped

1 tsp (5ml) garlic powder

1 tsp (5ml) fresh thyme, chopped

1/4 cup (60ml) egg substitute

1/3 cup (85ml / 36g) breadcrumbs (see recipe on pg 154)

nonfat cooking spray

1. In a large mixing bowl, combine all ingredients; mix well.
2. Coat loaf pan with nonfat cooking spray.
3. Spread meat mixture into loaf pan.
4. Preheat oven to 375°F (190°C).
5. Bake 35-45 minutes, or until internal temperature is 165°F (75°C).
6. Remove from oven and cool 10 minutes before slicing.

1 *serving*

- SERVING SIZE: 1 WRAP
- COUNTS AS:
  - 1 PROTEIN
  - 1 STARCH
  - 1 FAT

▸ *size according to plan*

meals in minutes

Chicken & Avocado Wraps

※ Ingredients

5 or 7oz (140 or 196g) plain, cooked chicken

2 Tbsp (30ml) salsa

1/8 ripe avocado, peeled, pitted and chopped

1 Tbsp (15ml) red onion, diced

1 1/2 tsp (7.5ml) pepper sauce (optional)

1/2 whole wheat flour tortilla

1. In a bowl combine, chicken, salsa, avocado, red onion and pepper sauce.
2. Place chicken salad on tortilla and roll.

Sultry ✿
Poultry

White Chicken Chili

1 *serving*

- SERVING SIZE: 1/2 RECIPE
- COUNTS AS:
  1 PROTEIN
  1 STARCH
  1 VEGETABLE

▶ *size according to plan*

☀ Ingredients

12 or 16oz (336 or 448g) ground white meat chicken breast

5 green onions, chopped

1/2 white onion, chopped

2 small tomatoes, chopped

1 cup (250ml / 70g) fresh mushroom slices

1/2 cup (125ml) dried cooked white beans

2 1/2 cups (625ml) low-sodium chicken broth

3 garlic cloves, minced

1-2 tsp (5-10ml) chili powder, to taste

1/4 tsp (1ml) lite salt

1/4 tsp (1ml) ground cumin

1 tsp (5ml) cilantro

dash of hot sauce

nonfat cooking spray

1. Coat large saucepan with nonfat cooking spray.

2. Add green and white onions and mushrooms to pan; sauté 2 minutes.

3. Add chicken, tomato, garlic, chili powder, salt, cilantro and cumin to pot. Cook until chicken is browned.

4. Add broth and beans. Bring to a boil, cover and reduce heat.

5. Simmer 30 minutes, or until reaches desired consistency. You may add a dash of hot sauce to reach your desired taste.

Sesame Chicken

1 *serving*

- SERVING SIZE: 2-3 SKEWERS
- COUNTS AS:
  1 PROTEIN
  1 FAT

▶ *size according to plan*

☀ Ingredients

6 or 8oz (168 or 224g) boneless-skinless, chicken breast

2 Tbsp (30ml) low-sodium teriyaki sauce

1 Tbsp (15ml) water

1 garlic clove, minced

1/8 tsp (.5ml) ground ginger

1 Tbsp (15ml) sesame seeds, toasted

1. For marinade, combine teriyaki sauce, water, garlic and ginger.

2. Stir in chicken. Let marinate for 20 minutes.

3. Thread chicken, accordion-style, onto skewers.

4. Place on broiler pan. Broil 4-5 inches (10-13cm) from heat for 3 minutes.

5. Turn over and broil another 3-4 minutes or until chicken is no longer pink.

6. Sprinkle with toasted sesame seeds.

Sultry ❖ Poultry

4 *servings*

- SERVING SIZE: 1/4 RECIPE
- COUNTS AS:
  1 PROTEIN
  1 STARCH
  2 VEGETABLES
  1 FAT

▶ *size according to plan*

family fare

Curry Chicken

☀ Ingredients

24 or 32oz (670 or 900g)
boneless-skinless, chicken breast

1 lime, juiced

1/2 cup (125ml / 63g) flour

freshly ground pepper

2 Tbsp (30ml) butter

5 green onions, chopped

1 Tbsp (15ml) curry powder

garlic powder to taste

1 cup (250ml) low-sodium beef
broth

1 small can low-sodium stewed
tomatoes

2 Tbsp (30ml) plain nonfat yogurt

1. Marinade chicken in lime juice, refrigerated, for approximately 20 minutes.
2. Season flour with pepper.
3. Lightly coat each piece of chicken in flour, shaking to remove excess.
4. In a nonstick skillet, sauté chopped onions in 1 Tbsp (15ml) butter until golden. Remove and set aside.
5. Sauté chicken in remaining butter until brown.
6. Add sautéed onions, curry powder, garlic powder, broth and stewed tomatoes to pan. Bring to a boil.
7. Cover and simmer on medium-low heat for 30 minutes, or until chicken is done. Season to taste.
8. Remove chicken from pan and stir yogurt into sauce.
9. Place chicken back in sauce.
10. Serve with rice if desired.

---

8 *servings*

- SERVING SIZE: 5 OR 7OZ (140 OR 196G) COOKED
- COUNTS AS:
  1 PROTEIN
  1 VEGETABLE

▶ *size according to plan*

family fare

Honey Mustard Glazed Chicken

☀ Ingredients

3-3 1/2 pounds (1.3-1.6kg)
boneless skinless chicken breast

2 lemons

1/3 cup (85ml) chipotle pepper
sauce

1/4 cup (60ml) honey mustard,
fat-free or lite

1 packet artificial sweetener

1. Remove the rind from one of the lemons and chop finely.
2. Juice the lemons and marinate the chicken in the lemon juice and half of the chipotle pepper sauce.
3. In a glass bowl or zip-top bag, marinate for at least 1 hour or up to 2 hours.
4. Remove chicken from marinade; discard the marinade.
5. Make the glaze from remaining chipotle pepper sauce, artificial sweetener, honey mustard and lemon zest.
6. Grill over medium high heat, about 8 minutes per side, brushing with glaze towards the end of cooking.

Sultry ❀
Poultry

Jerk Chicken

family fare

4 *servings*

■ SERVING SIZE: 5 OR 7OZ (140 OR 196G) COOKED CHICKEN

■ COUNTS AS:
1 PROTEIN
2 VEGETABLES
1 FAT

▸ *size according to plan*

☀ Ingredients

5 green onion, chopped

4 garlic cloves, chopped

4 fresh Scotch bonnet or Habanero chilies, seeded and chopped

2 Tbsp (30ml) fresh lime juice

2 Tbsp (30ml) fresh lemon juice

3 Tbsp (45ml) olive oil

2 Tbsp (30ml) low-sodium soy sauce

1 Tbsp (15ml) brown sugar

1 Tbsp (15ml) fresh thyme leaves

2 tsp (10ml) ground allspice

2 tsp (10ml) freshly ground pepper

3/4 tsp (4ml) freshly grated nutmeg

1/2 tsp (2.5ml) cinnamon

4 boneless-skinless, chicken breasts, each 6 or 8oz (168 or 224g)

1 Place onion and garlic into a blender. Add chilies.

2 Squeeze in fresh lime juice, lemon juice, soy sauce, olive oil, brown sugar, thyme, allspice, pepper, nutmeg and cinnamon. Blend until marinade is smooth.

3 Using 2 separate zip-top plastic bags, pour in marinade, dividing evenly among the bags.

4 Divide the chicken between the bags and seal, pressing out any excess air.

5 Place bags into a shallow pan and into the refrigerator and marinate for 24 hours. Turn bags occasionally to evenly coat chicken with marinade.

6 Let chicken stand at room temperature for 10 minutes before cooking.

7 Preheat grill to medium temperature. Grill and cook chicken until browned on all sides. Then, lower the heat and cover until chicken is cooked through.

Chicken with Broccoli & Ziti

1 *serving*

■ SERVING SIZE: 5 OR 7OZ (140 OR 196G) COOKED

■ COUNTS AS:
1 PROTEIN
1 STARCH
2 VEGETABLES
1 FAT
1/2 DAIRY

▸ *size according to plan*

☀ Ingredients

6 or 8oz (168 or 224g) boneless-skinless, chicken breast, cubed

garlic powder

1/3 cup (85ml / 53g) cooked pasta

1 cup (250ml / 184g) cooked broccoli

1 tsp (5ml) olive oil

1oz (28g) part-skim shredded mozzarella

nonfat cooking spray

1 Coat skillet with nonfat cooking spray. Season chicken with garlic powder.

2 Sauté chicken until cooked through.

3 Once chicken has been cooked, add broccoli and pasta.

4 Toss with oil and top with cheese, before serving.

Sultry ✤ Poultry

4 *servings*

- SERVING SIZE: 1/4 RECIPE
- COUNTS AS:
  1 PROTEIN
  1 FRUIT
  1 DAIRY

▶ *size according to plan*

family fare

Chicken Normandy

☼ Ingredients

4 boneless-skinless, chicken breasts, 6 or 8oz each (168 or 224g)

freshly ground pepper

2 medium granny smith apples, sliced

5 green onions and tops, sliced

2/3 cups (175ml) unsweetened apple juice

2 tsp (10ml) low-sodium chicken bouillon crystals

1 1/2 tsp (7.5ml) dried sage leaves

2/3 cup (175ml) fat-free half & half

2 tsp (10ml) flour

1/4 cup (60ml) artificial sweetener

nonfat cooking spray

1. Coat large skillet with nonfat cooking spray; heat over medium-high flame. Sauté chicken breast until brown, 3-5 minutes on each side.

2. Season to taste with pepper.

3. Add apples, onions, apple juice, bouillon and sage to skillet; heat to boiling.

4. Reduce heat and simmer, covered, until chicken is tender, 10-12 minutes. Remove chicken and apples to serving platter. Cover loosely to keep warm.

5. Continue simmering juice mixture until reduced and almost completely evaporated.

6. Combine half & half and artificial sweetener in glass measuring cup; pour into skillet.

7. Heat to boiling; boil, stirring constantly, until thickened, about 1 minute.

8. Pour over chicken and apples.

Chicken Patties

3 *servings*

- SERVING SIZE: 1 PATTY
- COUNTS AS:
  1 PROTEIN
  1 STARCH

▶ *size according to plan*

☼ Ingredients

1-1 1/2 pound (448 - 680g) ground white meat chicken breast

1 granny smith apple, chopped

5 green onions, chopped

1/3 cup (85ml / 36g) breadcrumbs (see recipe on pg 154)

1 tsp (5ml) mint, chopped

2 Tbsp (30ml) thyme, chopped

freshly ground pepper

1. Combine all the ingredients in large mixing bowl. Form into 3 patties.

2. For best results and taste place them in the refrigerator for about 30 minutes.

3. Cook in a skillet, heated over a medium flame, 5 minutes per side.

Sultry ❖ Poultry

Baked Chicken Parmesan

4 *servings*

family fare

- **SERVING SIZE: 1 CHICKEN BREAST**
- **COUNTS AS:**
  - 1 PROTEIN
  - 1 VEGETABLE
  - 1/2 DAIRY

▶ *size according to plan*

☀ Ingredients

- 1 1/2 or 2 pounds (672 or 896g) boneless-skinless, chicken breast
- 1/4 cup (60ml) egg substitute
- 1/2 cup (125ml / 54g) breadcrumbs (see recipe on pg 154)
- 1 1/2 cups (375ml) lite tomato sauce
- 2oz (56g) part-skim mozzarella cheese, shredded
- 1/4 tsp (1ml) basil
- 1/4 tsp (1ml) garlic powder
- 1/4 tsp (1ml) oregano

1. Rinse chicken breast and dip into the egg substitute.
2. Mix in another bowl the breadcrumbs, basil, oregano and garlic powder. Place next to egg substitute. Dip chicken from egg substitute into breadcrumbs and coat well.
3. Pour 1/2 cup (125ml) tomato sauce on the bottom of a baking pan.
4. Place breaded chicken breast in pan.
5. Using the remaining sauce, cover each chicken breasts.
6. Evenly sprinkle the shredded cheese over each chicken breast.
7. Cover pan with aluminum foil.
8. Bake in preheated oven 375°F (190°C) for 20 minutes.
9. Remove foil and continue baking for 10-15 minutes longer to allow cheese to melt and chicken is cooked through.
10. Serve with pasta or your favorite vegetable.

Lemon-Herb Marinated Chicken

1 *serving*

- **SERVING SIZE: 1 SERVING**
- **COUNTS AS:**
  - 1 PROTEIN
  - 1 FAT

▶ *size according to plan*

☀ Ingredients

- 1 Tbsp (15ml) canola oil
- 1 Tbsp (15ml) lemon juice
- 1/2 tsp (2.5ml) rosemary
- 1/2 tsp (2.5ml) lite salt
- 1/4 tsp (1ml) freshly ground pepper
- 6 or 8oz (168 or 224g) boneless-skinless chicken

1. Mix oil, lemon juice, rosemary, pepper and salt.
2. Pour over chicken.
3. Allow to sit 30 minutes.
4. Remove from marinade.
5. Grill or broil.
6. Serve hot, garnish with fresh lemon slices.

Sultry ❖ Poultry

Ginger Chicken & Apricots

8 *servings*

■ SERVING SIZE: 5 OR 7OZ
(140 OR 196G) COOKED,
AND 1/4 CUP (60ML) SAUCE
■ COUNTS AS:
 1 PROTEIN
 1 VEGETABLE
 1 FRUIT

▶ *size according to plan*

family fare

❉ Ingredients

3-3 1/2 pounds (1.3kg) boneless-
 skinless, chicken breast

1 tsp (5ml) ground ginger

1 1/2 cups (375ml) dried apricots

1 1/2 cups (375ml) boiling water

1 Tbsp (15ml) olive oil

1 Tbsp (15ml) butter

5 green onions, finely chopped

1 1/2 tsp (7.5ml) artificial
 sweetener

2 Tbsp (30ml) finely grated ginger

1 cinnamon stick roughly separated

8 green cardamom pod, lightly
 crushed

1/4 tsp (1ml) ground cloves

1/4 tsp (1ml) freshly ground
 pepper

1 1/2 cups (375ml) low-sodium
 tomato juice

1/3 cup (85ml) finely chopped fresh
 coriander

1 Place chicken breast in a bowl; sprinkle ginger over
   chicken, rubbing well to coat pieces evenly.

2 Cover and refrigerate for 1-12 hours.

3 Meanwhile cover apricots with boiling water; let stand
   for 30 minutes.

4 In a large, deep skillet, heat oil over medium-high
   flame. Brown chicken on all sides; transfer to a plate.

5 Drain off any fat; reduce heat to medium.

6 Melt butter; stir in onion, artificial sweetener, ginger,
   cinnamon stick, cardamom, cloves and pepper. Cook,
   stirring often until tender and golden, about
   8 minutes.

7 Stir in tomatoes, tomato juice, and apricots with their
   soaking water.

8 Bring to boil over high heat, stirring up brown bits;
   boil for 5 minutes or until tomatoes melt into the
   liquid.

9 Add the coriander.

10 Return chicken to pan and reduce heat to medium-
   low; cover and simmer, turning chicken once, until
   juices run clear when chicken is pierced, about
   20 minutes.

Chicken Sun-dried Tomato Pesto

4 *servings*

■ SERVING SIZE: 1 RECIPE
■ COUNTS AS:
 1 PROTEIN
 1 FAT
 2 VEGETABLES

▶ *size according to plan*

❉ Ingredients

4 skinless, boneless chicken
 breast halves, 6 or 8oz each

lite salt

freshly ground pepper

2 tsp (10ml) olive oil

1 (14.5oz / 400g) can diced
 tomatoes with green peppers
 and onions

1/4 cup (60ml) sun-dried tomato
 pesto

1 (14oz / 400gl) can artichoke
 hearts in water, drained and
 quartered

1 Season both sides of chicken breasts with salt and
   pepper.

2 Heat oil in a large skillet over medium-high heat.

3 Place chicken in skillet; cook, turning once to brown
   each side. Remove chicken from pan, and set aside.

4 Pour tomatoes into pan; cook for 1 minute, stirring
   constantly.

5 Stir in pesto and artichokes, and return chicken to pan.
   Cover, and reduce heat to medium.

6 Simmer for 5-10 minutes, or until chicken is cooked
   through.

Sultry ❀
Poultry

Turkey Kielbasa

6 *servings*

- SERVING SIZE: 1/6 OF RECIPE
- COUNTS AS:
  - 1 PROTEIN
  - 1 STARCH
  - 1 VEGETABLE

size according to plan

☼ Ingredients

1 bottle (12 oz / 375ml) dark beer or ale

2 Tbsp (30ml) Dijon-style mustard

1/2 tsp (2.5ml) caraway seeds

6 cup (1.5L) coarsely shredded cabbage

1-1 1/2 lb (448g-672g) turkey kielbasa or smoked turkey sausage (low-sodium), cut on the diagonal into 2-inch (5cm) pieces

1 Granny Smith apple (or Braeburn or Winesap), cut into 1/4-inch (1/2cm) wedges

1 can (16 oz / 448g) sweet potatoes, drained, cut into 1-1/2-inch (4cm) cubes

1 In a large deep skillet over high heat, combine beer, mustard and caraway seeds. Bring to boil.

2 Add cabbage, reduce heat to medium-low and cover. Simmer 5 to 8 minutes or until cabbage is crisp-tender.

3 Add turkey kielbasa, apple and sweet potatoes.

4 Increase heat to high and bring mixture to boil.

5 Reduce heat to medium-low, cover and simmer 3 to 5 minutes or until apple is crisp-tender and all ingredients are hot.

Turkey Waldorf Sandwich

1 *serving*

- SERVING SIZE: 1 RECIPE
- COUNTS AS:
  - 1 PROTEIN
  - 1 STARCH

size according to plan

☼ Ingredients

1 1/2 or 3oz (42-84g) cooked turkey breast, cubed

1/8 cup (30ml) diced celery

1/4 small tart red apple, cored and cut into small cubes

1/2 Tbsp (7.5ml) walnuts, chopped

1/4 Tbsp (4ml) reduced-calorie mayonnaise

1/4 Tbsp (4ml) nonfat yogurt, plain or vanilla

pinch of freshly grated nutmeg

pinch of ground cinnamon

1 lettuce leaf, washed, cleaned and crisp

2 slices reduced-calorie raisin bread

1 In medium bowl combine turkey, celery, apple, walnuts, mayonnaise, yogurt, nutmeg and cinnamon. Blend well.

2 Cover and refrigerate at least 1 hour to allow flavors to blend.

3 To serve, arrange a lettuce leaf on a bread slice. Spoon turkey mixture over lettuce leaf and top with another slice of bread.

Sultry ✦
Poultry

Lemon-Herb Roasted Turkey

10 *servings*

- SERVING SIZE: 4 OR 6OZ (112 OR 168G) COOKED SKINLESS TURKEY
- COUNTS AS:
  1 PROTEIN

▶ *size according to plan*

Can make 10-20 servings (depending on size of turkey)

family fare

☀ Ingredients

1 12-14 pound (5-6kg) fresh or frozen turkey, thawed

nonfat cooking spray

1/3 cup (85ml / 11g) chopped fresh sage

1/3 cup (85ml / 9g) chopped fresh rosemary

1/3 cup (85ml / 20g) chopped fresh parsley

1 Tbsp (15ml) lemon zest

3 Tbsp (45ml) olive oil

1/2 cup (125ml) low-sodium chicken broth

1 tsp (5ml) lite salt

3 Tbsp (45ml) lemon juice

2 Tbsp (30ml) honey, divided

2 lemons, quartered

1 Preheat oven to 325°F (160°C).

2 To prepare turkey, remove and discard giblets; rinse turkey inside and out with cold water, and pat dry.

3 Trim away any excess fat from the body. Starting around the neck, use your fingertips to loosen the skin of the bird from the flesh. Tuck wings under the body of the bird.

4 Place turkey on a broiler pan (or roasting pan with rack) coated with cooking spray. Combine sage, parsley, rosemary, lemon zest, olive oil and salt in a small bowl. Rub the herb mixture under the skin of the bird and along the cavity. Combine broth, 2 Tbsp (30ml) lemon juice and honey; pour half of mixture over the turkey. Stuff cavity of bird with lemon pieces.

5 Insert an oven-safe meat thermometer into the meaty part of the thigh, making sure not to touch the bone. Roast in oven for approximately 3 hours or until thermometer registers 180°F (80°C).

6 Halfway through roasting pour remaining lemon juice mixture over turkey. Remove bird from oven, cover loosely with foil and let stand 15-20 minutes, before carving.

Turkey Meatballs

4 *servings*

- SERVING SIZE: 4 or 6 MEATBALLS
- COUNTS AS:
  1 PROTEIN
  1 VEGETABLE

▶ *size according to plan*

family fare

☀ Ingredients

1 pound (448g) raw ground turkey breast

1/4 cup (60ml / 27g) breadcrumbs (see recipe on page 154)

2 Tbsp (30ml) egg substitute

2 tsp (10ml) low-sodium Worcestershire sauce

1 cup (250ml) low-sodium chicken broth

3 green onions, sliced

2 tsp (10ml) garlic powder

nonfat cooking spray

1 In a bowl, combine breadcrumbs, garlic powder, onions and Worcestershire sauce. Add turkey and egg; mix well to combine all ingredients. Shape into 16 meatballs.

2 Coat baking dish with nonfat cooking spray. Arrange meatballs in a baking dish. Pour broth over meatballs. Bake in 350°F (180°C).oven until no longer pink. Drain off any excess fat.

3 Serve meatballs over pasta for an additional starch serving.

Sultry ✤ Poultry

Rolled Turkey Divan

1 *serving*

- **SERVING SIZE: 1 RECIPE**
- **COUNTS AS:**
  - 1 PROTEIN
  - 2 VEGETABLES
  - 1/2 DAIRY

▶ *size according to plan*

❄ Ingredients

5 or 7oz (140 or 196g) turkey breast tenderloin

1/2 cup (125ml) low-sodium chicken broth

1 cup (250ml / 70g) fresh mushrooms, sliced

1/2 cup (125ml) skim milk

2 Tbsp (30ml) dry sherry

1/8 tsp (.5ml) ground nutmeg

dash of red pepper

8 broccoli spears, cooked and drained

1 Tbsp (15ml) cornstarch

1 Tbsp (15ml) cold water

1 Tbsp (15ml) parmesan cheese

nonfat cooking spray

1. Cut turkey into 2-4 equal portions. Place piece of turkey between 2 pieces of wax paper or plastic wrap. Working from center to the edges, pound the turkey lightly with a meat mallet until the tenderloin is 1/4 inch (1/2cm) thick. Repeat with remaining turkey.

2. For sauce, whisk together chicken broth, milk, sherry, nutmeg, pepper, cold water and cornstarch in a bowl; set aside.

3. Coat large skillet with nonfat cooking spray. Sauté mushrooms over medium heat until tender. Add to sauce mixture.

4. Divide broccoli among turkey slices, placing spears cross-wise near one end of each slice.

5. Spoon about 1 Tbsp (15ml) of the sauce over each portion of broccoli. Roll turkey over broccoli and sauce. Secure with a toothpick, if necessary.

6. Coat baking dish with nonfat cooking spray. Arrange turkey rolls, seam side down, in baking dish. Pour remaining sauce over turkey rolls. Sprinkle with Parmesan cheese.

7. Bake, uncovered, in a 350°F (180°C).oven for 30 minutes, or until turkey is no longer pink.

Turkey with Barbeque Sauce

1 *servings*

- **SERVING SIZE: 1 RECIPE**
- **COUNTS AS:**
  - 1 PROTEIN

▶ *size according to plan*

❄ Ingredients

5 or 7oz (140 or 196g) fresh turkey breast tenderloin

2 Tbsp (30ml) barbeque sauce

1 Tbsp (15ml) water

1/2 packet artificial sweetener

1/2 tsp (2.5ml) lemon juice

dash of garlic powder

1/8 tsp (.5ml) dried thyme, crushed

1. Place turkey breast in baking pan.

2. Combine barbeque sauce, water, lemon juice, artificial sweetener, garlic powder and thyme. Pour mixture over turkey. In a 350°F (180°C) oven bake turkey approximately 20 minutes or until cooked through.

Sultry ❖ Poultry

Spinach Stuffed Turkey

(4) servings

- **SERVING SIZE: 1/4 OF RECIPE**
- **COUNTS AS:**
  - 1 PROTEIN
  - 1 VEGETABLE
  - 1/2 DAIRY

▶ *size according to plan*

☀ Ingredients

2 garlic cloves, minced

1/2 cup (125ml / 80g) chopped onions

1 cup (250ml / 70g) button mushrooms, sliced

1 bag (10oz / 280g) baby spinach leaves

4oz (112g) reduced-fat shredded cheddar cheese

1-1 1/2 pound (448g) turkey breast cutlets

dash of lite salt

freshly ground pepper

1 Tbsp (15ml) flour

1/2 cup (125ml) low-sodium chicken broth

nonfat cooking spray

1. Coat skillet with nonfat. Heat over medium heat. Add garlic and onions; sauté 1-2 minutes, until tender.

2. Add mushrooms, tossing with other ingredients to combine; cook until mushrooms soften.

3. Next, add spinach and 1/2 cup (125ml) broth to pan; toss ingredients together to allow spinach to wilt and cook down. Remove from heat and allow to cool to room temperature. Stir in 1 Tbsp (15ml) flour.

4. Rinse off turkey cutlets and pat dry. Season with salt and pepper.

5. Divide spinach mixture evenly among turkey cutlets, forming a mound in the center of each cutlet. Sprinkle half of cheese over turkey. Gently roll turkey over spinach, securing with butcher's string or toothpicks, as needed.

6. Transfer stuffed turkey breasts to an oven safe skillet or sauté pan that has been sprayed with cooking spray.

7. Bake in a 350°F (180°C) oven for approximately 15 minutes. Top with remaining cheese and cook until all cheese is melted.

Turkey á la King

(1) serving

- **SERVING SIZE: 1 LOIN**
- **COUNTS AS:**
  - 1 PROTEIN
  - 2 VEGETABLES
  - 1 LA LITE

▶ *size according to plan*

meals in minutes

☀ Ingredients

5 or 7oz (140 or 196g) fresh turkey tenderloins

1/4 cup (60ml / 40g) frozen peas, thawed

1/2 cup (125ml / 35g) fresh mushrooms, sliced

1 green onion, sliced

1 packet L A Lite Cream of Mushroom soup mix

3/4 cup (200ml) boiling water

nonfat cooking spray

1. Chop turkey into 1-inch (2.5cm) pieces.

2. Spray medium skillet with cooking spray.

3. Add onion, mushrooms, and turkey to skillet. Sauté 5 minutes.

4. Add peas and turn heat to low flame, continue to sauté until turkey is cooked through.

5. While turkey is cooking, combine boiling water and soup mix. Whisk together with a fork until smooth to make a gravy.

6. Turn off heat and pour gravy over turkey, stir to combine.

7. Serve over rice or vegetables.

Sultry ❖ Poultry

1 *serving*

meals in minutes

■ SERVING SIZE: 1 RECIPE
■ COUNTS AS:
  1 PROTEIN
  3 VEGETABLES
  1 FRUIT (optional)

▶ *size according to plan*

Raspberry Turkey Delite

☀ Ingredients

1 cup (250ml / 70g) fresh mushroom slices

1/2 medium green pepper

5 green onions

5 or 7oz (140 or 196g) fresh ground turkey breast

3oz (90ml) white zinfandel wine (optional)

1 Tbsp (15ml) fat-free raspberry vinaigrette

nonfat cooking spray

1 Coat pan with nonfat cooking spray.

2 Sauté mushrooms, green peppers and whole green onions; set aside.

3 Form turkey into patty.

4 Place turkey patty in skillet and brown on each side.

5 Return vegetables to pan.

6 Pour wine into pan, simmer another 5 minutes, or until turkey is cooked through.

7 Serve hot, drizzle with raspberry vinaigrette, before serving.

---

4 *servings*

family fare

■ SERVING SIZE: 1/4 OF RECIPE
■ COUNTS AS:
  1 PROTEIN
  1 STARCH
  1 VEGETABLE

▶ *size according to plan*

Sloppy Joe

☀ Ingredients

1-1 1/2 pound (448g) ground turkey breast

1/2 cup (125ml / 80g) diced white onion

1/2 cup (125ml / 74g) diced green pepper

2 small tomatoes, diced

2 Tbsp (30ml) ketchup

1/2 tsp (2.5ml) garlic powder

1/4 tsp (1ml) paprika

2 tsp (10ml) vinegar

1 packet artificial sweetener

1 tsp (5ml) Worcestershire sauce

dash of hot sauce

dash of oregano

dash of red pepper flakes

4 slices lite bread

nonfat cooking spray

1 Coat Dutch oven with nonfat cooking spray. Brown ground turkey, onions and peppers. Add remaining ingredients.

2 Cook over low heat 10-15 minutes.

3 Serve over diet bread.

"So many recipes to choose from, something new every day."

- Morgan D.

Sultry ♣ Poultry

serving

■ **SERVING SIZE: 1 RECIPE**
■ **COUNTS AS:**
   1 PROTEIN
   1 STARCH
   2 VEGETABLES

▶ *size according to plan*

good source of fiber

Vegetable Stuffed Turkey Roll

☀ Ingredients

5 or 7oz (140 or 196g) turkey breast tenderloin

1/2 cup (125ml / 35g) mushrooms, sliced

1/4 medium carrot, shredded

1 stalk celery, thinly sliced

2 Tbsp (30ml) diced white onions

1/2 tsp (2.5ml) dried thyme, crushed

1/2 tsp (2.5ml) dried sage

1/4 tsp (1ml) lite salt

freshly ground pepper

1 slice whole wheat lite bread, toasted and cubed

1-2 Tbsp (15-30ml) water

nonfat cooking spray

1　Rinse turkey; pat dry. Place between 2 pieces of clear plastic wrap or wax paper. With a meat mallet, pound turkey to 1/2 inch (1cm) thickness.

2　Coat skillet with nonfat cooking spray. Add mushrooms, carrot, celery, onion, thyme, sage, salt and pepper; cook over medium heat until tender.

3　Add bread cubes and toss lightly to mix. Stir in enough of water to moisten. Spoon stuffing over pounded turkey.

4　Roll turkey over stuffing, tucking ends under; secure with string or a toothpick. Place on a rack in a shallow baking pan.

5　Bake in a 350°F (180°C)oven, covered loosely with foil, for 20-30 minutes. Remove foil. Bake 5-10 minutes more. Remove string. Let stand 10 minutes before slicing.

serving

■ **SERVING SIZE: 1 SANDWICH**
■ **COUNTS AS:**
   1 PROTEIN
   1 STARCH
   1 VEGETABLE
   1 LA LITE

▶ *size according to plan*

Open Faced Turkey Sandwich

☀ Ingredients

5 or 7oz (140 or 196g) fresh turkey tenderloins

1/4 tsp (1ml) lite salt

1/4 tsp (1ml) freshly ground pepper

1/4 tsp (1ml) onion powder

1/4 tsp (1ml) garlic powder

1 slice whole wheat lite bread

1 packet L A Lite Cream of Chicken soup mix

3/4 cup (200ml) boiling water

1/2 cup (125ml / 63g) green beans, cooked

nonfat cooking spray

1　Coat large baking sheet with nonfat cooking spray.

2　Place turkey on sheet, sprinkle with onion, pepper, salt and garlic.

3　Place in preheated 375°F (190°C) oven. Bake approximately 25 minutes, or until turkey is cooked through.

4　While turkey is cooking, combine boiling water and soup mix. Whisk together with a fork until smooth to make a gravy.

5　Remove turkey from oven and place on top of bread. Serve green beans on the side.

6　Top turkey and green beans with gravy.

Sultry ❖
Poultry

Turkey Chili

4 *servings*

family fare

■ SERVING SIZE: 1 1/2 CUPS
  (375ML)
■ COUNTS AS:
  1 PROTEIN
  3 VEGETABLES

▶ *size according to plan*

✳ Ingredients

1-1 1/2 pounds (448g) ground
  turkey breast

2 garlic cloves

1/2 cup (375ml) water

1 cup (250ml) low-sodium
  chicken broth

6 tomatoes, seeded and chopped

1/2 cup (125ml / 80g) raw white
  onions, chopped

1/2 cup (125ml / 128g) canned
  kidney beans, drained and rinsed

1/2 Tbsp (7.5ml) chili powder

1/2 tsp (2.5ml) cumin

1/2 tsp (2.5ml) paprika

1/2 tsp (2.5ml) lite salt

1/2 tsp (2.5ml) freshly ground
  pepper

nonfat cooking spray

1 Heat a pot over medium flame, coated with nonfat
   cooking spray.

2 Add garlic and cook until golden brown.

3 Add turkey breast with water.

4 Add in chopped vegetables, broth, beans and spices.

5 Simmer over medium-low heat for 45 minutes.

"The chili recipe is my favorite...so
tasty. Thought I would never be
able to eat it again but L A Weight
Loss proved me wrong."

- Gina H.

Basic Turkey Burger

1 *serving*

■ SERVING SIZE: 1 BURGER
■ COUNTS AS:
  1 PROTEIN

▶ *size according to plan*

✳ Ingredients

5 or 7oz (140 or 196g) fresh
  ground turkey breast

freshly ground pepper

dash of onion powder

1/8 tsp (.5ml) sage

nonfat cooking spray

1 Combine turkey and spices.

2 Shape into a patty.

3 Coat skillet with nonfat cooking spray. Brown both
   sides of the patty; turn down heat to low and finish
   cooking until juices run clear.

4 This burger is also great on the grill!

Sultry ✿
Poultry

6 *servings*

- SERVING SIZE: 2 OR 4OZ (56 OR 84G) COOKED DUCK WITH 2-3 TBSP (30-45ML) SAUCE
- COUNTS AS:
  1 PROTEIN
  1 VEGETABLE
  1 FRUIT

▶ *size according to plan*

family fare

Pineapple-Sauced Duck Breast

☀ Ingredients

2 cups (500ml) canned, crushed pineapple, with juice

1/4 cup (60ml) water

2oz (56g) dried cherries

1-2 packets artificial sweetener

2 Tbsp (30ml) red onion, minced

2 Tbsp (30ml) red bell pepper, diced

1 Tbsp (15ml) minced fresh ginger

1-2 garlic cloves, minced

1/2 jalapeño, seeded and minced

12 or 20oz (336 or 560g) duck breast, skinned

1/2 tsp (2.5ml) lite salt

1/2 tsp (2.5ml) freshly ground pepper

2 green onions, sliced

2 Tbsp (30ml) cilantro, chopped

nonfat cooking spray

1 In a small saucepan, combine pineapple in juice and next eight ingredients. Bring to a boil over medium-high heat; reduce heat. Simmer, uncovered, approximately 10-15 minutes, until slightly thickened and syrupy. Remove from heat and cool to room temperature.

2 Rinse duck breast and pat dry. Season with salt and pepper. Coat skillet with nonfat cooking spray; heat over medium flame.

3 Cook duck in skillet, about 4-6 minutes per side, or until cooked through. Remove from pan and let stand about 5 minutes, to allow juices to redistribute throughout the meat. Slice each breast into strips, or as desired.

4 Just before serving, add green onions and cilantro to pineapple sauce; stir to combine. Spoon sauce over duck slices.

California Turkey Burger

1 *serving*

- SERVING SIZE: 1 BURGER
- COUNTS AS:
  1 PROTEIN
  1 VEGETABLE
  1 FAT

▶ *size according to plan*

☀ Ingredients

cooked (see Basic Turkey Burger recipe on page 119)

2 Tbsp (30ml) mashed avocado

1 Tbsp (15ml) chopped green pepper

1 leaf lettuce

2 slices onion

1/8 cucumber, sliced

1 Spread avocado over turkey burger.

2 Sprinkle with chopped pepper.

3 Top with lettuce, cucumber and onion.

Sultry ✿ Poultry

1 *serving*

good source of fiber

Turkey - Broccoli Bake

☀ Ingredients

5 or 7oz (140 or 196g) fresh turkey tenderloins

1 cup (250ml / 184g) frozen chopped broccoli, thawed and drained

1 Tbsp (15ml) margarine, melted

1 tsp (5ml) garlic powder

1oz (28gm) reduced-fat shredded cheddar cheese

3 Melba toasts

nonfat cooking spray

1 Coat small casserole dish with nonfat cooking spray.

2 Chop turkey into 1-inch pieces.

3 Combine turkey, melted margarine, and broccoli in casserole dish and sprinkle with garlic powder.

4 Place in preheated 375°F (190°C) oven and bake 25-30 minutes, or until turkey is just opaque.

5 While turkey is baking, crumble Melba toasts in to small bowl. Add cheese to Melba mixture and toss well to combine.

6 Remove turkey from oven, sprinkle Melba mixture over casserole.

7 Place back in oven and bake another 10-15 minutes, or until turkey is cooked through and cheese has melted.

8 Serve immediately.

---

1 *serving*

good source of calcium

Turkey Melt

☀ Ingredients

2 slices light bread

1 Tbsp (15ml) Dijon mustard

4 or 6oz (112 or 168g) cooked turkey breast

1 slice tomato

1oz (28g) reduced-fat swiss cheese

nonfat cooking spray

1 Spread mustard over bread.

2 Place turkey, tomato, and cheese on one piece of bread. Top with other slice.

3 Coat small skillet with nonfat cooking spray.

4 Place sandwich in skillet over medium heat, cook 2 minutes, or until cheese begins to melt.

5 Flip sandwich over and cook on second side until cheese melted.

6 Serve immediately.

Sultry ✤ Poultry

Roast Turkey with Cider

8 *servings approx 8-10*

- SERVING SIZE: 4 OR 6OZ (112 OR 168G) COOKED TURKEY BREAST, SKIN REMOVED, 2 TBSP (30ML) GRAVY, AND 1/4 CUP (60ML) OF STUFFING
- COUNTS AS:
  1 PROTEIN
  1 STARCH
  1 VEGETABLE

▶ *size according to plan*

☀ Ingredients

12 pound (5.4kg) oven-ready turkey

freshly ground pepper

5 yellow onions, cut into wedges

4 garlic cloves

1 1/2 cups (375ml) dry cider

1 Tbsp (15ml) softened tub margarine

1 Tbsp (15ml) flour

3 Tbsp (45ml) fat-free half & half

Stuffing

1 Tbsp (15ml) olive oil

10 green onions, chopped

2 garlic cloves, crushed

1 cooking apple, peeled, cored and chopped

1/2 cup (125ml / 54g) fresh breadcrumbs (see recipe on pg 154)

3oz (84g) dried prunes, chopped

2 Tbsp (30ml) freshly chopped mint

1/4 cup (60ml) egg substitute

1 Preheat the oven to 375°F (190°C).

2 Rinse turkey inside and out; pat dry. Season the body cavity with pepper.

3 To make stuffing, heat olive oil in a pan over medium flame. Sauté the onion and garlic for 5 minutes or until softened.

4 Stir in the apple. Remove from the heat and add remaining stuffing ingredients, with seasoning to taste. Mix well to form a stiff consistency.

5 Stuff the neck cavity with prepared stuffing then fold the neck flap over and secure with skewers or trussing needle and twine.

6 Place the onion wedges and whole garlic cloves in the body cavity.

7 Weigh the turkey and calculate the cooking time allowing 18 minutes per pound (448g).

8 Place breast side down in the roasting pan; pour 1/2 cup (125ml) of the cider on top of the turkey. Place in the oven and roast for the calculated cooking time.

9 Twenty minutes before the end of the cooking time, turn the turkey over, pour over 1/2 cup (125ml) of the cider and continue to cook, loosely covered with aluminum foil.

10 Cook the turkey to an internal temperature of 180°F (80°C)

11 Remove from the oven, place turkey on a serving plate, loosely cover with aluminum foil and stand for 20 minutes before carving.

Gravy

1 Strain 1 cup (250ml) of the juices from the roasting pan into a saucepan and stir in the remaining cider, bring to a boil.

2 Cream the margarine with the flour, then gradually whisk into the cider mixture.

3 Cook for 2 minutes, adjust seasoning and stir in the fat-free half & half.

4 Heat gently for 1 minute; serve with the cooked turkey.

Sultry ❖ Poultry

Raspberry Glazed Duck

4 *servings*

family fare

- SERVING SIZE: 2 OR 4OZ (56 OR 84G) COOKED DUCK WITH 2-3 TBSP SAUCE
- COUNTS AS:
  1 PROTEIN
  1 FRUIT

size according to plan

☀ Ingredients

12 or 20oz (336 or 560g) duck breast, skinned

1 tsp (5ml) lite salt

2 tsp (10ml) cinnamon

1/4 tsp (1ml) ground ginger

2 packets artificial sweetener

1 Tbsp (15ml) sugar

1/2 cup (125ml) red wine

3 Tbsp (45ml) sugar-free raspberry jam

1/2 cup (125ml / 62g) fresh raspberries

nonfat cooking spray

1 Preheat broiler.

2 Coat large skillet with nonfat cooking spray and heat over medium-high flame.

3 Cook one side of duck breast until browned, about 5-10 minutes.

4 Meanwhile, while duck is cooking combine artificial sweetener, sugar, salt, ginger and cinnamon in small bowl.

5 Turn breasts over and cook other side until browned.

6 Remove duck from skillet. Sprinkle one side of duck with cinnamon mixture then set aside.

7 Combine red wine and jam in skillet and heat over medium heat, bring up to a low simmer and cook for 3 minutes. Add raspberries and cook 1 minute. Remove sauce from heat.

8 Place duck breasts in broiler pan and broil for about 2 minutes, or until cinnamon mixture begins to brown.

9 Remove duck from broiler and allow to rest 2-3 minutes. Slice thinly and top with sauce.

Spanish-Style Turkey Burger

1 *serving*

good source of calcium

- SERVING SIZE: 1 BURGER
- COUNTS AS:
  1 PROTEIN
  1 VEGETABLE
  1/2 DAIRY

size according to plan

☀ Ingredients

cooked "Basic Turkey Burger" (see recipe on page 119)

1/4 cup (60ml / 24g) chopped onions

1/4 cup (60ml / 37g) green peppers, chopped

1/2 tsp (2.5ml) hot sauce

1 Tbsp (15ml) salsa

1oz (28g) reduced-fat cheddar cheese

nonfat cooking spray

1 Spray small skillet with cooking spray.

2 Sauté onion, pepper and hot sauce, until vegetables are cooked.

3 Spread salsa over cooked turkey burger.

4 Top burger with vegetable mixture.

5 Place cheese over burger and melt under broiler.

6 Serve hot.

Sultry ❖ Poultry

Sassy
♣ Sides

A diverse collection of starches and side dishes can make the difference between a bland meal and a gourmet meal. You'll find plenty of ways in this section, to spruce up favorite sides such as potatoes, rice and mixed vegetables. Spicy Broccoli, Herbed Eggplant and Pineapple Stuffing are amongst the many fabulous recipes inside!

◁ Stuffed Summer Squash recipe can be found on page 148

Storage Tips

■ Root vegetables such as squashes and potatoes should be stored in a cool, well ventilated place at 50-60°F.

■ Corn and peas should be stored in a ventilated container.

■ Store dry ingredients such as rice and flours in a dry, cool storage area and in airtight containers once original packaging is opened.

Potatoes

■ **Russet potatoes** — Also known as the Idaho potato, the russet is long and slightly rounded. The skin is brown and rough and has many eyes. These are best for baked potatoes and French fries because of their low moisture content and high starch content.

■ **Round red potatoes** — These are also called boiling potatoes. They have a waxy flesh with less starch and more moisture than the russet, making them a good choice for boiling. These are also good for roasting, frying and mashing.

■ **Yukon gold potatoes** — These have a golden skin and the flesh ranges from buttery yellow to golden brown. These boiling potatoes have a moist texture. Yukon gold potatoes are great for making mashed potatoes.

■ **New potatoes** — These are young potatoes of any variety. Because they are younger than most potatoes, they have not converted all of their sugar into starch. This gives them a crisp and waxy texture and a very thin skin. They are small enough to be cooked whole; new potatoes can be oven roasted or boiled. New potatoes are also popular when making potato salad because they retain their shape better than an older potato.

■ **Sweet potatoes** — This large edible root is not actually a potato; the texture is often moister than a regular potato and the flavor is sweeter. There are many varieties of sweet potatoes, each with their own distinctive flavor.

■ **Yams** — Yams are not the same as a sweet potato, although canned sweet potatoes are commonly referred to as yams. They are similar in size and shape to sweet potatoes, but have more natural sugars and higher moisture content. Yams can be substituted for sweet potatoes in most recipes.

TIPS!

Steam vegetables in steaming rack or basket over 1-inch boiling water. Depending on size of vegetables, steam for 2 minutes or longer. Vegetables are best when they are still slightly crunchy.

Sassy
❖ Sides

Rice

- **Arborio rice** — This is an Italian grown grain with a high starch content. The grains are shorter and fatter than other types of short-grain rice. It is typically used in risotto due to its increased starch content, which provides a creamy texture.

- **Basmati rice** — Basmati is a long-grained rice with a very fine texture. It has a nut-like flavor and aroma because it is aged to decrease the moisture content. It is often found in Indian and Middle Eastern markets and cooking.

- **Brown rice** — This rice refers to the entire grain of rice with only the inedible husk removed. The bran coating gives it a light brown color, nutty flavor and chewy texture, and provides a higher fiber content than white rice. Brown rice takes longer to cook than white rice, although some quick cooking brown rices have recently become available in the market.

- **Long-grain rice** — This rice has a length that is four to five times that of its width. Both white and brown rice come in long-grain varieties. When cooked, long-grain rice produces a light product that separate easily.

- **Medium-grain rice** — This rice is shorter and moister than long-grain and not as starchy as short-grain. Medium-grain rice is fluffy immediately after cooking, but clumps once it cools.

- **Short-grain rice** — This rice has a fat, almost round grain. The grains have high starch content and, when cooked, it is moist and sticky. This variety is sometimes called glutinous rice (although it is gluten free) and is often seen in Asian cooking.

- **White rice** — This variety has had the husk, bran and germ removed. It is lower in fiber than brown rice, which still has the bran and germ.

Vegetables

Fresh vegetables provide the diet with a variety of vitamins and minerals; they are low in fat and provide fiber. Many vegetables also contain antioxidants, which may protect against certain types of cancers and other disease. Portion sizes are, unless noted, 1/2 cup (125ml) cooked or 1 cup (250ml) raw. Water loss during cooking is due to heat breaking down the cell membranes, leaving a more concentrated food item; this is why cooked vegetables have a smaller portion size than raw vegetables.

Basic Cooking Methods

- **Steaming** — Cooking vegetables over boiling water. Steaming is a preferred cooking method for vegetables as it will help retain the vegetables flavor and color. Steaming also helps vegetables to retain many nutrients that may be lost when vegetables are boiled.

- **Sautéing** — Cooking vegetables quickly in a small amount of fat in a skillet over direct heat. This works well for fast cooking vegetables such as spinach and other greens.

- **Boiling** — Cooking in boiling water or other liquid.

- **Grilling** — Cooking over hot coals or other direct heat source. This works best for larger chunks of vegetables such as eggplant, zucchini, onions and sweet peppers.

- **Blanching** — To place vegetables into boiling water briefly, then place in cold water to stop the cooking process; this method is used to set color and flavor while keeping vegetables crisp.

- **Roasting** — This is a dry heat method most often done in the oven in an uncovered pan; vegetables are cooked at extremely high temperatures to develop the natural sweetness and flavors.

Sassy
Sides

Cabbage with Apples

serving

- **SERVING SIZE: 1 RECIPE**
- **COUNTS AS:**
  2 VEGETABLES
  1 FRUIT

▸ *size according to plan*

good source of fiber

☀ Ingredients

1 cup (250ml / 70g) cabbage, shredded

5 green onions, thinly sliced

1/4 cup (60ml) water

1 Tbsp (15ml) lemon juice

1/4 cup (60ml) low-sodium chicken broth

1/4 tsp (1ml) caraway seeds

1 small apple, cored and cut into bite-size pieces

1 In a saucepan, combine cabbage, onion, water, lemon juice, broth and caraway seeds.

2 Bring mixture to boiling; reduce heat. Cover and simmer for 7-8 minutes, or until cabbage is nearly tender.

3 Stir in apple. Cook for 2-3 minutes more, or until apple is tender.

Garlic & Pepper Stir-Fry

servings

- **SERVING SIZE: 1/2 OF RECIPE**
- **COUNTS AS:**
  3 VEGETABLES

▸ *size according to plan*

☀ Ingredients

2 garlic cloves, minced

1/2 medium carrot, sliced

1/2 medium green pepper, sliced

1/2 medium red pepper, sliced

1/2 medium yellow or orange pepper, sliced

5 green onions, sliced

1 cup (250ml / 70g) fresh mushrooms, sliced

1 tsp (5ml) garlic powder (optional)

nonfat cooking spray

1 Preheat a wok or skillet over medium flame; coat with nonfat cooking spray. Add garlic and stir-fry for 1 minute.

2 Add carrot slices and stir-fry for 2 minutes. Add pepper strips and onion stir-fry for another 2 minutes.

3 Add mushrooms and garlic powder; stir-fry about 2 minutes more or until vegetables are crisp-tender.

"I never really cooked until I bought the L A Weight Loss cookbook—now I love getting creative in the kitchen."

- B. Garvett

Sassy
❖ Sides

Breaded Zucchini **Sticks**

2 *servings*

SERVING SIZE: 1/2 OF RECIPE
COUNTS AS:
1 STARCH
1 VEGETABLE

size according to plan

☼ Ingredients

2 cups (500ml / 226g) zucchini, cut into sticks

2/3 cup (175ml / 72g) breadcrumbs (see recipe on page 154)

dash of lite salt

freshly ground pepper

dash of seasoning blend

nonfat cooking spray

1 Combine breadcrumbs, pepper, salt and seasoning blend in small bowl.

2 Rinse off zucchini sticks in water and shake off excess water.

3 Roll in crumbs and place on a cookie sheet coated with nonfat cooking spray.

4 Bake at 375°F (190°C) for 20 minutes, until lightly browned.

Twice Baked **Potatoes**

8 *servings*

SERVING SIZE: 1/2 POTATO
COUNTS AS:
1 STARCH
1 FAT
1/2 DAIRY

size according to plan

family fare

☼ Ingredients

4 small potatoes, baked

4oz (112g) shredded reduced-fat cheddar cheese

2 Tbsp (30ml) skim milk

2 Tbsp (30ml) low-fat sour cream

2 tsp (10ml) garlic powder

1 Tbsp (15ml) chives, diced

nonfat cooking spray

1 Preheat oven to 325°F (160°C).

2 Slice a small hole on the top of each baked potato.

3 Using a spoon, remove the flesh of the potato and place into a medium mixing bowl.

4 Add milk, sour cream, garlic and chives to potato mixture.

5 Stir until well blended and smooth.

6 Add cheese and combine.

7 Spoon potato mixture back into the potato skins.

8 Place stuffed potatoes on a baking sheet that has been coated with nonfat cooking spray.

9 Bake 12-15 minutes, or until top of potato filling starts to brown.

Sassy
❖ Sides

Pineapple Stuffing

family fare

4 *servings*

- SERVING SIZE: 1/4 PAN
- COUNTS AS:
  - 1 STARCH
  - 1 FRUIT
  - 1 FAT

▶ *size according to plan*

☀ Ingredients

4 slices of lite bread

2 cups (500ml / 390g) canned, crushed pineapple, drained

1/4 cup (60ml) egg substitute

1/2 tsp (2.5ml) cinnamon

1/4 tsp (1ml) ginger

1/4 cup (60ml) lite margarine

nonfat cooking spray

1 Preheat oven to 350°F (180°C)

2 Dice bread in to 1-inch (2.5cm) cubes.

3 In medium bowl, mix bread and pineapple.

4 Add egg to moisten bread.

5 Mix in cinnamon and ginger.

6 Melt margarine in small microwave-safe bowl.

7 Pour half of the melted margarine over bread mixture and mix well.

8 Coat 8-inch (20cm) square baking pan with nonfat cooking spray.

9 Spread bread mixture evenly in the pan.

10 Pour remaining margarine over stuffing.

11 Bake 15 minutes; center of the dish will be firm when done.

Spaghetti Squash Parmesan

1 *serving*

- SERVING SIZE: 1 RECIPE
- COUNTS AS:
  - 1 STARCH
  - 1 VEGETABLE

▶ *size according to plan*

☀ Ingredients

1/2 cup (125ml / 78g) cooked spaghetti squash

2 Tbsp (30ml) lite tomato sauce

1 Tbsp (15ml) parmesan cheese

1 Place squash on microwave safe plate.

2 Top with sauce and cheese.

3 Heat 1-2 minutes until sauce is hot.

4 Serve hot.

"I'm eating healthier, feeling energized and loving it!"

- Paula R.

Sassy
❖ Sides

Garlic Grits

6 *servings*

SERVING SIZE:
1/3 CUP (85ML) COOKED

COUNTS AS:
1 STARCH

size according to plan

✳ Ingredients

3 1/2 cups (625ml) water

1/2 cup (125ml) skim milk

1/2 tsp (2.5ml) lite salt

1 cup (250ml / 156g) quick cooking grits (not instant!)

1 tsp (5ml) garlic powder

2 cloves roasted garlic, chopped

2 Tbsp (30ml) lite margarine

1/4 cup (60ml) water

1. Combine water, milk, and salt in medium pot. Bring to a boil.
2. Stir in grits slowly. Bring back to a boil, stirring for 1 minute.
3. Reduce heat to low. Add garlic powder, stir.
4. Cook, stirring occasionally, about 5-10 minutes.
5. Grits should have a thick, yet creamy texture.
6. More water may need to be added during cooking if grits appear too thick; try adding 1/4 cup (60ml) of water at a time.
7. Stir in margarine and roasted garlic just before serving.

Turnip Casserole

4 *servings*

SERVING SIZE:
1/2 CUP (125ML)

COUNTS AS:
1 VEGETABLE
1 FAT
1/2 DAIRY

size according to plan

good source of fiber

✳ Ingredients

2 cups (500ml) raw turnips

1 Tbsp (15ml) lite margarine

1 tsp (5ml) flour

1/4 cup (60ml) skim milk

1 tsp (5ml) fat-free cream cheese

nonfat cooking spray

1. Preheat oven to 350°F (180°C).
2. Peel and chop turnips; boil in water until tender. Drain and set aside.
3. Coat small casserole dish with nonfat cooking spray.
4. In small saucepan, combine margarine, flour and skim milk. Cook, stirring constantly, until smooth, over medium heat.
5. Place turnips in casserole dish.
6. Put pieces of fat-free cream cheese over turnips.
7. Pour sauce over casserole.
8. Bake at 350°F (180°C) for about 30-35 minutes or until browned.

Sassy
❖ Sides

Whole Wheat Rigatoni

3 *servings*

■ SERVING SIZE:
2/3 CUP (170ML)

■ COUNTS AS:
1 VEGETABLE
1 STARCH
1 FAT

▶ *size according to plan*

good source of fiber

☀ Ingredients

1 Tbsp (15ml) lite margarine

2 garlic cloves, minced

1 cup (250ml / 56g) raw spinach

1/2 cup (125ml / 90g) cooked
sliced artichoke hearts

1 cup (250ml /140g) cooked whole
wheat rigatoni

1 Tbsp (15ml) fat-free Italian
dressing

2 Tbsp (30ml) pine nuts

1 Tbsp (15ml) parmesan cheese

1 Melt margarine in small saucepan. Add garlic and
spinach; stir over low heat until spinach is wilted
down.

2 Add artichokes, pasta and dressing. Mix well.

3 Sprinkle with pine nuts and cheese. Serve immediately.

Croutons

2 *servings*

■ SERVING SIZE: 1/2 OF RECIPE

■ COUNTS AS:
1 STARCH

▶ *size according to plan*

☀ Ingredients

2 slices lite bread

nonfat cooking spray

garlic powder, to taste

1/4 tsp (1ml) lite salt

onion powder to taste

oregano to taste

1 Dice bread into 1-inch cubes.

2 Coat baking sheet with nonfat cooking spray. Place
bread cubes on sheet.

3 Next, coat the bread cubes with cooking spray. Sprinkle
with garlic powder, onion powder, oregano and salt.

4 Bake in 375°F (190°C) oven for 6-8 minutes, or until
bread is lightly browned and crisp.

Sassy
Sides

Curried Rice

1 *serving*

■ SERVING SIZE: 1/3 CUP (85ML)
■ COUNTS AS:
   1 STARCH
   1 FAT

▶ *size according to plan*

☀ Ingredients

1 tsp (5ml) dried minced onion

1/2 tsp (2.5ml) curry powder

freshly ground pepper

1/3 cup (85ml / 53g) cooked brown or white rice

1 Tbsp (15ml) slivered almonds, chopped

2 pimiento-stuffed olives or ripe olives, chopped (optional)

nonfat cooking spray

1 Coat small saucepan with nonfat cooking spray; add onion and sauté until soft.

2 Add curry powder and pepper; cook, stirring, for 30 seconds.

3 Stir in hot rice and almonds. Sprinkle with olives, if desired.

Noodles with Mushrooms

1 *serving*

■ SERVING SIZE: 1 RECIPE
■ COUNTS AS:
   1 STARCH
   1 VEGETABLE
   1/2 DAIRY

size according to plan

☀ Ingredients

1/3 cup (85ml / 46g) cooked egg noodles

1 cup (250ml / 70g) fresh mushrooms, sliced

1 Tbsp (15ml) flour

1 Tbsp (15ml) lemon juice

1 tsp (5ml) lemon zest

1/2 cup (125ml) skim milk

1 Tbsp (15ml) parsley, chopped

nonfat cooking spray

1 Coat skillet with nonfat cooking spray; add mushrooms and sauté until tender.

2 Stir in flour, lemon juice and lemon zest.

3 Gradually add milk. Heat to boiling, stirring constantly.

4 Cook approximately 5 minutes until slightly thickened.

5 Stir in noodles and parsley.

Sassy
❖ Sides

Cornbread

12 *servings*

- **SERVING SIZE:** 1/12th OF BREAD
- **COUNTS AS:**
  1 STARCH
  1 FAT

▶ *size according to plan*

☀ Ingredients

1 cup (250ml / 122g) cornmeal

1/2 cup (125ml / 62g) all-purpose flour

2 tsp (10ml) baking powder

2 tsp (10ml) sugar

1 cup (250ml) skim milk

1/4 cup (60ml) egg substitute

3 Tbsp (45ml) canola oil

nonfat cooking spray

1 Preheat oven to 425°F (220°C).

2 Coat 8-inch baking dish with nonfat cooking spray.

3 In medium bowl, combine cornmeal, flour, baking powder and sugar.

4 In separate bowl, combine milk, egg substitute and oil.

5 Add wet ingredients to dry ingredients, stirring, until just moistened.

6 Pour batter into prepared dish. Allow to rest 5 minutes before baking.

7 Bake about 15 minutes, or until lightly browned, and when a tooth pick is inserted into center comes out clean.

8 Cut into squares.

Zucchini-Tomato Bake

1 *serving*

- **SERVING SIZE:** 1 RECIPE
- **COUNTS AS:**
  2 VEGETABLES
  1/2 DAIRY

▶ *size according to plan*

☀ Ingredients

2 cups (500ml / 226g) zucchini, sliced

1/4 tsp (1ml) lite salt

1 tsp (5ml) Italian seasoning

1 small tomato, sliced

1 Tbsp (15ml) water

1oz (28g) part-skim mozzarella cheese

nonfat cooking spray

1 Coat baking dish with nonfat cooking spray. Place zucchini slices in baking dish.

2 Sprinkle with salt and Italian seasoning.

3 Place tomato slices on top of zucchini. Sprinkle with water.

4 Cover and bake in 350°F (180°C).oven for 10-15 minutes, or until tender.

5 Remove from oven and sprinkle with cheese. Bake uncovered 5-10 minutes, or until cheese is melted.

Sassy
❖ Sides

Ratatouille

2 servings

- SERVING SIZE: 1/2 OF RECIPE
- COUNTS AS:
  2 VEGETABLES
  1 FAT

size according to plan

☀ Ingredients

1 cup (250ml / 82g) diced
  eggplant

1 cup (250ml / 113g) sliced
  zucchini

1/2 medium green pepper,
  chopped

1 small tomato, chopped

2 Tbsp (30ml) lite margarine

1/4 tsp (1ml) lite salt

1/4 tsp (1ml) freshly ground
  pepper

1 garlic clove, crushed

1 Melt margarine in a large skillet.

2 Add garlic and sauté until tender.

3 Add remaining ingredients.

4 Cover and cook over medium heat, stirring
  occasionally, about 5 minutes.

Pickles

4 servings

- SERVING SIZE: 1/2 CUCUMBER
- COUNTS AS:
  2 VEGETABLES

size according to plan

☀ Ingredients

2 medium cucumbers, sliced or
  quartered

1/2 cup (125ml) water

1/2 cup (125ml) vinegar

1/4 tsp (1ml) dill

dash garlic powder

1 Combine cucumbers, water and vinegar in a sealable
  container.

2 Add dill and garlic powder. Toss to coat.

3 Let stand at least 2 hours before serving.

"My husband uses the cookbook
more than I do. He actually
started losing weight without
even trying."

- *Rosie M.*

Sassy
♣ Sides

Stir-Fried Oriental Style Vegetables

2 *servings*

- SERVING SIZE: 1/2 OF RECIPE
- COUNTS AS:
  2 VEGETABLES

▶ *size according to plan*

☀ Ingredients

1 Tbsp (15ml) brown sugar artificial sweetener

1 Tbsp (15ml) reduced-sodium soy sauce

1 Tbsp (15ml) vinegar

1 tsp (5ml) grated fresh ginger

2 green onions, sliced

1 tsp (5ml) garlic powder

1/2 cup (125ml / 35g) fresh mushrooms, sliced

1 cup (250ml / 70g) cabbage, shredded

1/2 medium green pepper, sliced

1/2 medium red pepper, sliced

1/2 cup (125ml / 16g) fresh bean sprouts

nonfat cooking spray

1. To make sauce, stir together artificial sweetener, soy sauce and vinegar. Set aside.

2. Coat a wok or skillet with nonfat cooking spray. Preheat skillet over medium-high flame. Stir-fry ginger for 30 seconds.

3. Add onions and garlic powder and stir fry for 1 minute. Add cabbage and stir-fry for 2 minutes. Add peppers and bean sprouts; stir-fry for another minute, or until vegetables are crisp-tender.

4. Pour sauce over vegetables and toss to coat all vegetables.

Cauliflower with Cheese

1 *serving*

- SERVING SIZE:
  1/2 CUP COOKED
- COUNTS AS:
  1 VEGETABLE
  1 DAIRY

▶ *size according to plan*

good source of calcium

☀ Ingredients

1 cup (250ml / 100g) raw cauliflower florets

1/4 cup (60ml) water

1oz (28g) low-fat cheddar cheese, shredded

1/2 cup (125ml) skim milk

1 drop red pepper sauce, if desired

1. Place cauliflower in a microwave safe dish. Pour water over cauliflower. Heat on high for 3-5 minutes or until tender. Drain and set aside.

2. In saucepan, heat remaining ingredients over medium heat, stirring frequently, until cheese is melted and mixture is smooth.

3. Pour over cauliflower before serving.

Sassy
❖ Sides

Sherried Mushrooms

1 serving

- **SERVING SIZE: 1 RECIPE**
- **COUNTS AS:**
  2 VEGETABLES

▶ *size according to plan*

☀ Ingredients

1 cup (250ml / 70g) fresh whole
  mushrooms

1 green onion, chopped

1/4 cup (60ml) low-sodium broth

pinch dried tarragon, crushed

1 Tbsp (15ml) dry sherry

1 tsp (5ml) cornstarch

1. Gently clean mushrooms with a damp paper towel or soft brush.

2. In a medium skillet, combine mushrooms, onion, broth and tarragon. Bring to boil; reduce heat and cover. Simmer for 10-12 minutes, or until mushrooms are just tender.

3. In a small bowl, whisk together sherry and cornstarch until smooth; stir into skillet.

4. Cook, stirring, until slightly thickened and bubbly. Continue to cook another 2 minutes before serving.

Zucchini & Peppers

1 serving

- **SERVING SIZE: 1 RECIPE**
- **COUNTS AS:**
  3 VEGETABLES
  1 FAT

▶ *size according to plan*

☀ Ingredients

1 cup (250ml / 113g) zucchini,
  sliced

1/2 medium green pepper,
  chopped

1 garlic clove, crushed

1/4 tsp (1ml) lite salt

1/8 tsp (.5ml) freshly ground
  pepper

1 tomato, cut into wedges

1 Tbsp (15ml) lite margarine

nonfat cooking spray

1. Coat large skillet with nonfat cooking spray. Add zucchini, pepper, garlic, salt and pepper.

2. Cover and cook over medium heat, stirring occasionally, until vegetables are crisp-tender, about 5 minutes.

3. Add tomato. Cover again and cook over low heat just until tomato is heated through, about 3 minutes. Add margarine and heat until melted.

Sassy
❖ Sides

Stewed Tomatoes

4 *servings*

- SERVING SIZE: 1/4 OF RECIPE
- COUNTS AS:
  1 VEGETABLE

▶ *size according to plan*

☀ Ingredients

4 tomatoes, chopped

5 green onions, finely chopped

1/2 medium green pepper, chopped

1 packet artificial sweetener

1/2 tsp (2.5ml) lite salt

freshly ground pepper

1 tsp (5ml) garlic powder

1/4 tsp (1ml) oregano

1. Combine all ingredients in medium saucepan.
2. Cover and heat to boiling; reduce heat.
3. Simmer, uncovered, 10-15 minutes.

Corn O'Brien

2 *servings*

- SERVING SIZE: 1/2 OF RECIPE
- COUNTS AS:
  1 STARCH
  1 VEGETABLE

▶ *size according to plan*

☀ Ingredients

1 cup (250ml / 164g) frozen, whole kernel corn

1 large celery stalk, diced

1/4 tsp (1ml) crushed red pepper

1/2 medium green pepper, diced

nonfat cooking spray

1. Cook corn by steaming or microwaving.
2. Coat skillet with nonfat cooking spray. Add celery, crushed red pepper and green pepper; sauté until tender.
3. Add corn. Cook over low heat, stirring occasionally, until corn is heated through.

Sassy
❖ Sides

Classic Mashed Potatoes

6 *servings*

- SERVING SIZE: 1/2 CUP (12ML)
- COUNTS AS:
  1 STARCH

▶ *size according to plan*

☀ Ingredients

3 small potatoes, cooked

1/4 cup (60ml) milk

2 Tbsp (30ml) lite margarine, melted

1/2 tsp (2.5ml) lite salt

1/2 tsp (2.5ml) garlic powder

freshly ground pepper

1. Remove skin from potatoes.
2. Chop potatoes into a large dice and place in large mixing bowl.
3. Add milk, melted margarine, salt, garlic powder and pepper.

   For creamy potatoes: Mix using electric mixer 1-2 minutes.

   For chunky potatoes: Use a masher to soften potatoes, mix well until all ingredients are combined.

Peas & Mushrooms

2 *servings*

good source of fiber

- SERVING SIZE:
  1/2 OF RECIPE
- COUNTS AS:
  1 STARCH
  1 VEGETABLE

▶ *size according to plan*

☀ Ingredients

1 cup (250ml / 70g) mushrooms, sliced

2 green onions, chopped

1/4 tsp (1ml) lite salt

1/2 tsp (2.5ml) garlic powder

1/8 tsp (.5ml) freshly ground pepper

1 cup (250ml / 144g) frozen peas, thawed

nonfat cooking spray

1. Coat skillet with nonfat cooking spray and heat over medium flame. Add mushrooms, onions, garlic powder, salt and pepper. Sauté until mushrooms are tender.
2. Add peas to skillet and heat through.
3. Heat well.
4. Season with hot pepper sauce (optional).

"With 'No-Fuss' foods, I'm eating healthier and liking it!"

- Paula R.

Sassy
❖ Sides

Garlic n' Herb Pita Chips

2 servings

- SERVING SIZE: 8 CHIPS EACH
- COUNTS AS:
  1 STARCH

▶ *size according to plan*

meals in minutes

☀ Ingredients

6-inch (15cm) whole wheat pita

nonfat cooking spray

1 tsp (5ml) garlic powder

1/4 tsp (1ml) lite salt

oregano or thyme, sprinkle to taste

1 Cut pita in to 8 small pieces; separate layers into 16 wedges.

2 Preheat oven to 375°F (190°C).

3 Spray cookie sheet with nonfat cooking spray, place pitas on sheet.

4 Spray pieces with nonfat cooking spray.

5 Sprinkle with garlic powder, salt and herbs, as desired.

6 Bake for 5 minutes, or until lightly browned.

7 Serve with dip or salsa.

Grilled Corn on the Cob

6 servings

- SERVING SIZE: 1 EAR
- COUNTS AS:
  1 STARCH

▶ *size according to plan*

family fare

☀ Ingredients

6 ears of corn

2 Tbsp (30ml) lite margarine

lite salt to taste

freshly ground pepper

1 Peel corn, remove silk, wash well and pat dry.

2 Preheat grill to medium.

3 Place each piece of corn on individual piece of aluminum foil.

4 Spread 1 tsp (5ml) of softened lite margarine over each piece of corn.

5 Sprinkle lightly with salt and pepper.

6 Wrap each piece of corn tightly in aluminum foil.

7 Place on grill; cook approximately 25 minutes, turning occasionally until corn is tender.

Sassy
❖ Sides

Italian-Style Beans

serving

■ SERVING SIZE: 1 RECIPE
■ COUNTS AS:
  2 VEGETABLES

▶ *size according to plan*

good source of fiber

☀ Ingredients

1 cup (250ml / 110g) fresh green beans

2 Tbsp (30ml) fat-free Italian dressing

1/2 tomato, chopped

1 Tbsp (15ml) grated parmesan cheese

1 Place green beans, dressing and tomato in small saucepan.

2 Cook, uncovered, over low heat until heated through.

3 Remove from heat. Sprinkle with parmesan cheese just before serving.

Broccoli with Cheese

serving

■ SERVING SIZE: 1 RECIPE
■ COUNTS AS:
  1 VEGETABLE
  1 DAIRY

▶ *size according to plan*

good source of calcium

☀ Ingredients

1 cup (250ml / 70g) raw broccoli florets

1/4 cup (60ml) water

1oz (28g) low-fat cheddar cheese, shredded

1/2 cup (125ml) skim milk

1 drop red pepper sauce, if desired

1 Place broccoli in microwave safe dish. Pour water over broccoli. Heat on high for 3-5 minutes or until tender. Drain and set aside.

2 In saucepan, heat remaining ingredients over medium heat, stirring frequently, until cheese is melted and mixture is smooth.

3 Pour over broccoli. Serve immediately.

Sassy
❖Sides

Creamy Cucumbers

2 *servings*

- SERVING SIZE:
  1/2 OF RECIPE
- COUNTS AS:
  3 VEGETABLES
  1/2 DAIRY

▶ *size according to plan*

good source of calcium

☀ Ingredients

1 medium cucumber, sliced

1 Tbsp (15ml) chopped onion

1 tomato, chopped

2 Tbsp (30ml) cilantro

1 tsp (5ml) ground cumin

1 cup (250ml) plain nonfat yogurt

1 tsp (5ml) lite salt

1 Mix cucumber, onion, and salt in a small bowl.

2 Allow mixture to sit for five minutes.

3 Remove excess water from cucumbers.

4 Transfer to a dry bowl.

5 Add tomato and cilantro to cucumber mixture.

6 Stir in yogurt and cumin.

7 Cover and refrigerate 1 hour before serving.

Spanish Rice

4 *servings*

- SERVING SIZE:
  1/2 CUP (125ML)
- COUNTS AS:
  1 STARCH
  1 VEGETABLE
  1/2 DAIRY

▶ *size according to plan*

family fare

☀ Ingredients

1 1/3 cup (330ml) water

1/2 medium green pepper, diced

1/2 cup (125ml / 80g) white or yellow onion, diced

1/2 celery stalk, diced

1/4 tsp (1ml) of lite salt

2 small tomatoes, chopped

2/3 cup (170ml / 126g) raw brown or white rice

1/4 tsp (1ml) chili powder

freshly ground pepper

dash of hot sauce

1 In a medium saucepan, combine water, green pepper, onion, celery and salt. Bring to a boil. Then reduce heat and cover. Simmer for 5 minutes.

2 Stir in tomatoes, rice, chili powder, pepper and hot sauce. Return to boil. Reduce heat to low; cover and simmer approximately 20 minutes, or until liquid is absorbed.

"This is a fantastic side dish with a turkey burger. Better than instant rice."

- Michele G.

Sassy
❖ Sides

Balsamic-Glazed Vegetables

9 *servings*

- **SERVING SIZE:**
  1/2 CUP (125ML) COOKED
- **COUNTS AS:**
  2 VEGETABLES

▶ *size according to plan*

❊ Ingredients

1 1/2 pounds (672g) of your choice baby carrots, yellow squash, broccoli, cauliflower, zucchini, sliced

1/2 cup (125ml) water

1/2 cup (125ml) balsamic vinegar

1 tsp (5ml) garlic or onion powder

1 Tbsp (15ml) butter

freshly ground pepper

chopped parsley leaves, for garnish

1. Place vegetables in a pan with water, garlic or onion powder and vinegar.

2. Bring to a boil and cover. Reduce heat to medium and cook 10 minutes. Remove lid and raise heat back up.

3. Allow the water to boil away and the vinegar to reduce and glaze the vegetables, about 5 minutes.

4. When the vegetables are glazed, to a rich brown color add the butter to the pan.

5. Turn vegetables to coat lightly with butter.

6. Season with black pepper. Garnish with parsley.

Creamed Spinach

4 *servings*

- **SERVING SIZE:**
  1/2 CUP (125ML)
- **COUNTS AS:**
  1 VEGETABLE
  1 FAT

▶ *size according to plan*

good source of fiber

❊ Ingredients

2 pounds (896g) fresh baby spinach

2 Tbsp (30ml) lite margarine

2 tsp (10ml) flour

3/4 cup (200ml) skim milk

1/4 tsp (1ml) freshly ground pepper

dash of nutmeg

1. Cut and discard tough stems from spinach. Rinse and lightly pat dry.

2. Bring 2 quarts (2L) water to boil.

3. Add the spinach, bringing back to a boil and cook exactly 3 minutes.

4. Drain in colander; press spinach with hands to remove any excess moisture.

5. Chop spinach fine.

6. Melt margarine in a saucepan, add flour and cook, stirring until a light golden brown.

7. Slowly add milk, stirring with a wire whisk, until mixture thickens.

8. Add spinach, pepper and nutmeg; toss together and serve.

Sassy
❖ Sides

Ginger Carrots

6 *servings*

- SERVING SIZE: 1/2 CUP (125ML)
- COUNTS AS:
  1 VEGETABLE

▶ *size according to plan*

☀ Ingredients

1 pound (448g) carrot, peeled, sliced on an angle

1 Tbsp (15ml) lite margarine

2 Tbsp (30ml) artificial sweetener

2 Tbsp (30ml) fresh squeezed orange juice

2 Tbsp (30ml) grated ginger

1. In a pot of water, bring carrots to a boil and cook for approximately 5 minutes, or until fork tender. Drain.

2. In a sauté pan, over low heat, add margarine and artificial sweetener.

3. Stir for approximately 2 minutes, or until artificial sweetener begins to brown.

4. Add orange juice, ginger and carrots.

5. Simmer for approximately 5 minutes, or until liquid slightly thickens.

6. Serve immediately.

Lemon Green Beans

4 *servings*

- SERVING SIZE:
  1/2 CUP (125ML)
- COUNTS AS:
  2 VEGETABLES

▶ *size according to plan*

good source of fiber

☀ Ingredients

1 pound (448g) fresh green beans, cleaned and trimmed

1/4 cup (60ml / 37g) green or yellow peppers, chopped

2 Tbsp (30ml) fresh dill

1 fresh green onion, sliced, thinly

1 tsp (5ml) fresh garlic, ground

2 tsp (10ml) olive oil

2 Tbsp (30ml) lemon juice

1. Place beans in 4 quarts (4L) of boiling water.

2. Cook green beans for 4-5 minutes in boiling water.

3. Drain beans and run cold water over them to stop cooking process.

4. Place green beans in a bowl; add the peppers, dill, onion, garlic, olive oil and lemon juice.

5. Toss together until coated and serve.

Sassy
❖ Sides

Spicy Broccoli

2 servings

- SERVING SIZE:
  1/2 CUP (125ML)
- COUNTS AS:
  1 VEGETABLE
  1 FAT

▶ *size according to plan*

good source of fiber

☀ Ingredients

2 cups (500ml / 140g) raw broccoli florets

2 tsp (10ml) oil

1 tsp (5ml) crushed red pepper flakes

4 garlic cloves, chopped

1. Simmer broccoli, covered, in 1-inch (2.5cm) of water for 5-7 minutes, until tender. Drain broccoli and return skillet to heat.
2. Heat skillet over high flame.
3. Add oil, crushed pepper and garlic.
4. Add broccoli to spiced oil and toss to combine.
5. Serve immediately.

Green Beans with Mushrooms

7 servings

- SERVING SIZE: 1/2 CUP (125ML)
- COUNTS AS:
  2 VEGETABLES

▶ *size according to plan*

☀ Ingredients

1 1/4 pounds (560g) green beans, trimmed and halved

1 tsp (5ml) olive oil

1 Tbsp (15ml) lite margarine

1 green onion, chopped

1 cup (250ml / 70g) Portobello mushroom caps, sliced

1/2 cup (125ml) dry sherry

freshly ground pepper

1. Simmer green beans in water for about 5 minutes, until crisp-tender.
2. Drain green beans and return skillet to medium heat.
3. Add oil and margarine to the pan.
4. Add onions and sauté 2-3 minutes.
5. Add mushrooms and season with black pepper.
6. Sauté mushrooms with onions, about 3-5 minutes; add green beans back to the skillet.
7. Heat green beans through and add sherry.
8. Cook for 1-2 minutes.

Sassy
❖ Sides

Peppers & Mushrooms

- **SERVING SIZE:**
  1 CUP (250ML)
- **COUNTS AS:**
  2 VEGETABLES

▶ *size according to plan*

meals in minutes

☀ **Ingredients**

3 Tbsp (45ml) low-sodium vegetable broth

1 onion, cut into wedges

2 garlic cloves, crushed

1 green bell pepper, cut into 1/4 inch (1/2cm) strips

1 sweet red pepper, cut into 1/4 inch strips (1/2cm)

1/2 pound (224g) mushrooms, sliced

3 sweet chili peppers, chopped

6 cilantro leaves, chopped

freshly ground pepper

1 Tbsp (15ml) fresh parsley, chopped

1 Heat broth in a skillet; add onion and garlic and sauté until onion is translucent.

2 Add peppers, mushrooms and cilantro.

3 Stir-fry until peppers are tender.

4 Add freshly ground pepper and cook 1 minute.

5 Sprinkle with parsley and serve.

Herbed Eggplant

- **SERVING SIZE:**
  1/2 CUP (125ML)
  1 VEGETABLE

▶ *size according to plan*

family fare

☀ **Ingredients**

1 medium eggplant

2 tomatoes, chopped

1/4 cup (60ml / 40g) chopped onion

2 tsp (10ml) coriander

2 tsp (10ml) parsley

1 tsp (5ml) cilantro

nonfat cooking spray

1 Cut eggplant in half and bake at 325°F (160°C).for 20 minutes, or until soft. Remove eggplant from oven.

2 Mash eggplant with fork or potato masher.

3 Coat medium skillet with nonfat cooking spray and heat over medium flame.

4 Sauté onions until translucent.

5 Stir in tomato and cilantro; cook 1-2 minutes.

6 Stir in eggplant. Cook 4-5 minutes or until all liquid has evaporated.

7 Remove from heat and sprinkle with coriander and parsley.

Sassy
❖ Sides

Vegetables in Peanut Sauce

2 *servings*

- SERVING SIZE: 1/2 OF RECIPE
- COUNTS AS:
  1/2 PROTEIN
  2 VEGETABLES

▸ *size according to plan*

☼ Ingredients

1/4 pound (112g) bean sprouts

1/4 head (112g) cabbage, shredded

1/4 pound (112g) fresh spinach

1/4 cup (60ml) water

1 tsp (5ml) skim milk or plain, enriched soymilk

1/4 tsp (1ml) red pepper flakes or chili powder

2 packets brown sugar artificial sweetener

2 Tbsp (30ml) peanut butter

1 Bring a large pot of water to a boil; add cabbage and cook 1 minute.

2 Then add spinach, cook 1 minute. Add bean sprouts and cook another minute.

3 Drain vegetables.

4 To make sauce, bring another 1/4 cup (60ml) water to a boil in small sauce pan.

5 Add milk, red pepper, artificial sweetener and peanut butter.

6 Mix well until ingredients form a smooth sauce.

7 Bring to a boil and remove from heat.

8 Place vegetables on platter, top with sauce.

Sweet Cole Slaw

1 *serving*

- SERVING SIZE: 1 RECIPE
- COUNTS AS:
  2 VEGETABLES

▸ *size according to plan*

☼ Ingredients

1 cup (250ml / 70g) shredded cabbage

1/4 cup (60ml / 30g) shredded carrot

1 Tbsp (15ml) chopped sweet pepper

1 Tbsp (15ml) rice vinegar

1 packet artificial sweetener

1/2 tsp (2.5ml) low-sodium soy sauce

1 Combine all ingredients in a bowl.

2 Toss together to mix well.

3 Chill at least 30-60 minutes before serving.

"The cookbook is great because it gives you the food exchange for every recipe."

- F. Grove

Sassy
❖ Sides

Grilled Tomatoes & Eggplant

4 *servings*

- SERVING SIZE:
  2 TOMATO HALVES,
  1/2 CUP (125ML) COOKED EGGPLANT
- COUNTS AS:
  2 VEGETABLES
  1 FAT

▸ *size according to plan*

✳ Ingredients

1 pound (448g) eggplant, trimmed
  and cut crosswise into 1-inch
  (2.5cm) slices

1 pound (448g) tomatoes, sliced

freshly ground pepper

3 Tbsp (45ml) chopped parsley

1 Tbsp (15ml) olive oil

1 large garlic clove, pressed

3 Tbsp (45ml) shredded lite or
  reduced-fat Romano cheese

nonfat cooking spray,
  olive oil flavored

1 Spray both sides of eggplant and tomato slices with olive-oil flavored, nonfat cooking spray.

2 Sprinkle with freshly ground pepper to taste.

3 Grill eggplant slices until brown and tomato halves are charred.

4 Combine parsley, olive oil and garlic in a small bowl; pour over eggplant and tomatoes.

5 Top with grated cheese.

Stuffed Summer Squash

family fare

8 *servings*

- SERVING SIZE:
  1/4 OF A ZUCCHINI
  1/4 OF A SQUASH
- COUNTS AS:
  2 VEGETABLES

▸ *size according to plan*

✳ Ingredients

2 large yellow summer squash

2 large zucchini

2 heads radicchio, roughly
  chopped

6oz (168g) baby spinach

1 Tbsp (15ml) balsamic vinegar

1 Tbsp (15ml) olive oil

1 tsp (5ml) minced garlic

freshly ground pepper

nonfat cooking spray

1 In a medium bowl, whisk together the oil, vinegar, garlic and freshly ground pepper. Set aside.

2 Cut summer squash and zucchini in half lengthwise.

3 With a melon-baller or small spoon, scoop out center of each section, leaving only the skins. Reserve the flesh for another use.

4 Coat large saucepan with nonfat cooking spray. Heat over medium flame and add radicchio.

5 Stir and cook for 30 seconds; next add baby spinach, cover and turn off heat

6 Allow to steam for 1 minute, or until just wilted.

7 Season with pepper, to taste.

8 Drizzle inside of squash and zucchini shells with marinade, then stuff with radicchio and baby spinach.

9 Prepare grill and preheat to medium high.

10 Placed stuffed shells on grill and cook for 2-3 minutes or until bottoms are crisp-tender and slightly charred and filling is heated through.

Sassy
✤ Sides

Buttermilk Biscuits

12 *dozen biscuits*

- SERVING SIZE: 1 BISCUIT
- COUNTS AS:
  1 STARCH
  1 FAT

▶ *size according to plan*

family fare

☀ Ingredients
2 1/2 cups (625ml / 315g) all purpose flour

1 Tbsp (15ml) sugar

1 Tbsp (15ml) artificial sweetener

1/2 tsp (2.5ml) baking powder

1/2 tsp (2.5ml) salt

4 Tbsp (60ml) cold butter, cubed

4 Tbsp (60ml) cold lite margarine, cubed

1/4 cup (60ml) warm water

1 package active dry yeast

3/4 cup (200ml) warm low-fat buttermilk

nonfat cooking spray

1 In large bowl, combine flour, sugar, artificial sweetener, baking powder and salt.

2 Cut in butter and margarine to flour mixture, using a pastry blender or 2 knives, until mixture resembles coarse crumbs, set aside.

3 Place warm water in a small bowl; sprinkle in yeast and stir until dissolved.

4 Add yeast mixture and warm buttermilk to flour mixture, stir until blended well.

5 Turn out dough onto a floured surface. Knead dough until smooth. Form into a ball.

6 With a rolling pin, roll out dough to 3/4 to 1 inch (2-2.5cm) thickness.

7 Cut biscuits with a 2 or 2 1/2 (5-6cm) inch biscuit cutter.

8 Place biscuits onto a baking sheet coated with nonstick cooking spray. Cover biscuits and let rest until doubled in size, about 30-45 minutes.

9 Meanwhile, preheat oven to 400°F (200°C).

10 Bake in oven for approximately 15 minutes or until lightly browned.

Glazed Carrots

4 *servings*

- SERVING SIZE:
  6 CARROTS
- COUNTS AS:
  1 VEGETABLE
  1 FAT

▶ *size according to plan*

family fare

☀ Ingredients
24 cooked baby carrots

2 packets artificial sweetener

1 Tbsp (15ml) grated orange peel

1 Tbsp (15ml) orange juice

4 Tbsp (60ml) lite margarine

dash of cinnamon

1 Melt margarine in small saucepan. Add orange peel and juice.

2 Add carrots and artificial sweetener; cook over low heat, stirring occasionally, until carrots are glazed and heated through.

3 Sprinkle with cinnamon.

Sassy ♣ Sides

Cauliflower & Potatoes

1 *serving*

- **SERVING SIZE: 1 RECIPE**
- **COUNTS AS:**
  1 STARCH
  2 VEGETABLES

▶ *size according to plan*

☀ Ingredients

1 cup (250ml / 100g) raw cauliflower

1/2 potato, peeled

1/4 tsp (1ml) cumin seeds

1/4 tsp (1ml) ginger

1 garlic clove

1/4 cup (60ml) water

1/4 tsp (1ml) turmeric

1/4 tsp (1ml) red chili powder

1 tomato, diced

1/2 tsp (2.5ml) garam masala

1/2 tsp (2.5ml) coriander powder

1/2 tsp (2.5ml) parsley

nonfat cooking spray

1 Chop cauliflower and potato into a large dice.

2 Heat a medium sauté pan coated with nonfat cooking spray.

3 Sauté cumin seeds for 1 minute.

4 Add ginger, garlic and potatos.

5 Cook 1-2 minutes, stirring continuously, over medium high heat.

6 Add water, remaining spices and tomato.

7 Simmer for 5 minutes while stirring.

8 Add cauliflower and continue to cook 1 minute on medium high. Lower heat and cover.

9 Allow to simmer 10-15 minutes, or until cauliflower and potatoes are tender.

10 Garnish with parsley.

11 Serve hot.

Rosemary Rigatoni

3 *servings*

- **SERVING SIZE:**
  1/3 CUP (85ML)
- **COUNTS AS:**
  1 STARCH
  1 FAT

▶ *size according to plan*

☀ Ingredients

3 Tbsp (45ml) lite margarine

2 Tbsp (30ml) fresh rosemary, chopped

1 Tbsp (15ml) lemon zest

1 tsp (5ml) lemon juice

1 cup (250ml / 140g) cooked rigatoni

1/4 tsp (1ml) lite salt

1 Melt margarine in small saucepan. Add lemon zest, lemon juice, and rosemary; mix well.

2 Add pasta and stir until coated with margarine.

3 Sprinkle with salt.

Sassy
❖ Sides

Fancy Rice

6 servings

- **SERVING SIZE:**
  3/4 CUP (200ML)
- **COUNTS AS:**
  1/2 PROTEIN
  1 STARCH

▶ *size according to plan*

☀ Ingredients

1 Tbsp (15ml) olive or canola oil

1oz (28g) low-sodium Canadian bacon, diced

1/2 cup (125ml / 80g) onion, diced

1/2 medium green pepper, diced

1 celery stalk, diced

2 garlic cloves, minced

3 cups (750ml / 495g) cooked black-eyed peas

1 cup (250ml / 15g) cooked rice

1/4 tsp (1ml) lite salt

1/8 tsp (.5ml) freshly ground pepper

1/8 tsp (.5ml) cayenne pepper

1 Heat 1 tbsp olive oil in a Dutch oven over medium-high flame. Add Canadian bacon and cook for approximately 2-3 minutes or until lightly browned.

2 Next add onion, green pepper, celery and garlic. Cook, stirring, until just tender.

3 Add black-eyed peas, rice and seasonings; toss to combine.

4 Reduce heat to medium, and cook until heated through. Add a small amount of water if becomes too dry or starts to burn.

Stir-Fried Asparagus

1 serving

- **SERVING SIZE:**
  1 CUP (250ML) COOKED
- **COUNTS AS:**
  2 VEGETABLES

▶ *size according to plan*

good source of fiber

☀ Ingredients

1 1/2 cups (375ml / 201g) fresh asparagus

1 tsp (5ml) cornstarch

1 tsp (5ml) cold water

1/4 cup (60ml) low-sodium chicken broth

1/2 cup (125ml / 35g) fresh mushrooms, sliced

1 tsp (5ml) garlic powder

nonfat cooking spray

1 Cut asparagus on an angle 1/2-inch (2.5cm) pieces.

2 Mix cornstarch and cold water; reserve.

3 Coat skillet with nonfat cooking spray. Heat skillet over medium-high flame.

4 Add asparagus and mushrooms; sprinkle with garlic powder. Stir-fry until asparagus is crisp-tender, about 3 minutes.

5 Stir in broth; heat to boiling.

6 Stir cornstarch mixture; cook and stir until thickened, about 10 seconds.

Sassy ❖ Sides

8 *servings*

- SERVING SIZE:
  1/2 CUP (125ML)
- COUNTS AS:
  1 STARCH

▶ *size according to plan*

good source of fiber

Succotash

☀ Ingredients

1 package (16oz / 448g) frozen lima beans

1 package (16oz / 448g) frozen whole kernel corn

1/4 tsp (1ml) lite salt

1 cup (250ml) water

1 tomato, diced

1/2 cup (125ml / 80g) diced white onion

1 In medium saucepan, combine corn, lima beans, salt and water.

2 Bring to a boil and then reduce heat.

3 Add tomato and onion to mixture; simmer 5 minutes until all vegetables are tender.

"Easy-Appetizing-Flavorful"
- Paula R.

---

3 *servings*

- SERVING SIZE:
  1/3 CUP (85ML)
- COUNTS AS:
  1 STARCH

▶ *size according to plan*

family fare

Lemon Pilaf

☀ Ingredients

2 tsp (10ml) dried minced onion

1-2 garlic cloves, finely chopped

1/2 cup (125ml / 96g) raw brown or white rice

1 cup (250ml) low-sodium chicken broth

1 tsp (5ml) lemon zest, minced

nonfat cooking spray

1 Coat saucepan with nonfat cooking spray. Sauté onion and garlic until soft.

2 Add remaining ingredients. Heat to boiling, stirring once or twice. Reduce heat to low and cover tightly.

3 Simmer approximately 20 minutes, or until all liquid is absorbed.

4 Remove from heat; fluff with fork and serve.

Sassy
❖ Sides

Fried Cabbage

serving

■ SERVING SIZE: 1 RECIPE
■ COUNTS AS:
  3 VEGETABLES

size according to plan

good source of fiber

☀ Ingredients

2 cups (500ml / 140g) cabbage, shredded

5 green onions, chopped

1/4 tsp (1ml) onion powder

1/8 tsp (.5ml) lemon pepper

1/4 tsp (1ml) lite salt

nonfat cooking spray

1 Tbsp (15ml) water

1. Coat skillet with nonfat cooking spray; heat over low flame.

2. Add all ingredients to skillet.

3. Cover and cook over low until all vegetable are tender.

4. Add water, 1 Tbsp (15ml) at a time, if mixture becomes dry while cooking.

5. Serve hot.

Asparagus with Dijon Sauce

servings

■ SERVING SIZE: 1/2 CUP (125ML)
  COUNTS AS:
  1 VEGETABLE

☀ Ingredients

1 pound (448g) frozen asparagus spears, thawed

1 cup (250ml) low-sodium chicken broth

2 Tbsp (30ml) Dijon mustard

2 Tbsp (30ml) grated reduced-fat romano cheese

nonfat cooking spray

1. Coat large skillet with nonfat cooking spray. Heat over high flame.

2. Add asparagus to pan. Pour broth over asparagus and reduce heat; cover and steam over medium heat until crisp-tender, about 4 minutes.

3. Remove asparagus to serving plate with slotted spoon; keep warm.

4. Add mustard to skillet; increase heat to high and bring to a boil, stirring constantly.

5. Pour over asparagus; sprinkle with cheese.

Sassy
❖ Sides

Breadcrumbs

6 *servings*

- SERVING SIZE: 1/3 CUP (85ML)
- COUNTS AS:
  1 STARCH

▶ *size according to plan*

☀ Ingredients

6 slices lite bread

1/4 tsp lite salt

1/2 tsp (2.5ml) onion powder

1/2 tsp (2.5ml) garlic powder

1/4 tsp (1ml) oregano

1/4 tsp (1ml) basil

1. Toast bread lightly to remove any moisture.
2. Allow toast to cool.
3. Crumble toast into crumbs over large plate.
4. Mix salt, onion powder, oregano, basil and garlic powder into crumb mixture.
5. Adjust seasonings to taste.

---

family fare

Pad Thai Noodles

8 *servings*

- SERVING SIZE:
  1/2 CUP (125ML) COOKED
- COUNTS AS:
  1 STARCH
  1 VEGETABLE

▶ *size according to plan*

☀ Ingredients

1 package (6.75oz / 190g) dry rice noodles

1 cup (250ml / 83g) raw bean sprouts

1 Tbsp (15ml) chopped red pepper

3 green onions, chopped

1 Tbsp (15ml) chopped white onion

1 tsp (5ml) lemon juice

1 Tbsp (15ml) low-sodium soy sauce

1 tsp (5ml) rice wine vinegar

1/4 tsp (1ml) sugar

1 clove minced garlic

2 Tbsp (30ml) chopped peanuts

1 egg

nonfat cooking spray

1. Soak noodles in hot water for 15-20 minutes, or until soft. Drain and set aside.
2. Coat wok with nonfat cooking spray. Heat over medium-high flame.
3. Add red pepper, white onion and garlic; sauté for 1 minute. Remove from wok and set aside.
4. Place egg in wok and scramble. Add onion and pepper mixture back to wok. Add noodles, bean sprouts, soy sauce and vinegar. Heat through.
5. Add green onion, lemon juice, sugar and peanuts. Mix well.

Sassy
❖ Sides

Tandoori Cauliflower

6 *skewers*

SERVING SIZE: 1 RECIPE
COUNTS AS:
1 VEGETABLE
1 FAT
1/2 DAIRY

size according to plan

family fare

✳ Ingredients

2 cups (500ml) plain nonfat yogurt

1 1/2 pounds (672g) cauliflower

3 garlic cloves, minced

1 1/2 Tbsp (30ml) ginger, freshly grated

2 Tbsp (30ml) olive oil

1 tsp (5ml) cayenne pepper

1/2 tsp (2.5ml) freshly ground pepper

1 tsp (5ml) cumin, ground

1/2 tsp (2.5ml) coriander, ground

2 tsp (10ml) fresh lemon juice

2 Tbsp (30ml) whole wheat flour

1. Wrap the yogurt in cheesecloth, twist and suspend from a wooden spoon over a bowl.

2. Leave suspended in the refrigerator for 24 hours to drain the excess liquid from the yogurt.

3. Using a small grinder, blend the garlic, ginger and oil until you get a paste like substance. Place this mixture into a bowl.

4. Add cayenne, pepper, coriander, cumin, yogurt, lemon juice and flour to thicken into a paste.

5. Separate the cauliflower into florets. Using a fork, prick florets in several places.

6. Place cauliflower into a plastic bag and pour the yogurt marinade overtop. Refrigerate for a minimum of 2 hours.

7. Soak some bamboo skewers in water for a minimum of 30 minutes.

8. Preheat the grill to medium high.

9. Remove the cauliflower and divide them among the skewers. Place the skewers on the middle burner and cook using indirect heat for 25 minutes with the lid closed.

10. Lift the lid and turn the heat up to high.

11. Move florets over to sit directly over the heat. This will crisp the outside of the florets.

12. Remove from heat once crisp and serve hot.

Corn with Basil

4 *servings*

SERVING SIZE:
1/2 CUP (125ML) COOKED
COUNTS AS:
1 STARCH

size according to plan

✳ Ingredients

1 (10oz / 280g) package frozen, whole kernel corn

5 green onions, chopped

1 large celery stalk, thinly sliced

1 garlic clove, minced

1 tsp (5ml) fresh basil, chopped, or 1/4 tsp (1ml) dried basil leaves

nonfat cooking spray

1. Cook corn by steaming or microwaving.

2. Coat skillet with nonfat cooking spray. Cook and stir corn, onion, celery and garlic, over low heat, until onion is tender about 10 minutes.

3. Stir in basil; reduce heat.

4. Cover and cook until corn is tender, 3 minutes.

Sassy
❖ Sides

Marinated Cucumbers

1 *serving*

- SERVING SIZE: 1 RECIPE
- COUNTS AS:
  1 VEGETABLE

▶ *size according to plan*

☀ Ingredients

- 1 Tbsp (15ml) apple cider vinegar
- 1 Tbsp (15ml) water
- 1/2 packet artificial sweetener
- 1/4 tsp (1ml) freshly ground pepper
- 1/4 tsp (1ml) dill, minced
- 1/4 medium cucumber, peeled and thinly sliced

1. Stir together vinegar, water, artificial sweetener and pepper until dissolved.
2. Stir in dill and set aside.
3. Add cucumbers to marinade. Toss and chill before serving.

Green Onions & Carrots

1 *serving*

- SERVING SIZE: 1 RECIPE
- COUNTS AS:
  2 VEGETABLES

▶ *size according to plan*

☀ Ingredients

- 5 green onions, chopped
- 2 thin slices fresh ginger, finely chopped
- 1 garlic clove, finely chopped
- 1/2 medium carrot, shredded
- 1/4 tsp (1ml) lite salt
- 1/8 tsp (.5ml) fresh ground pepper
- nonfat cooking spray

1. Coat pan with nonfat cooking spray; add onion, ginger and garlic; stir fry for approximately 2 minutes, or until onions are crisp-tender.
2. Stir in carrots and salt; sprinkle with pepper.

"The recipes taste as good as in the picture!"

- Sandy S.

Sassy
❖ Sides

Peas & Onions

2 *servings*

■ SERVING SIZE:
1/2 OF RECIPE

■ COUNTS AS:
1 STARCH

▶ *size according to plan*

good source of fiber

※ **Ingredients**

1/2 cup (125ml) water

1/2 tsp (2.5ml) lite salt

1 cup (250ml / 144g) frozen peas, thawed

1/2 cup (125ml / 80g) sliced white onion

1/4 tsp (1ml) dried thyme leaves

1. In small saucepan, bring water and salt to a boil.
2. Add peas, onions and thyme.
3. Heat to boiling; reduce heat. Cook, uncovered, 5 minutes or until onions are tender.
4. Drain before serving.

Apple Chutney

6 *servings*

■ SERVING SIZE: 1/6 OF RECIPE

■ COUNTS AS:
1 FRUIT

▶ *size according to plan*

※ **Ingredients**

2 tart apples, peeled, cored and finely chopped

1/8 yellow onion, quartered

1/2 (1 inch / 2.5cm) piece fresh ginger root, peeled

2 Tbsp (30ml) and 1/4 tsp white wine vinegar

1 Tbsp (15ml) and 1/2 tsp (2.5ml) white sugar

1 Tbsp (15ml) and 1/2 (2.5ml) tsp brown sugar

1/8 tsp (.5ml) cinnamon

1/8 tsp (.5ml) white pepper

1/8 tsp (.5ml) ground cardamom

1/8 tsp (.5ml) ground nutmeg

1. In a saucepan, mix the apples, onion, ginger, vinegar, white sugar, brown sugar, cinnamon, white pepper, cardamom and nutmeg.
2. Bring to a boil, reduce heat and cover.
3. Simmer 30 minutes, stirring frequently, until the apples are tender. Mix in some water if necessary to keep the ingredients moist.
4. Remove the onion and ginger, and store in the refrigerator until ready to serve.

Sassy
❖ Sides

Veal ♣ Deal Plus

From delectable Veal Involtini and Tangy Glazed Pork Chops to Stuffed Lamb and Buffalo Burgers, this unique section truly has something for everyone. No matter what your favorite dish, you'll find many new and easy ways to create delightful meals that will keep the whole family coming back for seconds every time.

Mediterranean Veal Chops recipe can be found on page 169

Cuts of Veal

Veal is a term used to describe a young calf or cow that is approximately 1-3 months old. When shopping for veal, choose a piece that has a somewhat pale pink flesh; veal that is turning red means that the calf was likely older than 3 months. The texture should be firm, finely grained and smooth.

- **Roast** — A large cut of meat that is large enough to serve multiple people. Popular roasts include loin, shoulder, rib, breast and crown roasts.

- **Breast** — Cuts from the breast region of a young calf, such as a boneless breast roast.

- **Shanks** — Cuts from the front leg of the calf. It is a very flavorful cut, but because of large amounts of connective tissue, it can be a tough cut of meat. Moist heat methods such as braising or stewing are used to prepare shank cuts. Osso buco is a popular dish made with veal shanks.

- **Round** — Cuts of meat from the leg. Popular cuts from the leg include cutlets, round steaks, rump roasts and round roasts.

- **Chops** — Cuts of meat usually from the rib section and may also include part of the rib. Chops may also come from the loin.

- **Ground Veal** — This can come from various parts of the calf, so the fat content will vary depending on which cuts are ground. Ground veal is often used in conjunction with other ground meats to make dishes such as meatballs or meatloaves.

- **Loin** — A tender cut that comes from either side of the backbone. The loin may be cut into steaks, chops or roasts.

Basic Veal Roast

Place roast (4-5 pounds) (1.8 - 2.3kg) into shallow pan and roast at 325°F (160°C), until internal temperature reads 150° (65°C). Remove from oven and allow to rest for 10 minutes to allow juices to redistribute throughout the roast. Slice and serve.

TIP!

For more tender cuts of veal, choose loin roast, rib roast, rump roast and loin chop.

The less tender cuts, great for marinating, are shanks, shoulder roasts, breasts and riblets.

Lamb

Lamb is the meat from a sheep that is less than 1 year old. Meat from an animal that is older than 2 years is called mutton; mutton has a stronger flavor, but is less tender than lamb. Lamb is traditionally tender, with the exception of leg cuts. Baby lamb, which is from an animal younger than 8 weeks, should be pale pink when raw; other lamb cuts should be reddish-pink.

Lamb is a staple in many cultures, especially in Greece, Turkey, the Middle East, North Africa, India and beyond. Common flavors and spices you may see in lamb recipes include rosemary, lemon, garlic, mint and thyme, as well as cumin, coriander, cinnamon and turmeric.

Cuts

- **Roast** — A large cut of meat that is large enough to serve multiple people. Popular roasts include shoulder, shank leg, loin, loin eye and crown roasts.

- **Chops** — Cut of meat usually from the rib section; it may also include part of the rib. Chops may also come from the shoulder, rib or loin.

- **Ground Lamb** — Ground lamb can come from various parts of the lamb; therefore, the fat content will vary depending on which cuts are ground.

- **Legs** — Any cut of meat from the leg area. Leg cuts, such as a shank, are flavorful cuts of meat, but may be very tough. These are best suited for moist cooking methods, such as braising.

- **Loin** — A tender cut that comes from either side of the backbone. The loin may be cut into chops or roasts.

- **Rib** — A cut of meat from the rib section. It is a tender cut that may available as chops or roasts.

Fresh Pork Cuts

Place roast (4-5 pounds) (1.8-2.2kg) into shallow pan and roast at 325°F (160°C). until internal temperature reads 150°F (65°C). Remove from oven and allow to rest for 10 minutes to allow juices to redistribute throughout the roast. Slice and serve.

- **Chops** — Cut of meat from the rib section and will usually also include part of the rib.

- **Ground Pork** — Ground pork can come from various parts of a pig, so the fat content will vary depending on which cuts are used. Ground pork is often used in conjunction with other ground meats to make meatballs and meatloaves.

- **Loin** — Cut from either side of the backbone, from the shoulder to the leg, of the pig. This is a tender cut of meat that can be cut in to chops, tenderloin or roasts.

- **Ribs** — A cut of meat that is long and narrow, taken from the lower portion of the loin. This cut is usually a fatty cut of pork. These include "baby-back" ribs, spare ribs and country style ribs.

- **Roast** — A large cut of meat that is large enough to serve multiple people. Popular roasts include loin roasts, crown roasts and rib roasts.

 TIP!

Cooking in a small amount of fat in a skillet over direct heat works well for pork cutlets and chops.

Pork and Pineapple **Stir-Fry**

- **SERVING SIZE: 1 RECIPE**
- **COUNTS AS:**
  1 PROTEIN
  3 VEGETABLES
  1 FRUIT

▶ *size according to plan*

good source of fiber

☀ Ingredients

4 or 6oz (112 or 168g) pork tender loin

2 tsp (10ml) cornstarch

2 tsp (10ml) low-sodium soy sauce

1 cup (250ml) low-sodium chicken broth

1/8 tsp (.5ml) ground cumin

3 green onions, diced

1 cup (250ml / 83g) bean sprouts

3/4 cup (200ml / 115g) fresh pineapple, cut into bite-size chunks

1/2 small tomato, diced

1 cup (250ml / 47g) shredded romaine

nonfat cooking spray

1 Partially freeze meat. Thinly slice across the grain into bite-size strips. Set aside.

2 Mix chicken broth, cornstarch, soy sauce and cumin. Set aside.

3 Coat skillet or wok with nonfat cooking spray. Add pork and stir fry until no longer pink; set aside.

4 Over medium heat, add green onion and stir fry 1 minute. Add bean sprouts and stir fry another minute, or until vegetables are tender.

5 Add pork to vegetable mixture. Stir soy sauce mixture into pork and vegetables. Cook and stir until thickened.

6 Add tomato and pineapple. Toss to coat with sauce. Heat through.

7 Serve over shredded romaine lettuce.

BBQ Pulled **Pork**

- **SERVING SIZE: 3 OR 5OZ (84 OR 140G) COOKED**
- **COUNTS AS:**
  1 PROTEIN
  1 VEGETABLE

▶ *size according to plan*

family fare

☀ Ingredients

2-3 pounds (896g-1360g) pork loin, diced

1 can (16oz / 996g) low-sodium stewed tomatoes

2/3 cup (175ml) barbeque sauce

1/2 cup (125ml) water

1 onion, diced

2 Tbsp (30ml) vinegar

1/2 green pepper, diced

3 packets artificial sweetener

4 garlic cloves, minced

1/3 cup (85ml) hot water

1 Preheat oven to 375°F (190°C).

2 In a large casserole dish, combine all ingredients.

3 Bake 3-4 hours, or until pork is tender enough to be shredded with a fork.

4 Stir casserole every 30 minutes, if liquid evaporates, add additional hot water, 1/3 cup (85ml) at a time.

5 Once pork is tender, remove from oven. Use 2 large forks to shred all pork.

Veal ✤
Deal Plu

Sausage Patties

12 *servings*

- **SERVING SIZE: 2 PATTY**
- **COUNTS AS:**
  - 1 PROTEIN
  - 1 STARCH

▸ *size according to plan*

☀ Ingredients

10 green onions, finely chopped

1/2 cup (125ml / 54g) breadcrumbs (see recipe on pg 154)

1/2 cup (125ml) skim milk

2-3 pounds (996g-1360g) ground lean pork

1 tsp (5ml) white pepper

1/4 tsp (1ml) freshly ground pepper

1/4 tsp (1ml) ground cayenne

1 tsp (5ml) finely chopped fresh thyme

1 tsp (5ml) finely chopped fresh sage

nonfat cooking spray

1. Coat skillet with nonfat cooking spray and heat over medium heat.

2. Cook onion, stirring occasionally, until softened and beginning to brown. Remove from heat and cool 10 minutes.

3. While onions are cooling, stir together bread crumbs and milk in a large bowl and let stand until crumbs absorb the milk.

4. Add onions and remaining ingredients to crumb mixture and stir with a fork until blended well.

5. Preheat oven to 250°F (120°C).

6. Form sausage patties into 1/2-inch (1.5cm) thick patties, with dampened hands, and arrange on a wax paper lined tray.

7. Make into 12 patties.

8. Coat heavy skillet with nonfat cooking spray; heat over medium-high flame. Cook patties, turning once, until browned and just cooked through, about 4-6 minutes per batch.

9. Transfer to shallow baking pan and keep warm, covered with foil, in oven while cooking remaining batches.

Pork & Sauerkraut

8 *servings*

- **SERVING SIZE: 3 OR 5OZ (84 OR 140G) COOKED PORK WITH 1/2 CUP (125ML) SAUERKRAUT**

- **COUNTS AS:**
  - 1 PROTEIN
  - 1 VEGETABLE

▸ *size according to plan*

8-12 servings, depending on weight of meat

☀ Ingredients

1 pork loin (2-3 pounds / .89-1.3kg loin)

2 large cans sauerkraut, low-sodium if available

2 apples, peeled, cored and chopped

2 garlic cloves, minced

1/4 cup (60ml) apple juice

nonfat cooking spray

1. Cut pork loin into large chunks.

2. Spray casserole dish with nonfat cooking spray.

3. Combine pork, sauerkraut, apples, juice and garlic in casserole dish.

4. Cover dish and bake in a preheated 300°F (150°C) oven for approximately 1 hour.

5. Stir after 1 hour and cover, bake additional 30 minutes.

6. Remove cover, turn up heat to 350° (180°C), and bake 30-45 minutes or until pork is cooked.

Veal ♣ Deal Plus

Pork Tenderloin & Peppers

2 *servings*

- SERVING SIZE: 1/2 OF RECIPE
- COUNTS AS:
  1 PROTEIN
  2 VEGETABLES

▶ *size according to plan*

☀ Ingredients

1/2 tsp (2.5ml) dried thyme leaves

2 garlic cloves, crushed

8 or 12oz (224 or 336g) pork tenderloin

1/3 cup (85ml) water

1/2 medium red pepper, cut into 1/4-inch (1/2cm) strips

1/2 medium green pepper, cut into 1/4-inch (1/2cm) strips

1/2 medium yellow pepper, cut into 1/4-inch (1/2cm) strips

3 green onions, thinly sliced

1/4 tsp (1ml) lite salt

1 Tbsp (15ml) cold water

2 tsp (10ml) cornstarch

nonfat cooking spray

1. Mix together thyme and garlic; rub over pork.

2. Coat large skillet with nonfat cooking spray. Add pork to skillet and cook until no longer pink.

3. Remove pork and cover loosely with foil to keep warm.

4. Add water, peppers, onion and salt to skillet; cover and simmer, until vegetables are tender.

5. Mix cold water and cornstarch; stir into pepper mixture. Cook, stirring, until slightly thickened.

6. Cut pork into strips and add back to vegetable mixture. Heat through and serve.

Roast Pork with Rosemary

6 *servings*

- SERVING SIZE: 3 OR 5OZ COOKED PORK
- COUNTS AS:
  1 PROTEIN

▶ *size according to plan*

family fare

☀ Ingredients

1 or 2 pounds (448 or 896g) pork loin roast

1 tsp (5ml) lite salt

1 tsp (5ml) freshly ground pepper

3 Tbsp (45ml) dried rosemary leaves, crushed

3 garlic cloves, crushed

1. Sprinkle meat with salt and pepper; rub with rosemary and garlic.

2. Place pork roast in roasting pan. Roast, uncovered, in a 325°F (160°C). oven until internal temperature of 160° (70°C), about 30 minutes per pound.

Veal ❖
Deal Plus

serving

- **SERVING SIZE: 1 RECIPE**
- **COUNTS AS:**
  1 PROTEIN
  1 STARCH
  1 FAT

▶ *size according to plan*

meals in minutes

Pork **Piccata**

☀ Ingredients

4 or 6oz (112 or 168g) pork tenderloin

1/3 cup (85ml / 36g) breadcrumbs (see recipe on pg 154)

1/4 tsp (1ml) lite salt

1 Tbsp (15ml) capers

freshly ground pepper

1 tsp (5ml) garlic powder

1 Tbsp (15ml) lite margarine

1 Tbsp (15ml) lemon juice

1 Tbsp (15ml) dry white wine

nonfat cooking spray

1 With a meat mallet, pound tenderloin to 1/4 inch (1/2cm) thickness.

2 Mix together breadcrumbs, salt, pepper and garlic powder. Dampen meat lightly with water, then coat with breadcrumb mixture.

3 Coat skillet with nonfat cooking spray. Heat skillet over medium flame. Add pork to skillet and cook, turning once, until done, about 7-8 minutes.

4 Remove pork from skillet; add lemon juice, margarine, capers and wine into skillet; heat to boil and serve over pork.

❖ Veal or chicken could be substituted for pork.

---

 serving

- **SERVING SIZE: 1 COOKED PORK CHOP**
- **COUNTS AS:**
  1 PROTEIN

▶ *size according to plan*

Italian **Pork Chops**

☀ Ingredients

4 or 6oz (112 or 168g) boneless pork loin chop

2 Tbsp (30ml) fat-free Italian dressing

1 Tbsp (15ml) parmesan cheese

1 Tbsp (15ml) hot water

nonfat cooking spray

1 Use fork to pierce holes in pork chop to tenderize.

2 Place pork chop in plastic sandwich bag and pour salad dressing over chop. Place in fridge and allow to marinate 1 hour.

3 Coat medium skillet with nonfat cooking spray.

4 Over high heat, brown both sides of pork chop.

5 Turn down heat and continue to cook approximately 10 minutes, turning occasionally.

6 Add hot water, 1 Tbsp (15ml) at a time, to prevent pork from sticking to pan.

7 Sprinkle with cheese just before serving.

Veal ❖ Deal Plus

Roast Lamb

1 *serving*

- SERVING SIZE: 1 LOIN
- COUNTS AS:
  1 PROTEIN

▶ *size according to plan*

good source of fiber

☀ Ingredients

4 or 6oz (112 or 168g) lamb loin

One of the following rubs:

Rosemary Garlic Rub

2 tsp (10ml) dried rosemary, crushed

1 garlic clove, minced

1/8 tsp (.5ml) lite salt

freshly ground pepper

OR

Lemon Thyme Rub

2 tsp (10ml) dried thyme

1 Tbsp (15ml) lemon zest

1 Tbsp (15ml) lemon juice

1/8 tsp (.5ml) lite salt

nonfat cooking spray

1 Preheat broiler.

2 Rinse lamb; pat dry. Combine ingredients for one of the herbal rubs in a small bowl.

3 Liberally apply the herbs to the loin, pressing the rub into the surface. Allow to rest 5-10 minutes.

4 Spray a broiler pan with nonfat cooking spray; place loin on pan.

5 Cook until desired doneness, approximately 7-11 minutes for medium rare or 15-19 minutes for medium; or to a temperature of 145°F (60°C).for medium rare or 160°F (70°C).for medium.

Pork al'Orange

1 *serving*

- SERVING SIZE: 1 RECIPE
- COUNTS AS:
  1 PROTEIN
  1 FRUIT

▶ *size according to plan*

☀ Ingredients

1 Tbsp (15ml) water

1/3 cup (85ml) orange juice

1 tsp (5ml) cornstarch

1 tsp (5ml) low-sodium soy sauce

1/4 tsp (1ml) ground ginger

2 tsp (10ml) dried onion

4 or 6oz (112 or 168g) pork tenderloin

nonfat cooking spray

1 Mix water, orange juice, cornstarch, soy sauce, ginger and onion in saucepan. Cook sauce over medium heat until thickened. Set aside.

2 Coat skillet with nonfat cooking spray. Add pork; cook until pork is no longer pink. Add sauce to pan, heat through.

Veal ♣
Deal Plus

4 *servings*

- SERVING SIZE: 3 OR 5OZ (84 OR 140G) COOKED LAMB WITH 1-2 TBSP (15-30ML) SAUCE
- COUNTS AS:
  1 PROTEIN
  2 VEGETABLES

▶ *size according to plan*

family fare

Stuffed Lamb

✳ Ingredients

1 or 1 1/2 pound (448 or 672g) lamb roast, untied

1/4 tsp (1ml) lite salt

1/8 tsp (.5ml) freshly ground pepper

2 medium carrot, diced

2 large celery stalks, diced

1/2 cup (125ml / 80g) yellow onion, diced

3 Tbsp (45ml) fresh mint, chopped

3 Tbsp (45ml) lemon juice

1/2 cup (375ml) water

1 Tbsp (15ml) cornstarch

1 Tbsp (15ml) cold water

nonfat cooking spray

1. Season lamb with salt and pepper.
2. Spray skillet with nonfat cooking spray. Add carrots, celery and onion; cook, stirring often, until vegetables are tender.
3. Stir in mint and lemon juice.
4. Spread vegetable mixture evenly over lamb. Roll lamb over stuffing; secure with butchers string.
5. Place lamb in roasting pan with rack, sprayed with nonfat cooking spray.
6. Bake in 325°F (160°C).oven, uncovered, for approximately 40-45 minutes for medium, or until desired doneness.
7. Remove meat from pan; cover loosely with foil to keep warm.
8. Place roasting pan on stovetop. Add 1/2 cup (125 ml) water to pan; heat to a boil.
9. In a small bowl, mix cornstarch and cold water; add to roasting pan and heat until thickened.
10. To serve, slice meat and top with sauce.

Tangy Glazed Pork Chops

1 *serving*

- SERVING SIZE: 1 RECIPE
- COUNTS AS:
  1 PROTEIN
  1 VEGETABLE

▶ *size according to plan*

✳ Ingredients

4 or 6oz (112 or 168g) pork chop (bone and fat removed), size according to plan

1 cup (250ml / 130g) zucchini, sliced

1 Tbsp (15ml) ketchup

2 tsp (10ml) low-sodium soy sauce

1 Tbsp (15ml) water

1/8 tsp (.5ml) ground ginger

dash garlic powder

nonfat cooking spray

1. Coat skillet with nonfat cooking spray. Cook pork chop over medium heat, about 10 minutes, or until meat is tender and no longer pink.
2. Meanwhile, steam zucchini for 5-6 minutes, or until crisp-tender.
3. Mix ketchup, soy sauce, water, ginger and garlic powder. Pour over pork chops in skillet; cover and heat through.

Veal ✿
Deal Plus

Lamb Kabobs

1 *serving*

- **SERVING SIZE: 1 RECIPE**
- **COUNTS AS:**
  1 PROTEIN
  3 VEGETABLES

▶ *size according to plan*

☀ Ingredients

4 or 6oz (112 or 168g) boneless lamb, cut into 1-inch (2.5cm) cubes

1/4 cup (60ml) lemon juice

1/2 tsp (2.5ml) dried oregano leaves

1/8 tsp (.5ml) pepper

1/2 medium green pepper, cut into 1-inch (2.5cm) pieces

5 green onions

1 cup (250ml / 82g) eggplant, cut into 1-inch (2.5cm) pieces

1 Place lamb cubes into non-metal bowl.

2 In a separate bowl, mix lemon juice, oregano and pepper; toss lamb cubes with marinade.

3 Cover and refrigerate lamb for 30 minutes to 2 hours.

4 Preheat broiler.

5 Thread lamb cubes onto long metal skewer(s), leaving space between each. Broil 3-inches (8cm) from heat and cook until desired level of doneness. Turn and brush with reserved marinade while cooking.

6 Meanwhile, prepare vegetables onto 2 or 3 more skewers, alternating the green pepper, onion and eggplant, leaving space between each piece. Broil until vegetables are crisp-tender; brush with marinade while cooking.

Veal & Mushrooms

meals in minutes

1 *serving*

- **SERVING SIZE: 1 RECIPE**
- **COUNTS AS:**
  1 PROTEIN
  1 VEGETABLE

▶ *size according to plan*

☀ Ingredients

5 or 7oz (140 or 196g) veal cutlet, unbreaded

1 cup (250ml / 70g) fresh mushrooms, sliced

1 garlic clove, minced

1 tsp (5ml) garlic powder

1 Tbsp (15ml) water

1 tsp (5ml) flour

1/8 tsp (.5ml) lite salt

freshly ground pepper

1 Tbsp (15ml) fresh parsley, chopped

2 Tbsp (30ml) dry white wine

nonfat cooking spray

1 Pound veal to 1/4-inch (1/2cm) thickness.

2 In skillet coated with nonfat cooking spray, sauté garlic, mushrooms and garlic powder, until tender.

3 Add veal to skillet and cook through. Remove veal and vegetables; keep warm.

4 In a small bowl, mix water and flour, until dissolved.

5 Add water-flour mixture, salt and pepper to meat juices in skillet and stir until thickened.

6 Add parsley and wine; heat through.

7 Before serving, drizzle veal and mushrooms with sauce.

Veal ✤
Deal Plus

4 servings

- **SERVING SIZE: 1 CHOP AND APPROXIMATELY 1/2 CUP (125ML) SAUCE**
- **COUNTS AS:**
  1 PROTEIN
  2 VEGETABLES

▶ *size according to plan*

family fare

Mediterranean Veal Chops

☀ Ingredients

4 boneless veal chops, 5 or 7oz (140-196g) each

1/4 tsp (1ml) lite salt

1/8 tsp (.5ml) freshly ground pepper

2 tsp (10ml) olive oil

1 garlic clove, minced

1 cup (250ml / 56g) baby spinach

1/4 cup (60ml) white wine

1 cup (250ml / 49g) grape tomatoes, halved

1 cup (250ml / 168g) artichoke hearts, roughly chopped

1 Tbsp (15ml) capers, rinsed

2 Tbsp (30ml) lemon juice

nonfat cooking spray

1. Preheat oven to 350°F (180°C).

2. Trim any excess fat from chops. Season with salt and pepper.

3. Coat a large oven-proof skillet with nonfat cooking spray. Heat over a medium-high flame.

4. Add chops to pan; sear chops on each side until lightly browned, about 3-4 minutes per side. Remove from pan; set aside.

5. Add olive oil and garlic to skillet; heat over a medium flame. Cook for 1 minute — do not allow garlic to burn.

6. Add spinach to pan; pour wine over spinach leaves. Toss together to wilt spinach.

7. Next add tomatoes, artichokes, and capers. Cook until heated through, about 3 minutes.

8. Return veal chops to pan; spoon spinach-artichoke sauce over chops.

9. Cover pan loosely with foil and place in the oven. Finish cooking in oven, approximately 25 minutes.

10. Remove from oven; sprinkle each chop with lemon juice just before serving. Allow to rest 5-10 minutes.

---

1 serving

- **SERVING SIZE: 1 VEAL CUTLET WITH VEGETABLES**
- **COUNTS AS:**
  1 PROTEIN
  1 STARCH
  2 VEGETABLES

▶ *size according to plan*

meals in minutes

Veal Swiss Steak

☀ Ingredients

5 or 7oz (140 or 196g) veal cutlet, unbreaded

1 Tbsp (15ml) flour

1/2 tsp (2.5ml) dry mustard

1/4 tsp (1ml) lite salt

1/2 small tomato, diced

1/4 tsp (1ml) garlic powder

1 cup (250ml) water

1/2 medium green pepper, sliced into strips

5 green onions, thinly sliced

1. If necessary, pound veal 1/4-inch (1/2cm) thick, with a meat mallet.

2. In a small dish, combine flour, dry mustard, and salt.

3. Coat each side of the veal with flour mixture.

4. Coat skillet with nonfat cooking spray. Cook veal over medium-high heat until browned; remove from pan and keep warm.

5. Add tomatoes, onion, green pepper, garlic powder and water. Bring to a boil; reduce heat.

6. Cover and simmer until vegetables are tender.

7. Return veal to pan to heat through before serving.

Veal ✤ Deal Plus

Italian-Style Veal

1 serving

- SERVING SIZE: 1 CUTLET WITH VEGETABLES AND CHEESE
- COUNTS AS:
  1 PROTEIN
  4 VEGETABLES
  1/2 DAIRY

▶ *size according to plan*

meals in minutes

☀ Ingredients

5 or 7oz (140 or 196g) veal cutlet, unbreaded

1/2 (125ml / 35g) cup fresh mushrooms, sliced

1/2 cup (125ml / 80g) white onion, finely chopped

1/2 medium red pepper, chopped

1/2 large celery stalk, finely chopped

1 garlic clove, minced

1 small tomato, seeded and diced

1/4 tsp (1ml) dried basil, crushed

1/8 tsp (.5ml) crushed red pepper (optional)

1oz (28g) reduced-fat mozzarella cheese, shredded

nonfat cooking spray

1 Coat oven-safe skillet with nonfat cooking spray. Brown both sides of veal over medium high heat. Remove from pan and keep warm.

2 Add mushrooms, onion, red pepper, celery and garlic to pan. Cook until tender.

3 Add tomatoes, basil, oregano and red pepper (optional); toss to combine.

4 Return veal to pan. Simmer until meat is heated through.

5 Top veal and vegetables with cheese. Broil, 3 inches (8cm) from heat, until cheese is melted.

Dijon Lamb Chops

1 serving

- SERVING SIZE: 1 RECIPE
- COUNTS AS:
  1 PROTEIN
  3 VEGETABLES

▶ *size according to plan*

meals in minutes

☀ Ingredients

4 or 6oz (112 or 168g) boneless lamb chop(s)

1 Tbsp (15ml) Dijon mustard

1/2 tsp (2.5ml) dried thyme

1/4 tsp (1ml) lite salt

1/2 medium carrot, sliced into thin strips

1 cup (250ml / 130g) zucchini, sliced into thin strips

1 cup (250ml / 100g) cauliflower florets

nonfat cooking spray

1 Preheat broiler.

2 In a small bowl, mix mustard, thyme and salt.

3 Place lamb chop on broiler pan, coated with nonfat cooking spray. Brush lamb chop with half of the marinade.

4 Broil chop, 3-inches (8cm) from heat, about 6 minutes. Turn chop over and brush with remaining marinade. Broil another 5-8 minutes.

5 Meanwhile, steam vegetables lightly until tender. Season to taste.

6 Serve vegetables with lamb chop.

Veal ♣
Deal Plus

4 *servings*

■ SERVING SIZE: 1/4 OF THE
RECIPE OR 1 INVOLTINI
■ COUNTS AS:
   1 PROTEIN
   1 VEGETABLE
   1/2 DAIRY

● *size according to plan*

family fare

Veal Involtini

❋ **Ingredients**

1 1/4–1 3/4 pounds (560-784g)
   veal scaloppini

1/8 tsp (.5ml) lite salt

1/8 tsp (.5ml) freshly ground
   pepper

1 cup (250ml / 56g) baby spinach
   leaves, rinsed

4oz (112g) lite mozzarella cheese,
   sliced thin

2 tsp (10ml) olive oil

2-3 garlic cloves, crushed

1 cup (250ml) white wine

1 Preheat oven to 350°F (180°C).

2 Rinse veal; pat dry. Season with salt and pepper.

3 Arrange veal scaloppini on a cutting board. Onto each
   veal cutlet, place a few spinach leaves, 3-4 per piece.
   Top spinach with a slice of mozzarella.

4 Roll each veal scaloppini, enclosing spinach and cheese.
   Secure with a toothpick or with some butcher's string.

5 Heat an oven-proof skillet over a medium-high flame.
   Add olive oil and garlic, sauté 30 seconds.

6 Add veal rolls (involtini) to pan, sear until lightly brown
   on all sides, about 2 minutes per side. Pour wine over
   veal.

7 Put pan in oven to finish cooking, about 15 minutes.
   Remove from oven, loosely cover with foil; allow to rest
   5-10 minutes before serving.

---

1 *serving*

■ SERVING SIZE: 1 RECIPE
■ COUNTS AS:
   1 PROTEIN
   2 VEGETABLES

size according to plan

Veal Goulash

❋ **Ingredients**

5 or 7oz (140 or 196g) veal, any
   boneless cut, such as a chop,
   cubed, into bite-sized pieces

1/8 tsp (.5ml) lite salt

freshly ground pepper

1/2 cup white onion, sliced

1 small tomato, seeded and diced

1/2 Tbsp (7.5ml) flour

1/4 cup (60ml) low-sodium beef
   broth

1 Tbsp (15ml) lemon juice

1/2 tsp (2.5ml) paprika

1/4 tsp (1ml) caraway seeds

nonfat cooking spray

1 Season veal cubes with salt and pepper.

2 Spray skillet with nonfat cooking spray; brown veal
   over medium-high heat.

3 Add onion and tomato; cook, uncovered,
   approximately 15 minutes.

4 Sprinkle veal and vegetables with flour. Stir, while
   cooking, for about 1 minute.

5 Stir in beef broth, lemon juice, paprika and caraway
   seeds.

6 Cover and reduce heat. Simmer 20 minutes or until
   veal is tender.

Veal ❖
Deal Plus

Balsamic Lamb Chops

4 *servings*

- **SERVING SIZE: 1/4 OF RECIPE**
- **COUNTS AS:**
  1 PROTEIN

▸ *size according to plan*

☼ Ingredients

1 tsp (5ml) dried rosemary

1/4 tsp (1ml) dried basil

1/4 tsp (1ml) dried oregano

1/2 tsp (2.5ml) dried thyme

freshly ground pepper

1 or 1 1/2 pounds (448 or 672g)
  boneless lamb chops

1 Tbsp (15ml) olive oil

2 shallots, minced

1-2 garlic cloves, minced

1/3 cup (85ml) balsamic vinegar

2/3 cup (170ml) low-sodium
  chicken broth

1/3 cup (85ml) water

1 tsp (5ml) butter

nonfat cooking spray

1. Combine rosemary, basil, oregano, thyme and pepper in a small bowl. Rub herb mixture onto lamb chops, on both sides; allow to rest 15-30 minutes, covered.

2. Heat olive oil in a large skillet or grill pan over medium-high flame.

3. Cook chops, approximately 3-4 minutes per side, for medium-rare doneness, or to desired temperature. Remove from pan and set aside, keeping warm.

4. Coat the same pan with nonfat cooking spray, allowing pan to reheat. Add shallots and garlic; cook until golden brown.

5. Next, add in balsamic vinegar, stirring constantly, scraping to remove any browned bits from the bottom of the pan. Add in chicken broth and water, stirring to combine, and continue to cook approximately 5 minutes or until slightly thickened and reduced by half.

6. Remove sauce from heat and stir in butter.

7. Drizzle each chop with sauce; garnish with fresh rosemary and lemon slices.

Buffalo Burgers

4 *servings*

- **SERVING SIZE: 1 BURGER PATTY**
- **COUNTS AS:**
  1 PROTEIN

▸ *size according to plan*

☼ Ingredients

1 - 1 1/2 pounds (448-672g)
  ground buffalo

1/2 jalapeño, seeded and minced

1/8 tsp (.5ml) lite salt

freshly ground pepper

dash of garlic powder

1. Combine all ingredients in a large bowl, mix until just combined.

2. Form into 4 patties. Cover and refrigerate until ready to use.

3. Preheat grill or broiler. Cook burgers for approximately 6 minutes on each side, or until desired doneness.

Veal ✤
Deal Plu

Veal Meatloaf

SERVING SIZE: 1/4 RECIPE
COUNTS AS:
1 PROTEIN
1 FAT
1 STARCH

size according to plan

☀ Ingredients

1 or 1 1/2 pounds (125ml)
  ground veal

1/2 cup (125ml) egg substitute

1/2 cup (125ml) dry bread crumbs

1/4 cup (60ml) warm water

1/2 (1oz) envelope dry onion
  soup mix

1 large carrot, grated

1 small shiitake mushroom, sliced

1 Preheat oven to 350°F (180°C).

2 In a bowl, mix the ground veal, egg substitute, dry bread crumbs, water, soup mix, carrots and shiitake mushrooms. Transfer to a 9 x 5 inch (23 X 13cm) loaf pan.

3 Bake 1 hour in the preheated oven, or to a minimum internal temperature of 160°F (70°C).

Venison Chili

SERVING SIZE:
1 CUP (250ML)
COUNTS AS:
1 PROTEIN
2 VEGETABLES

size according to plan

family fare

☀ Ingredients

1 Tbsp (15ml) canola or other
  vegetable oil

4 garlic cloves

2 cups (500ml / 320g) chopped
  yellow onion

1 cup (250ml / 148g) chopped
  green pepper

1 jalapeño, seeded and chopped

2 pounds (896g) ground venison

2 Tbsp (30ml) chili powder

1 tsp (5ml) ground cumin

1 tsp (5ml) cayenne pepper

1 (28oz / 784g) can diced
  tomatoes, no salt, undrained

3 cups (750ml) low-sodium chicken
  or beef broth

2 Tbsp (30ml) tomato paste, no salt

nonfat cooking spray

1 Coat large pot with nonfat cooking spray; heat over medium flame. Add oil and garlic, sauté until just golden.

2 Add onion, green pepper and jalapeño; cook until soft.

3 Stir in venison, chili powder, cumin and cayenne. Cook the meat and spices with the vegetables, stirring, until browned, about 5-6 minutes.

4 Add tomatoes and liquid, broth and tomato paste to chili base; stir to combine. Bring to a boil; reduce heat and simmer at least 30-45 minutes before serving.

Veal ✤
Deal Plus

Under
the
✿ Sea

There are lots of delicious recipes found Under the Sea and you'll find plenty to choose from inside the *L A Lite Cookbook*! From mouthwatering Ginger Salmon to Citrus Grilled Swordfish, you'll want to dive in to our unique seafood blends. Plus, you'll also discover the numerous health benefits of a variety of fish and the healthiest methods for selection, preparation and cooking.

Shrimp Fried Rice recipe can be found on page 183

How to select fish

When purchasing whole fish look for:

- Clear, bright eyes, not sunken eyes.
- Bright red gills.
- Intact scales that are firmly attached to the skin; scales should not be missing.
- Moist, shiny skin, but not slimy.
- Tail should be stiff and the flesh should be firm.
- Should not smell!
- Refrigerate fish for only 1 or 2 days.

When purchasing fish filets, look for:

- White fish should have a white translucent color with no discoloration.
- Flesh should be firm.
- Should not smell!
- Refrigerate fish for only 1 or 2 days.

How to purchase frozen fish:

- Frozen hard with no signs of thawing.
- Packaging should not be damaged.
- No evidence of freezer burn.

When purchasing shellfish/mollusks:

- Clear, bright eyes for crabs or lobsters.
- Shellfish should not smell!
- Check mollusks before cooking for freshness: avoid broken shells. Also the fish or shellfish should be alive — make sure they are responsive if pressure is applied to their shells.
- Once cooked, discard any mollusks which shells do not open after adequate cooking.
- Refrigerate shellfish on ice, for only 1-2 days maximum.

TIP!

Fish is a good source of potassium, vitamins, and other minerals. Potassium in your diet will help regulate blood pressure and proper muscle functions.

Cuts of fish

■ **Whole dressed** — A whole fish with tail and head still attached, though typically your fish monger will have cleaned it already.

■ **Pan dressed** — A whole fish with head, tail and fins removed.

■ **Filets** — To filet a fish is to remove the filets from the bones. Typically, it is sold in a full length or may be cut into individual servings.

■ **Steaks** — A cross-cut piece of the body of a larger fish. Steaks may contain small pieces of the backbone.

Basic cooking methods

It is important to cook fin fish thoroughly, but do not overcook it. Proper cooking allows the fish to develop the flavors and soften the connective tissue. Cooking fish at too high a temperature and cooking it too long will destroy the flavor, texture, and moisture of the fish. Fish is fully cooked when the flesh becomes opaque. White fish should also flake easily with pressure from a fork. Fish should be cooked to an internal temperature of 130° - 145° (55 - 65°C)..

Common methods for cooking fish

■ **Poaching** — Fish simmered in liquid, serve hot or cold.

■ **Steaming** — Fish is cooked from the steam of boiling water or any other liquid.

■ **Broiling or Grilling** — Fish is cooked by dry heat from above, as in the oven or under a salamander or a grill.

■ **Oven baking** — Fish is baked in an oven and basted usually with a small amount of fat or liquid, and sometimes in a pouch of paper or foil.

■ **Pan-frying** — Cooking fish quickly in a small amount of fat on a skillet over direct heat.

TIP!

• Fish offers the same quality and quantity of protein as meat but often with fewer calories. Fish is generally low in cholesterol and is healthy for the heart.

1 *serving*

- SERVING SIZE: 1 FILET
- COUNTS AS:
  1 PROTEIN

▶ *size according to plan*

meals in minutes

Poached **Fish**

☀ Ingredients

2 cups (500ml) water

1 cup (250ml) white wine

1/4 tsp (1ml) lite salt

1/4 tsp (1ml) dried thyme

1/4 tsp (1ml) dried tarragon

1 tsp (5ml) peppercorns

4 sprigs of parsley

1 bay leaf

5 or 7oz (140 or 196g) filet of
fish, such as cod or halibut

1 Heat water, wine, salt, thyme, tarragon, peppercorns,
parsley and bay leaf to a boil, in a deep skillet; reduce
heat. Cover and simmer 5 minutes.

2 Place fish in skillet; add water, if necessary, to cover.
Again, heat to boiling; then reduce heat.

3 Simmer fish, uncovered, until it flakes easily with a
fork.

4 Carefully remove fish with slotted spatula, allowing to
drain.

---

1 *serving*

- SERVING SIZE: 1 FILET
- COUNTS AS:
  1 PROTEIN
  1 STARCH

▶ *size according to plan*

meals in minutes

Oven Fried **Fish**

☀ Ingredients

5 or 7oz (140 or 196g) fish
filet, such as flounder or
tilapia

1/2 cup (125ml / 54g)
breadcrumbs (see recipe on
page 154)

1/8 tsp (.5ml) lite salt

1/8 tsp (.5ml) paprika

dash of dried dill

freshly ground pepper

butter flavor cooking spray

nonfat cooking spray

1 Preheat oven to 350°F (180°C).

2 In a shallow bowl, combine breadcrumbs, salt, paprika,
dill and pepper.

3 Rinse fish in cold water. Lightly pat dry.

4 Dip fish filet into breadcrumb mixture, coating each
side.

5 Coat baking pan with nonfat cooking spray. Place fish
on baking sheet. Spray fish with nonfat butter spray.

6 Bake fish, uncovered, until easily flakes, approximately
20 minutes.

Under
the ✤ Sea

Vegetable Stuffed Sole

1 *serving*

- SERVING SIZE:
  1 STUFFED FILET
- COUNTS AS:
  1 PROTEIN
  2 VEGETABLES

▶ *size according to plan*

※ Ingredients

5 or 7oz (140 or 196g) sole filet

1/4 tsp (1ml) lite salt

1/2 tsp (2.5ml) dried dill

1/4 tsp (1ml) freshly ground pepper

1/2 medium carrot, cut into strips

1/2 medium red pepper, cut into strips

1/4 cup (60ml) dry white wine

nonfat cooking spray

1. Preheat oven to 350°F (180°C) Coat a small baking dish with nonfat cooking spray.

2. In a small bowl, mix salt, dill and pepper; season filets with spice mixture. Place in baking dish.

3. Place carrot and pepper strips in the middle of the sole filet.

4. Roll fish, enclosing the vegetables; secure with toothpicks, if necessary. Place seam side down in baking dish. Pour wine over fish.

5. Cover with aluminum foil and bake until opaque, approximately 20 minutes, or until fish flakes easily with a fork.

Baked Stuffed Fish

1 *serving*

- SERVING SIZE: 2 FILET PIECES
  WITH STUFFING
- COUNTS AS:
  1 PROTEIN
  1 STARCH
  2 VEGETABLES

▶ *size according to plan*

※ Ingredients

5 or 7oz (140 or 196g) fish filet, such as tilapia or flounder

1 slice diet bread, toasted and cut into cubes

1 garlic clove, minced

1 tsp (5ml) dried minced onion

1/2 cup (125ml / 35g) mushrooms, chopped

1/2 medium carrot, shredded

1 Tbsp (15ml) lemon juice

1/4 tsp (1ml) dried marjoram

1/4 tsp (1ml) freshly ground pepper

1/4 cup (60ml) lemon juice

nonfat cooking spray

nonfat butter spray

1. Preheat oven to 350°F (180°C) oven. Coat baking dish with nonfat cooking spray.

2. Cut filet into 2 pieces; set aside.

3. Coat skillet with nonfat cooking spray. Add garlic, onions and mushrooms; sauté until tender.

4. Add in carrots, lemon juice, marjoram and pepper; gently toss with bread to combine.

5. Spoon stuffing on top of one piece of filet. Top with remaining piece of filet.

6. Season filet with butter spray; sprinkle with lemon juice. Bake, uncovered, until fish flakes easily with fork, or approximately 30 minutes.

Under the ✿ Sea

Ginger Salmon

1 *serving*

- SERVING SIZE: 1 FILET WITH SAUCE
- COUNTS AS:
  1 PROTEIN
  1 VEGETABLE

▸ *size according to plan*

☀ Ingredients

4 or 6oz (112 or 168g) salmon filet

1/2 Tbsp (7.5ml) brown sugar artificial sweetener

1/2 Tbsp (7.5ml) low-sodium soy sauce

1/2 Tbsp (7.5ml) dry white wine

1/2 Tbsp (7.5ml) lemon juice

1/2 tsp (2.5ml) garlic minced

1/4 tsp (1ml) fresh ginger, grated

dash of red pepper sauce

5 green onions, sliced

nonfat cooking spray

1. Coat skillet with nonfat cooking spray and heat over medium flame. Add salmon to pan.

2. Cook salmon for 4 minutes on each side.

3. Remove salmon from pan; cover loosely with foil to keep warm.

4. Combine remaining ingredients in a small bowl.

5. Reduce heat to low. Add sauce to skillet and sauté for 1 minute.

6. Return salmon to pan and cook until heated through.

> "Cooking is so easy now with the L A Weight Loss Cookbook."
>
> *- Mandy M.*

Broiled Ginger Scallops

1 *serving*

- SERVING SIZE: 1 RECIPE
- COUNTS AS:
  1 PROTEIN

▸ *size according to plan*

☀ Ingredients

4 or 6oz (112 or 168g) scallops

2 Tbsp (30ml) low-sodium soy sauce

1 garlic clove, minced

1 Tbsp (15ml) ginger, minced

2 Tbsp (30ml) lemon juice

1 Tbsp (15ml) brown sugar artificial sweetener

nonfat cooking spray

1. Arrange scallops in a single layer in a baking dish.

2. Heat soy sauce in a small saucepan, over a medium flame. Add garlic, ginger, lemon juice, and brown sugar; simmer 2-3 minutes. Allow to cool to room temperature.

3. Pour cooled sauce over scallops. Cover and refrigerate at least 2 hours.

4. Preheat broiler.

5. Remove scallops from marinade. Place scallops, in a single layer, on a broiler pan coated with nonfat cooking spray.

6. Broil 4 inches (10cm) from heat until opaque, approximately 6-8 minutes, turning once during cooking.

Under the ✿ Sea

Shrimp Jambalaya

serving

- **SERVING SIZE: 1 RECIPE**
- **COUNTS AS:**
  - 1 PROTEIN
  - 1 STARCH
  - 3 VEGETABLES

▶ *size according to plan*

✳ Ingredients

1/2 cup (125ml / 80g) white onion, chopped

1/2 medium green pepper, chopped

1 garlic clove, minced

5 or 7oz (140 or 196g) fresh shrimp, peeled and deveined

1 cup (250ml) low-sodium chicken broth

1/4 tsp (1ml) lite salt

1/8 tsp (.5ml) freshly ground pepper

1/8 tsp (.5ml) ground thyme

1/8 tsp (.5ml) hot pepper sauce

1 bay leaf

1 small tomato, seeded and chopped

2 1/2 Tbsp (37.5ml) uncooked brown rice

nonfat cooking spray

1. Coat a saucepan oven, over medium heat, with nonfat cooking spray. Add onion, green pepper and garlic; cook until tender.

2. Add shrimp; cook until opaque and turning pink. Remove shrimp and vegetables from pan; set aside.

3. Next, add rice, chicken broth, salt, pepper, thyme, hot pepper sauce, bay leaf and tomato. Heat to boiling. Reduce heat; cover and simmer, until rice is tender.

4. Return shrimp and vegetables to saucepan oven. Cover again, and cook until heated through.

"The Shrimp Jambalaya is my favorite, flavorful & easy."

- J. DeBow

Boiled Lobster Tails

serving

- **SERVING SIZE: 1 TAIL**
- **COUNTS AS:**
  - 1 PROTEIN

▶ *size according to plan*

✳ Ingredients

2 quarts (2L) water

1/4 tsp (1ml) lite salt

1 lobster tail, with shell, to yield 4 or 6oz (112 or 168g) cooked

nonfat cooking spray

lemon juice (optional)

1 tsp (5ml) butter (optional)

1. Bring water and salt to a boil in a large pot. Add lobster tail.

2. Return water to boiling. Cover and reduce heat; simmer 10 minutes. Drain.

3. Slice thin under-shell of tail down the middle and gently open tail; trim away shell, as needed. Pull meat out of tail to expose.

4. Place tail on broiler rack. Season with nonfat cooking spray.

5. Broil 3-inches (8cm) from heat until hot, approximately 2-3 minutes.

6. Serve with lemon and 1 tsp (5ml) of melted butter, to count as 1 fat, as desired.

Under the ❖ Sea

Lemon Shrimp Stir-fry

1 *serving*

- SERVING SIZE: 1 RECIPE
- COUNTS AS:
  - 1 PROTEIN
  - 3 VEGETABLES
  - 1 FRUIT

▸ *size according to plan*

❉ Ingredients

5 or 7oz (140 or 196g) fresh or fresh-frozen shrimp, peeled and deveined

1 Tbsp (15ml) cornstarch

1 tsp (5ml) artificial sweetener

1 Tbsp (15ml) low-sodium soy sauce

freshly ground pepper

1/2 cup (125ml) water

1/2 tsp (2.5ml) lemon zest, minced

1 1/2 Tbsp (22.5ml) lemon juice

1 large celery stalk, sliced on the bias

1/2 medium green or red pepper, sliced

1/2 cup (125ml / 35g) mushrooms, sliced

3 green onions, sliced

1/4 cup (60ml / 8g) fresh bean sprouts

nonfat cooking spray

1. In a bowl, combine cornstarch, artificial sweetener, soy sauce, pepper, water, lemon zest and lemon juice. Stir to combine; set aside.

2. Spray skillet or wok with nonfat cooking spray. Preheat over medium-high flame. Add celery and cook for 1 minute. Add green pepper and mushrooms and cook for another minute. Finally, add green onion. Stir-fry all vegetables for 1-3 minutes or until crisp-tender. Remove from pan and set aside.

3. Add shrimp to skillet or wok. Stir-fry for 2-3 minutes or until shrimp turns pink. Move shrimp to side(s) of skillet or wok, to keep warm.

4. Add sauce to center of pan; cook, stirring, until slightly thickened.

5. Return vegetables to pan. Add bean sprouts. Cook and stir for 1 minute or until heated through.

6. If desired, serve stir-fry over 1/3 cup (85ml / 55g) brown rice equals 1 Starch.

Steamed Crab

1 *serving*

- SERVING SIZE:
  2 CUPS (500ML)
- COUNTS AS:
  - 1 PROTEIN
  - 1 STARCH

▸ *size according to plan*

❉ Ingredients

4 or 6oz (112 or 168g) fresh crab meat, picked for shells

1/2 cup (125ml) water

1/2 cup (125ml) white wine

2-3 slices lemon

1 tsp (5ml) peppercorns

1/8 tsp (.5ml) lite salt

1 bay leaf

nonfat cooking spray

1. Under a light stream of water, rinse crab in a fine sieve or strainer.

2. Add water, wine, lemon, peppercorns, salt and bay leaf to a medium saucepan. Place steamer basket in pan.

3. Add crab to basket. Gently steam until heated through, about 10 minutes.

4. Serve hot or cold with cocktail sauce, red pepper or other desired condiment.

Under the ❖ Sea

Baked Crab & Broccoli

serving

good source of fiber

- **SERVING SIZE: 1 RECIPE**
- **COUNTS AS:**
  - 1 PROTEIN
  - 2 STARCH
  - 2 VEGETABLES
  - 1/2 DAIRY

▶ *size according to plan*

☀ Ingredients

1 cup (250ml / 70g) broccoli florets, trimmed

4 or 6oz (112 or 168g) fresh crab meat, rinsed and picked for shells

1 cup (250ml / 70g) fresh mushrooms, sliced

1 garlic clove, minced

1/2 cup (125ml) skim milk

1 Tbsp (15ml) flour

freshly ground pepper

1oz (28g) reduced-fat sharp cheddar cheese, shredded

3 slices Melba toast, finely crushed

1. Steam broccoli until crisp-tender, drain.

2. Arrange broccoli and crab meat in a casserole dish, coated with nonfat cooking spray. Set aside.

3. Spray skillet with nonfat cooking spray. Sauté mushrooms and garlic until tender. Sprinkle vegetables with flour and pepper. Stir in milk.

4. Cook sauce, stirring, until thickened. Add cheddar cheese; stir until melted.

5. Spoon sauce on top of broccoli and crabmeat. Cover with foil.

6. Bake at 400°F (200°C) for 15-20 minutes, until bubbling. Sprinkle with Melba toast crumbs; return to oven and bake again until golden brown.

Shrimp Fried Rice

serving

- **SERVING SIZE: 1 RECIPE**
- **COUNTS AS:**
  - 1 PROTEIN
  - 1 STARCH
  - 3 VEGETABLES

▶ *size according to plan*

☀ Ingredients

5 or 7oz (140 or 196g) peeled and deveined raw shrimp

1/2 medium green pepper, diced

2 green onion, diced

1/2 medium carrot, diced

1/2 stalk celery, diced

dash of garlic powder

dash of onion powder

1/4 tsp (1ml) ground ginger

1 Tbsp (15ml) low-sodium soy sauce

1/4 tsp (1ml) lite salt

1/3 cup (85ml / 53g) cooked brown rice

1 egg white, scrambled

nonfat cooking spray

1. Spray skillet or wok with nonfat cooking spray. Over medium-high heat, cook shrimp until pink. Remove from pan; set aside.

2. Return pan to flame. Stir-fry vegetables in wok until crisp-tender.

3. Season vegetables with garlic powder, onion powder, ginger, soy sauce and salt.

4. Add rice, scrambled egg white, and shrimp back to wok. Toss to combine; allow to heat through before serving.

Under the ✿ Sea

Tangy Shrimp Skewers

1 *serving*

- SERVING SIZE: 2-3 SKEWERS
- COUNTS AS:
  - 1 PROTEIN
  - 2 VEGETABLES
  - 1 FRUIT

▶ *size according to plan*

☼ Ingredients

5 or 7oz (140 or 196g) fresh or fresh-frozen raw shrimp

1/2 cup (125ml / 90g) pineapple chunks, canned in juice (drain and reserve juice)

1/2 medium red pepper, cut into 1 inch pieces

1/4 red onion, cut into 1-inch (2.5cm) pieces

2 Tbsp (30ml) low-sodium soy sauce

2 Tbsp (30ml) water

1 tsp (5ml) ginger, minced

1-2 garlic clove(s), minced

nonfat cooking spray

1 Preheat broiler or grill.

2 In a small saucepan, combine reserved pineapple juice, soy sauce, ginger and garlic, over a medium flame. Cook, stirring, until slightly thickened.

3 Thread shrimp, pineapple, pepper and onions, onto metal skewers, alternating the ingredients.

4 Place skewers onto grill or broiler pan (coated with nonfat cooking spray). Cook, brushing with sauce, approximately 4-5 minutes per side or until shrimp are opaque and cooked through.

Pan Seared Lemon-Pepper Grouper

1 *serving*

- SERVING SIZE: 1 FILET
- COUNTS AS:
  - 1 PROTEIN

▶ *size according to plan*

☼ Ingredients

5 or 7oz (140 or 196g) of fresh grouper

2 Tbsp (30ml) pepper-herb mix (recipe on page 224)

1 Tbsp (15ml) lemon juice

1 tsp (5ml) lemon zest

nonfat cooking spray

1 Combine lemon zest and pepper-herb mix together.

2 Sprinkle herb mixture over both sides of fish.

3 Coat medium skillet with nonfat cooking spray.

4 Fry fish over high heat for 1 minute on each side.

5 Turn down heat to low and cook on each side 5-7 minutes, or until fish flakes with a fork.

6 Drizzle lemon juice over fish, serve hot.

Under the ❖ Sea

Orange Sesame Salmon

1 *serving*

- SERVING SIZE: 1 FILET
- COUNTS AS:
  - 1 PROTEIN
  - 2 FRUITS
  - 1 FAT

* *size according to plan*

☀ Ingredients

4 or 6oz (112 or 168g) raw salmon filet

1/3 cup (85ml) orange juice

1/2 cup (125ml / 95g) canned mandarin oranges, drained

2 tsp (10ml) sesame seeds

1/4 tsp (1ml) ginger

nonfat cooking spray

1. Sprinkle ginger over salmon filet.
2. Coat medium skillet with nonfat cooking spray.
3. Place salmon in skillet and sear each side 2 minutes over high heat.
4. Pour orange juice over salmon and reduce heat.
5. Simmer 15 minutes, flipping occasionally to cook evenly.
6. Next, add oranges and sesame seeds, cooking another 1-2 minutes or until oranges are warmed through.
7. Serve hot over rice or salad.

Salmon Stuffed Tomatoes

1 *serving*

- SERVING SIZE:
  2 STUFFED TOMATOES
- COUNTS AS:
  - 1 PROTEIN
  - 2 VEGETABLES

size according to plan

☀ Ingredients

4 or 6oz (112 or 168g) fresh salmon filet

2 small whole tomatoes

1 tsp (5ml) olive oil

2 tsp (10ml) white wine vinegar

2 tsp (10ml) lemon juice

1/4 tsp (1ml) lite salt

1 Tbsp (15ml) chopped cilantro

1. Cook salmon filet, as desired; chill.
2. Chop cooked salmon into small pieces.
3. In medium bowl combine salmon, oil, vinegar, lemon juice, salt and cilantro. Mix well. Chill.
4. While salmon mixture is chilling, cut tops off of tomatoes. Remove seeds and flesh from tomatoes. Chop 1/4 cup of tomato flesh; discard rest.
5. Mix diced tomato into salmon salad.
6. Fill hollowed tomatoes with salmon mixture.
7. Serve chilled, garnish with chopped parsley, if desired.

Under the ♣ Sea

Curried Salmon

1 *serving*

- **SERVING SIZE: 1 FILET**
- **COUNTS AS:**
  1 PROTEIN
  2 VEGETABLES
  1/2 DAIRY

▸ *size according to plan*

meals in minutes

☀ Ingredients

4 or 6oz (112 or 168g) fresh salmon filet

2 Tbsp (30ml) fat-free evaporated milk

2 Tbsp (30ml) skim milk

2 tsp (10ml) curry powder

1/2 carrot, thinly sliced

1/8 tsp (.5ml) ground ginger

1/8 tsp (.5ml) lite salt

1/8 tsp (.5ml) coriander

1 packet artificial sweetener

1/2 small tomato, diced

1 In a small saucepan, combine evaporated milk, skim milk, curry powder, ginger, salt, coriander and artificial sweetener. Heat over medium heat.

2 Chop salmon into small pieces. Add to curried milk mixture.

3 Bring mixture to a simmer; reduce heat to low.

4 Add carrot and tomato and cook 5-10 minutes, or until salmon is cooked.

5 Serve hot over rice or vegetables.

Citrus Grilled Swordfish

1 *serving*

- **SERVING SIZE:
  1 SWORDFISH STEAK**
- **COUNTS AS:**
  1 PROTEIN
  1 FRUIT

▸ *size according to plan*

meals in minutes

☀ Ingredients

5 or 7oz (140 or 196g) raw swordfish steak

1/4 cup (60ml) orange juice

1 Tbsp (15ml) lemon juice

1 Tbsp (15ml) lime juice

1 tsp (5ml) low-sodium soy sauce

1/4 tsp (1ml) lite salt

1 tsp (5ml) chopped cilantro

1 Tbsp (15ml) chives

1/4 tsp (1ml) onion powder

1/4 tsp (1ml) garlic powder

1/4 tsp (1ml) white pepper

1/4 tsp (1ml) freshly ground pepper

2 slices orange

1 Sprinkle swordfish with salt, pepper, cilantro, chives, garlic powder and onion powder.

2 In a small bowl, combine juices and soy sauce; brush steak with marinade and set aside.

3 Place steak on grill. Cook steak for 5 minutes per side, or until cooked through. Baste steak with citrus marinade while cooking.

4 Garnish with fresh orange. Squeeze juice for orange wedges over fish for a fresh burst of flavor.

Under the ❖ Sea

Salmon with Green Beans

4 *servings*

- SERVING SIZE: 3 OR 5 OUNCES COOKED (84 OR 140G) SALMON, 1/2 CUP (125ML) GREEN BEANS, 1/4 RECIPE GLAZE
- COUNTS AS:
  1 PROTEIN
  1 VEGETABLE

size according to plan

☼ Ingredients

4 salmon filets, 4 or 6oz (112 or 168g) each,

1/2 tsp (2.5ml) black pepper

1/2 cup (125ml) dry white wine

1/2 cup (125ml) balsamic vinegar

2 Tbsp (30ml) fresh orange juice

2 tsp (10ml) lemon juice

2 packets artificial sweetener

1 pound (448g) green beans, trimmed

nonfat cooking spray

1. Preheat a cast iron pan or heavy bottomed skillet over medium-high flame coated with nonfat cooking spray.

2. Season filets with pepper to taste, then spray with nonfat cooking spray.

3. Cook salmon until just cooked through, about 3 minutes on each side.

4. While salmon cooks, bring wine, vinegar, juices and artificial sweetener to a boil over high heat, in a small saucepan.

5. Cook glaze 3 or 4 minutes, until reduced and thickened.

6. Remove from heat. Stir in 1/2 tsp (2.5ml) coarse black pepper.

7. In a second skillet, bring 1/2-inch (1.5cm) water to a boil with green beans and pieces of orange rind and/or lemon rind.

8. Cover the green beans and cook 3-4 minutes.

9. Drain the beans and toss and season with pepper.

10. Drizzle glaze over salmon filets. Serve with green beans on the side.

Caesar Shrimp Skewers

1 *serving*

- SERVING SIZE: 1 SERVING
- COUNTS AS:
  1 PROTEIN
  1 VEGETABLE
  1 FAT

size according to plan

☼ Ingredients

1 Tbsp (15ml) fat-free Caesar dressing

2 Tbsp (30ml) lemon juice

1 Tbsp (15ml) lite margarine, melted

1 tsp (5ml) garlic powder

1 green onion, chopped

1/4 tsp (1ml) lite salt

5 or 7oz (140 or 196g) fresh shrimp peeled and deveined

1 yellow squash, cubed

kabob skewers

nonfat cooking spray

1. In a small bowl, combine dressing, lemon juice, margarine, chopped onion and half of the garlic powder.

2. Place shrimp and squash on skewers.

3. Spray finished kabobs with cooking spray, then sprinkle with salt and remaining garlic powder.

4. Place skewers on grill.

5. Brush with dressing and turn while grilling.

6. Cook until squash begins to soften. Continue to brush with dressing frequently during cooking.

7. Serve hot over rice.

Under the ❖ Sea

Herb Stuffed Salmon

8 *approx servings*

- **SERVING SIZE: 3 OR 5OZ COOKED (84 OR 100G)**
- **COUNTS AS:**
  1 PROTEIN

▸ *size according to plan*

family fare

☀ Ingredients

freshly ground pepper

1 Tbsp (15ml) olive oil

2 pounds (896g) salmon filets, skin on, scaled and pin bones removed

2 lemons

bunch fresh dill

bunch fresh marjoram

bunch fresh basil

nonfat cooking spray

1. Preheat the oven to 400°F (200°C).

2. Cut 5 lengths of string and lay them out on the work surface next to each another, with less than 1-inch space between each.

3. Sprinkle pepper over the work surface, then drizzle with olive oil.

4. Lay 1 salmon filet onto work surface, skin side down. Sprinkle pepper over the salmon, then, using fine grater or microplane, grate the zest of 1 lemon over top. Next, season with the marjoram, dill and basil.

5. Season the flesh side of the other salmon filet with pepper, and grate the second lemon.

6. Place 1 filet on top of the other, thin end to thick, then tie them together and trim the strings.

7. Put the fish on a baking sheet coated with nonfat cooking spray.

8. Bake for about 20 minutes, or until fish is flaky.

Fish Tacos

1 *serving*

- **SERVING SIZE: 2 TACOS**
- **COUNTS AS:**
  1 PROTEIN
  1 STARCH
  1 VEGETABLE
  1/2 DAIRY

▸ *size according to plan*

good source of calcium

☀ Ingredients

5 or 7oz (140 or 196g) mahi-mahi

1 tsp (5ml) hot sauce

1 tsp (5ml) cilantro

1/4 tsp (1ml) chili powder

1/2 whole wheat flour tortilla

1/4 cup (60ml / 18g) shredded lettuce

1/2 tomato, seeded and diced

1 Tbsp (15ml) salsa

1 Tbsp (15ml) fat-free sour cream

1oz (28g) reduced-fat shredded cheddar cheese

1. Sprinkle fish with hot sauce, cilantro and chili powder.

2. Bake in preheated 375°F (190°C) oven until flaky, approximately 15-20 minutes.

3. Slice tortilla in half.

4. Place fish in tortilla. Top with condiments and vegetables.

Under the ❖ Sea

servings

SERVING SIZE: 1/4 RECIPE
COUNTS AS:
1 PROTEIN
2 VEGETABLES

▶ *size according to plan*

good source of calcium

Spinach **Stuffed Sole**

☀ Ingredients

1.5 - 2 pounds (672-896g) sole filets

1 tsp (5ml) olive oil

1/2 pound (224g) fresh mushrooms, sliced

1/2 pound (224g) fresh spinach, chopped

1/4 tsp (1ml) oregano leaves, crushed

1 garlic clove, minced

2 Tbsp (30ml) sherry

4oz (112g) part-skim mozzarella cheese, grated

nonfat cooking spray

1 Preheat oven to 400°F (200°C).

2 Coat a baking dish with nonfat cooking spray.

3 Heat oil in skillet; sauté mushrooms about 3 minutes or until tender.

4 Add spinach and continue cooking about 1 minute, or until spinach is beginning to wilt.

5 Remove from heat; drain liquid into prepared baking dish.

6 Add oregano and garlic to drained vegetables; stir to mix ingredients.

7 Divide vegetable mixture evenly among filets, placing filling in center of each filet.

8 Roll filet around mixture and place seam-side down in prepared baking dish.

9 Sprinkle with sherry, then grated mozzarella cheese.

10 Bake fish for 15-20 minutes, or until flaky.

---

servings

SERVING SIZE: 4 OR 6OZ (112 OR 168G) COOKED TROUT
COUNTS AS:
1 PROTEIN
1 VEGETABLE

▶ *size according to plan*

family fare

Baked **Trout**

☀ Ingredients

2 pounds (896g) trout filet

3 Tbsp (45ml) lime juice (about 2 limes)

1 medium tomato, chopped

5 green onions, chopped

3 Tbsp (45ml) cilantro, chopped

1/2 tsp (2.5ml) olive oil

1/4 tsp (1ml) freshly ground pepper

1/4 tsp (1ml) cayenne pepper (optional)

nonfat cooking spray

1 Preheat oven to 350°F (180°C).

2 Rinse fish and pat dry.

3 Place in baking dish coated with nonfat cooking spray.

4 In a separate dish, mix remaining ingredients together and pour over fish.

5 Bake for 15-20 minutes or until flaky.

Under the ♣ Sea

Scallops & Mushrooms

1 *serving*

- **SERVING SIZE: 1 RECIPE**
- **COUNTS AS:**
  - 1 PROTEIN
  - 2 VEGETABLES

▶ *size according to plan*

☀ Ingredients

12 medium Portabella mushroom caps

1 Tbsp (15ml) low-sodium soy sauce

1 garlic clove, finely diced

1 green onion, finely diced

6 or 8oz (168 or 224g) large scallops

freshly ground pepper

nonfat cooking spray

1. Preheat oven to 325°F (160°C) degrees.

2. Marinate the mushrooms in the soy sauce, garlic and green onion. Let sit for 30 minutes.

3. Grill or broil mushrooms 2 minutes per side; then bake in the oven for 10 minutes. Allow mushrooms to cool slightly before cutting into thin strips.

4. Pat the scallops dry, then season with pepper.

5. Sear the scallops in a large skillet that has been coated with nonfat cooking spray over high heat for about 1 minute per side, or until browned.

6. Add mushrooms. Cook for 1 minute longer, or until warmed through.

Red Snapper

5 *servings*

family fare

- **SERVING SIZE: 4 OR 6OZ (112 OR 168G) COOKED**
- **COUNTS AS:**
  - 1 PROTEIN
  - 1 STARCH
  - 2 VEGETABLES

▶ *size according to plan*

☀ Ingredients

2 Tbsp (30ml) low-sodium chicken broth

1 green bell pepper, seeded and cut into thin strips

1 yellow bell pepper, seeded and cut into thin strips

1 onion, sliced

1 garlic clove, crushed

1 can (14.5oz / 406g) canned, diced tomatoes, no salt added

1/4 cup (60ml) sliced pimento-stuffed olives

1/4 cup (60ml) green pepper sauce

2 Tbsp (30ml) lime juice

1 pound (448g) red snapper filets

1/4 cup (60ml) chopped cilantro

1 cup (250ml / 158g) cooked yellow rice

1. In a large skillet, over medium heat, heat the broth to a simmer. Cook peppers and onion until tender-crisp; add garlic.

2. Add diced tomatoes with liquid, olives, green pepper sauce, lime juice and red snapper filets.

3. Heat to boiling; reduce heat to low.

4. Cover and simmer 5-10 minutes, stirring occasionally until fish is tender.

5. Stir in chopped cilantro.

6. Serve with yellow rice.

> "The L A Lite Cookbook recipes are such a delight. I savor the dishes bite by bite."
> — *Lynn K.*

Under the ✣ Sea

Tuna Tostadas

2 *servings*

■ SERVING SIZE: 1 TOSTADA
■ COUNTS AS:
  1 PROTEIN
  1 STARCH
  1 VEGETABLE
  1/2 DAIRY
  1 FAT

size according to plan

meals in minutes

☀ Ingredients

12oz (336g) water-packed, low-sodium tuna, well drained

1-2 tsp (5-10ml) pepper sauce

1 small tomato, seeded and chopped

1/2 cup (125ml / 80g) chopped onions

1/2 cup (125ml) finely chopped cilantro

1/4 cup (60ml) fat-free sour cream

2 Tbsp (30ml) fresh lime juice

1/4 ripe avocado, halved and pitted

corn tortilla, cut in half

2oz (56g) reduced-fat Mexican-style cheese

nonfat cooking spray

1 In a bowl, combine tuna and 1 tsp (5ml) pepper sauce and mix.

2 Add tomato, onion, cilantro, sour cream and lime juice. Blend and chill.

3 With a spoon, scoop the avocados into a bowl and mash with a fork; add remaining pepper sauce, blend.

4 Preheat oven to 350°F (180°C).

5 Spray tortilla lightly with nonfat cooking spray on both sides. Place on a baking sheet; bake until crisp.

6 To assemble, spread half of avocado mixture on each tortilla.

7 Add 1/2 of tuna mixture to each tortilla half.

8 Top each tostada with 1oz (28g) cheese.

Swordfish in Lemon Sauce

4 *servings*

■ SERVING SIZE: 3 OR 5OZ (84 OR 140G) COOKED
■ COUNTS AS:
  1 PROTEIN

size according to plan

family fare

☀ Ingredients

4 swordfish steaks, 4 or 6oz each (112 or 168g each)

6 whole black peppercorns

2 garlic cloves, peeled

1 tsp (5ml) dried oregano

1/4 tsp (1ml) dried basil

1/3 cup (85ml) fresh lemon juice

3 Tbsp (45ml) low-sodium vegetable broth

nonfat cooking spray

1 Wash fish and dry with paper towels.

2 In a small bowl, crush peppercorns, garlic, oregano and basil. Add lemon juice and broth.

3 Place fish in a shallow dish.

4 Add the marinade; turn to coat both sides.

5 Cover and set aside for 1 hour, turning once.

6 Coat broiling pan with non stick cooking spray and broil 4 inches (10cm) from heat.

7 Broil 4-5 minutes per side, brushing with marinade.

Under
the ♣ Sea

Mango Prawns

4 *servings*

- **SERVING SIZE: 1/4 RECIPE**
- **COUNTS AS:**
  - 1 PROTEIN
  - 1 FRUIT
  - 1 FAT

▸ *size according to plan*

☀ Ingredients

20 or 24oz (560 or 672g) uncooked prawns

1 egg white

2 tsp (10ml) cornstarch

1 tsp (5ml) sesame oil

1/2 tsp (2.5ml) white pepper

1 pound (448g) mango

2 cups (500ml) water

1 Tbsp (15ml) fresh ginger, finely chopped

1 Tbsp (15ml) sesame oil

1 Tbsp (15ml) dry sherry

2 Tbsp (30ml) green onion, finely chopped, for garnish

1 garlic clove, minced

1. Peel the prawns, then wash them and pat them dry.

2. Combine the prawns with the egg white, cornstarch, sesame oil and pepper. Mix well and leave in the refrigerator for 20 minutes.

3. Peel the mangos and cut the flesh into cubes.

4. Add water to a saucepan, bring to a boil.

5. Remove the saucepan from heat, immediately add the prawns, stirring vigorously to prevent them from sticking.

6. After 2 minutes, when the prawns turn white, quickly drain the prawns in a stainless steel colander.

7. Heat the wok or large frying pan over high flame.

8. Add the oil, when slightly smoking, add the ginger and garlic and fry for 10 seconds.

9. Then return the prawns to the wok or pan, together with dry sherry, and pepper.

10. Stir-fry the mixture for 1 minute.

11. Add the mango pieces and stir gently for 1 minute to warm the mango.

12. Garnish with green onions and serve.

Sautéed Sea Scallops

2 *servings*

- **SERVING SIZE: 1/2 OF RECIPE**
- **COUNTS AS:**
  - 1 PROTEIN
  - 1 VEGETABLE

▸ *size according to plan*

☀ Ingredients

8 or 12oz (224 or 336g) fresh sea scallops

6 mushrooms, sliced

1/2 green pepper, diced

1 tomato, diced

1/4 cup (60ml) dry white wine

2 green onions, chopped

1 tsp (5ml) dill, dried

1. Rinse scallops and pat dry with a paper towel.

2. Place mushrooms, green pepper, tomato and wine in a large skillet; cook 5 minutes until vegetables are tender.

3. Add onions, scallops and dill.

4. Cook another 5 minutes until scallops are opaque.

Under the ❖ Sea

Lemon Baked Flounder

 serving

- **SERVING SIZE: 1 FILET**
- **COUNTS AS:**
  1 PROTEIN
  1 FAT

▶ *size according to plan*

meals in minutes

☼ Ingredients

5 or 7oz (140 or 196g) flounder filet

1 Tbsp (15ml) lite margarine, melted

1 Tbsp (15ml) lemon juice

1 tsp (5ml) all purpose flour

2 tsp (10ml) fresh parley, chopped

1/4 tsp (1ml) freshly ground pepper

1/4 tsp (1ml) paprika

nonfat cooking spray

1 Rinse filet thoroughly in cold water; pat dry with paper towels and set aside.

2 Pre-heat oven to 350°F (180°C)

3 Combine melted margarine and lemon juice in a small bowl.

4 Combine flour, chopped parsley, and pepper in a shallow container.

5 Dip filet in margarine mixture, then dredge in flour mixture.

6 Transfer filet to a baking sheet that has been coated with nonfat cooking spray and drizzle any remaining margarine mixture over fish.

7 Sprinkle filets with paprika.

8 Bake in oven for 15 minutes, or until fish is golden brown and flakes easily when tested with a fork.

Tuna Melt

 serving

- **SERVING SIZE:**
  1 TUNA MELT
- **COUNTS AS:**
  1/2 PROTEIN
  1 STARCH
  1 FAT
  1/2 DAIRY

▶ *size according to plan*

meals in minutes

☼ Ingredients

1 6oz can (168g) low-sodium tuna, drained

1 Tbsp (15ml) lite mayonnaise

1/2 English muffin

1oz (28g) lite shredded cheese

1 Mix tuna with mayo.

2 Place tuna on top of English muffin.

3 Sprinkle sandwich with cheese.

4 Place in sprayed skillet over medium heat and cover until cheese is melted.

5 Serve hot.

Under the ❖ Sea

Tilapia Italiano

1 *serving*

- **SERVING SIZE: 1 FILET**
- **COUNTS AS:**
  - 1 PROTEIN
  - 2 VEGETABLES

▸ *size according to plan*

☀ Ingredients

5 or 7oz (140 or 196g) tilapia
  filet

1 tsp (5ml) crushed garlic

1/4 tsp (1ml) lemon pepper

1/2 tsp (2.5ml) oregano

dash of lite salt

2 tomatoes, diced

nonfat cooking spray

1 Rinse tilapia under cold water and pat dry with paper towels.

2 Coat skillet with nonfat cooking spray.

3 Sauté garlic over medium heat for 1 minute.

4 Sprinkle fish with oregano, lemon pepper and salt.

5 Add fish to pan, sauté on each side until opaque. Remove from pan and keep warm.

6 Add tomatoes to pan, heat over medium-high flame until reduced by half.

7 Return fish to pan and heat.

8 Serve hot.

Spiced Shrimp & Rice

1 *serving*

- **SERVING SIZE: 1 RECIPE**
- **COUNTS AS:**
  - 1 PROTEIN
  - 1 STARCH
  - 1 VEGETABLE

▸ *size according to plan*

☀ Ingredients

5 or 7oz (140 or 196g) raw
  shrimp, peeled and deveined

5 green onions, sliced

1 garlic clove, minced

1/4 tsp (1ml) grated ginger

2 cardamom pods

2 whole cloves

1/2 stick cinnamon

1 cup (250ml) hot water

1/3 cup (85ml / 64g) cooked rice

1 green chile, sliced

1/2 tsp (2.5ml) garam masala

1/4 tsp (1ml) chili powder

1 Tbsp (15ml) cilantro, chopped

nonfat cooking spray

1 Coat a medium saucepan with nonfat cooking spray; heat over a medium high flame.

2 Cook shrimp, turning once, until pink, approximately 5 minutes. Remove from saucepan and set aside.

3 Add onion, garlic and ginger to saucepan. Cook, stirring, until onion is translucent.

4 Add cardamom, cloves and cinnamon stick; cook and stir for 1 minute.

5 Return shrimp to sauce pan. Next add water, rice, green chile, garam masala and chili powder.

6 Bring to a boil. Reduce heat to low and cover; cook for 20 minutes, or until most of the water is absorbed.

7 Remove cardamom pods and cinnamon sticks. Garnish with cilantro, before serving.

Under
the ❖ Sea

Shrimp Creole

4 *servings*

- SERVING SIZE:
  APPROX 1 1/2 CUPS
- COUNTS AS:
  1 PROTEIN
  2 VEGETABLES

size according to plan

family fare

✴ Ingredients

1 Tbsp (15ml) canola oil

1-2 garlic cloves, minced

1/2 cup (125ml / 80g) onion, diced

1/2 cup (125ml / 74g) green pepper, chopped

1 celery stalk, diced

2 Tbsp (30ml) flour

1/2 cup (125ml / 122g) tomato sauce, low-sodium or no salt added

1-2 cups (250-500ml) water

dash of hot pepper sauce

2-3 tomatoes, seeded and chopped

1 1/2 or 3/4 pounds (672 or 784g) shrimp, peeled and deveined

1. Heat a large skillet coated with oil over a medium flame. Add garlic, onion, pepper and celery; sauté until tender.

2. Sprinkle with flour. Stir to coat all vegetables. Cook, until flour is lightly browned, approximately 5 minutes.

3. Add tomato sauce, water and hot pepper sauce. Stir to combine.

4. Bring to a boil; reduce heat.

5. Add tomatoes and shrimp. Cook, stirring occasionally, until shrimp are pink and cooked through.

Ginger Poached Cod

1 *serving*

- SERVING SIZE: 1 RECIPE
- COUNTS AS:
  1 PROTEIN
  2 VEGETABLES

size according to plan

✴ Ingredients

2 cups (500ml) water

2 Tbsp (30ml) fresh ginger, thinly sliced

1 small tomato, seeded and chopped

1/4 cup (60ml / 30g) white onion, sliced

5 or 7oz (140 or 196g) cod filet

1 cup (250ml / 70g) bok choy, leaves and stems, chopped

lite salt and pepper, to taste

1. In a large saucepan, simmer sliced ginger, tomato and onion in 2 cups (500ml) of water, over medium heat, until onions are tender.

2. Reduce heat to low; add fish and poach for 3-4 minutes, until just becoming opaque.

3. Add bok choy; gently stir while cooking, for approximately 1-2 minutes, allowing bok choy to wilt.

4. Serve immediately.

Under the ✤ Sea

Go Meatless

Vegetarian diets are those that exclude animal products, mainly that of meat, fish or poultry origin. There are several types of diets classified under this term, though the basis of all these diets are plant-based foods, including protein, fruits, vegetables and starches. For vegetarians, the *L A Lite Cookbook* is a fantastic resource of unique food preparation, combinations, storage and more!

◀ Vegetable Ziti Bake recipe can be found on page 208

Complete Proteins and Complementary Proteins

Protein is built of amino acids; there are essential and nonessential amino acids. Essential amino acids cannot be made in the body, therefore it is essential to get these from foods. Nonessential amino acids can be made in the body, so it is not pertinent to eat foods containing them. An example of an essential amino acid is tryptophan; tyrosine is a nonessential amino acid.

A complete protein is one that contains all the essential amino acids for the human body and in approximately the adequate amount needed. Most animal proteins are considered complete (with the exception of gelatin). Most plant-based proteins tend to be limiting only in one or two amino acids, such as vegetables, grains and legumes; some plant proteins, like corn, are known to be incomplete, while soy protein is complete.

As you can tell, most vegetable proteins are of lower quality than animal proteins, but if you pair your foods correctly to replace the missing "links" or amino acids, you can somewhat create a complete protein. The foods that supply the missing links to each other are complementary proteins; the strategy of combining two protein foods in a meal is called mutual supplementation. Some examples would be peanut butter and toast and rice and black beans.

But this is not a necessary action for you to achieve optimal health; in most instances, a vegetarian person will obtain the necessary and essential amino acids over the course of one day, provided he/she eats a variety of foods, such as grains, seeds, legumes, etc.

TIP!

Ever come across a recipe that called for dried herbs when you'd rather use fresh ones? Feel free to use the fresh herbs, just triple the amount that the recipe calls for that specific herb. Better yet, try to add in the herbs in the final cooking stages so their unique flavor stays bold.

Glossary of Vegetarian Cooking

- **Tofu** — Also known as soybean curd or bean curd; produced from curdled soy milk as extracted from ground, cooked soybeans, in which the curds are drained and pressed, similarly done as in cheese-making; it has a bland, nutty flavor that tends to take on the flavor of what it is cooked with or in; may be firm or soft.

- **Tempeh** — A fermented soy bean cake, similar in texture to soft tofu, though with a slightly nutty texture.

- **Seitan** — A protein rich meat substitute made from wheat gluten; it has a firm texture that is chewy and meat-like; also called "wheat meat"; also picks up the flavors that is cooked in or with; can be found in cakes or tubs.

- **Miso** — A fermented soybean paste and comes in many flavors; its flavor is influenced by the amount of salt, amount of aging, and koji (mold cultivated in barley, rice or soybean); can be used in many different menu items, soups, salads, entrees and dips; it is high in protein and B vitamins.

- **Textured Vegetable Protein** — Typically found in powdered form, this is produced by grinding soy beans and extruding them to obtain just protein; appears as a flour and easily prepared by mixing with water; may also be found flaked or in frozen form; make sure to use low fat version — it is basically defatted soy flour.

- **Edamame** — Japanese name for soybeans; may be fresh or fresh-frozen; may be eaten in the pod or out of the pod; generally steamed or boiled as an appetizer in Japanese restaurants.

TIP!

Want to keep your spices lasting longer? First, move your spice rack from above your stove. Store your spices in a cool, dark place. Humidity, light and heat are all flavor losing factors in your spice rack. To make the most of your spices, stash them in an airtight container or in the freezer in tightly sealed containers.

Preparing

Use an electric coffee grinder to grind up nuts, seeds and spices. It saves time preparing and cooking so you don't have to crush them yourself. Just make sure to clean it out before you put coffee beans in, or your coffee will go nuts!

When buying garlic for cooking always looks for heads that are firm with plenty of flaky paper covering.

Storing

Once you open the tofu package, rinse and cover the leftover with water to store in your refrigerator. Change the water daily and use the food within 7 days.

Keep your fresh herbs staying fresh longer in the refrigerator. Place any stem bunches in water. Store loose leaves in perforated bags in the coldest part of your fridge. Remember to shake them before you store them. To absorb extra moisture place a paper towel in the bag under the herbs.

Cooking

To help the oil heat faster when using a wok, add the oil so that it circles around the sides before reaching the bottom.

When stir-frying vegetables, cook them according to density. Stir-fry the densest veggies, such as carrots and eggplant, first because they take the longest. Green leafy vegetables require less cooking time.

Go Meatless

serving

- **SERVING SIZE: 1 RECIPE**
- **COUNTS AS:**
  2 VEGETABLES
  1/2 - 1 PROTEIN

▶ *size according to plan*

good source of fiber

Red Kidney Bean Curry

☀ Ingredients

1 cup (250ml / 177g) cooked red kidney beans

1/4 cup (60ml / 40g) white onions, chopped

1/2 green chili, sliced

1/2 tsp (2.5ml) ginger, grated

1/2 tsp (2.5ml) turmeric

1/2 tsp (2.5ml) cumin seeds

1 small tomato, seeded and chopped

1 Tbsp (15ml) lemon juice

1/2 tsp (2.5ml) garam masala

1/4 tsp (1ml) lite salt

1 Tbsp (15ml) chopped cilantro

nonfat cooking spray

1. Coat skillet with nonfat cooking spray. Add onion, chili, ginger, turmeric and cumin seeds. Cook, stirring, until onion is soft and lightly browned. Add tomato; cook until soft.

2. Add beans to onion mixture; toss to combine. Add lemon juice, garam masala and salt. Cook, stirring, uncovered for 5 minutes.

3. Garnish with cilantro.

---

servings

- **SERVING SIZE: 1 CUP (250ML) BEANS AND 1/3 CUP (85ML) RICE**
- **COUNTS AS:**
  1/2 - 1 PROTEIN
  1 STARCH

▶ *size according to plan*

family fare

Red Beans & Rice

☀ Ingredients

1 Tbsp (15ml) olive or canola oil

2 garlic cloves, minced

2 celery stalks, chopped

1 cup (250ml) onion, chopped

1 medium green pepper, chopped

1 jalapeño, seeded and deveined, chopped

1 pound (448g) dried red beans, rinsed and picked over

2 quarts (2L) low-sodium chicken or vegetable broth

1/4 tsp (1ml) freshly ground pepper

1/4 cup (60ml) flat leafed Italian parsley, chopped

2 cups (500ml / 330g) rice, cooked

1. Place beans in a large bowl; cover with water by one inch. Soak overnight. Drain and set aside.

2. In large soup pot, heat olive oil over medium flame. Add garlic, celery, onion and peppers. Sauté until soft, about 10 minutes.

3. Add broth and beans. Bring to a boil over medium-high heat. Reduce heat.

4. Continue to cook over low heat until beans are soft, about 2 hours. Stir occasionally while cooking.

5. Garnish with parsley and serve over hot cooked rice.

❖ Go
Meatless

Scrambled Tofu

4 servings

- SERVING SIZE: 1/4 OF RECIPE
- COUNTS AS:
  - 1/2 PROTEIN
  - 1 VEGETABLE

▶ *size according to plan*

☀ Ingredients

1/2 cup (125ml / 80g) onion, finely chopped

1 pound (448g) firm tofu, crumbled

1 Tbsp (15ml) low-sodium soy sauce

1 tsp (5ml) basil or cilantro

1/4 tsp (1ml) garlic powder

1/4 tsp (1ml) freshly ground pepper

nonfat cooking spray

1. Sauté onions in a skillet coated with nonfat cooking spray until tender; next, add remaining ingredients.
2. Cook until tofu starts to brown and heated through.
3. Serve with toast.

Indian-Style Chickpeas

4 servings

- SERVING SIZE: 1/4 OF RECIPE
- COUNTS AS:
  - 1/2 PROTEIN
  - 3 VEGETABLES

▶ *size according to plan*

☀ Ingredients

1 medium onion

3 garlic cloves, coarsely chopped

1 Tbsp (15ml) cumin seeds

1 Tbsp (15ml) turmeric

2-inch (5cm) long piece of fresh peeled ginger, chopped

1/2 cup (125ml) lite tomato sauce

chilies, cayenne powder, or chopped fresh jalapeños (optional and to taste)

2 carrots, diced

1 can (15.5oz / 434g) chickpeas, rinsed and drained

1. Place the first 6 ingredients and pepper (optional) in a blender and blend until smooth, add water if it is too thick to mix properly.
2. Pour the paste into a saucepan on medium high heat and stir until it begins to darken and gains aroma.
3. Stir constantly to prevent burning.
4. Add the diced carrots and stir the mixture to coat the carrots with the paste; add a small amount of water if there is no liquid at the bottom of the pan and allow the vegetables to steam until nearly done.
5. Add chickpeas and mix well, heating through.

Vegetarian Chili

10 *servings*

- **SERVING SIZE:** 1 CUP (250ML)
- **COUNTS AS:**
  - 1/2 PROTEIN
  - 2 VEGETABLES

▶ *size according to plan*

☀ Ingredients

1 large onion, finely chopped

1 green pepper, seeded and finely chopped

6 cups (1.5L) canned low sodium stewed tomatoes

2 cups (500ml / 480g) canned pinto beans, drained and rinsed

2 cups (500ml / 512g) canned kidney beans, drained and rinsed

1/8 tsp (.5ml) ground cloves

dash of allspice

2 Tbsp (30ml) chili powder

1 Tbsp (15ml) cumin

nonfat cooking spray

1 Sauté onion and green pepper in a Dutch oven coated with nonfat cooking spray.

2 Add the remaining ingredients and simmer until flavors are blended.

3 Heat and serve.

Jalapeño Red Bean Burgers

4 *servings*

- **SERVING SIZE:** 1 PATTY
- **COUNTS AS:**
  - 1/2 PROTEIN
  - 1 STARCH
  - 1 VEGETABLE

▶ *size according to plan*

good source of fiber

☀ Ingredients

1 can (16oz / 448g) kidney beans, drained and rinsed

1 small onion, finely chopped

1 small tomato, chopped

1 jalapeño chili, seeded and chopped

1 garlic clove, finely minced

1 tsp (5ml) chili powder

1/4 cup (60ml) barbecue sauce

1/3 cup (85ml / 36g) bread crumbs (see recipe on pg 154)

nonfat cooking spray

1 In a bowl, mash beans with a fork.

2 Add first 7 ingredients.

3 Add bread crumbs, enough so that mixture can be formed into patties that hold together.

4 Make 4 patties.

5 Grill in a skillet coated with nonfat cooking spray, until heated through.

"Try this with the sweet cole slaw."

✿ Go Meatless

BBQ Tofu

1 *serving*

- SERVING SIZE: 1 RECIPE
- COUNTS AS:
  1 PROTEIN

▶ *size according to plan*

☀ Ingredients

1/2 or 1 cup (125 or 250ml) firm tofu

1 Tbsp (15ml) low-sodium soy sauce

1 packet artificial sweetener

1 tsp (5ml) water

1/2 tsp (2.5ml) dry mustard

1 garlic clove, minced

1 tsp (5ml) onion powder

nonfat cooking spray

1. Cut tofu into strips.

2. In medium bowl, combine soy sauce, artificial sweetener, water, mustard, garlic and onion powder.

3. Marinade tofu in sauce 1 hour.

4. Cook tofu in wok that has been coated with nonfat cooking spray until heated through.

Pizza Bagel

1 *serving*

- SERVING SIZE: 1 RECIPE
- COUNTS AS:
  1 STARCH
  1 VEGETABLE
  1 DAIRY

size according to plan

good source of calcium

☀ Ingredients

1/2 small bagel

1 small tomato

fresh basil

2oz (56g) part-skim shredded mozzarella cheese

1. Cut tomato in to 2-3 slices.

2. Place tomato on bagel.

3. Sprinkle basil and cheese on top of tomato.

4. Place on baking sheet and place in 375°F (190°C) oven, until cheese is melted.

❖ Go
Meatless

4 *servings*

■ SERVING SIZE:
  1/2 OR 3/4 CUP (125 OR
  200ML) COTTAGE CHEESE

■ COUNTS AS:
  1 PROTEIN

▶ *size according to plan*

good source of calcium

Cheesy Delight

☼ Ingredients

2 cups (500ml) 1% cottage cheese

1 cup (250ml) boiling water

1 envelope sugar free flavored gelatin*

1 In a small bowl, combine gelatin powder and 1/4 cup (60ml) water, allow to soften.

2 In a blender, combine cottage cheese, gelatin mixture and remaining water. Process until smooth.

3 Divide into serving cups and refrigerate until firm.

4 Serve with fresh fruit.

*Unflavored gelatin can be used in place of fruit flavored, add 1 tsp vanilla extract and artificial sweetener to add flavor.

Vegetarian Pepper Quesadillas

2 *servings*

■ SERVING SIZE: 1 RECIPE
■ COUNTS AS:
  1 STARCH
  2 VEGETABLES
  1/2 DAIRY

☼ Ingredients

1/2 green pepper, chopped

1/2 red pepper, chopped

10 small green onions, chopped

2oz (56g) reduced-fat shredded cheese, such as cheddar

1 corn or flour tortilla

salsa

lite salt

freshly ground pepper

cumin

1 Sauté onion and pepper in skillet.

2 Stir in salt, pepper and cumin.

3 Remove from heat.

4 Spoon cheese onto tortilla. Top with pepper mixture.

5 Place on baking sheet and bake in 350°F (180°C) oven for 5-10 minutes until cheese is melted.

6 Top with salsa before serving.

❖ Go
Meatles

Meatless Sloppy Joe

family fare

4 *servings*

- SERVING SIZE: 1/4 RECIPE
- COUNTS AS:
  1 PROTEIN

▸ *size according to plan*

✸ Ingredients

1/2 cup (125ml / 48g) green onion, chopped

1/2 cup (125ml / 74g) green pepper, chopped

1 tsp (5ml) garlic, minced

3/4 cup (200ml / 53g) fresh mushroom, sliced

1/2 cup (125ml) reduced-sodium ketchup

2/3 cup (170ml) water

2 Tbsp (30ml) brown sugar artificial sweetener

1 Tbsp (15ml) mustard

1 tsp (5ml) celery seed

1/2 tsp (2.5ml) chili powder

12oz (336g) textured vegetable protein

nonfat cooking spray

1. Coat medium saucepan with nonfat cooking spray; heat over medium flame until hot.

2. Sauté onion, green pepper, and garlic until tender, 5-8 minutes. Stir in mushroom, ketchup, water, brown sugar, mustard, celery seed and chili powder; heat to boiling.

3. Stir in vegetable protein; reduce heat and simmer, covered, 10 minutes.

4. Season to taste with lite salt and pepper.

Tofu-Bacon

4 *servings*

- SERVING SIZE: 1/4 RECIPE
- COUNTS AS:
  1/2 PROTEIN
  1 VEGETABLE

▸ *size according to plan*

✸ Ingredients

1/3 cup (85ml) low-sodium soy sauce

2 Tbsp (30ml) water

1 Tbsp (15ml) nutritional yeast flakes

1 Tbsp (15ml) maple syrup

1/2 Tbsp (7.5ml) liquid smoke

8oz (224g) extra-firm tofu

1. Mix the soy sauce, water, yeast flakes, maple syrup and liquid smoke together in a shallow, flat container.

2. With a cheese slicer, shave the tofu into thin slices.

3. Marinate in the mixture for 24 hours.

4. To cook, heat a nonfat griddle over medium-high heat.

5. Fry the tofu slices until golden brown and almost crispy on both sides, scraping underneath the slices as you turn them with a sturdy spatula.

6. Serve hot.

✿ Go Meatless

Mediterranean Pasta Bake

1 *serving*

- SERVING SIZE: 1 RECIPE
- COUNTS AS:
  - 1 STARCH
  - 2 VEGETABLES
  - 1 FAT
  - 1/2 DAIRY

▶ *size according to plan*

☀ Ingredients

2 garlic cloves, minced

2 Tbsp (30ml) onion, diced

1/4 cup (60ml / 28g) thinly sliced zucchini

1/2 tomato, diced

1 tsp (5ml) flour

1/4 cup (60ml) skim milk

1 Tbsp (15ml) tomato paste

1/3 cup (85ml / 53g) cooked pasta

1oz (28g) lite feta cheese

9 kalamata olives, halved

nonfat cooking spray

1. Coat medium skillet with nonfat cooking spray. Sauté garlic and onion over medium heat for 1 minute.
2. Add zucchini and tomato; cook until zucchini is tender.
3. Sprinkle flour into zucchini mixture and mix well.
4. Stir in milk and tomato paste; heat to a simmer.
5. Toss in pasta. Top with cheese and olives.

Eggplant Parmigiana

2 *servings*

- SERVING SIZE: 1/2 OF RECIPE
- COUNTS AS:
  - 1 STARCH
  - 2 VEGETABLES
  - 1 DAIRY

▶ *size according to plan*

good source of calcium

☀ Ingredients

1/2 cup (125ml) lite tomato sauce

1 small tomato

1/2 cup (125ml) water

1 tsp (5ml) dried onion

1 tsp (5ml) garlic powder

dash of dried parsley flakes

dash of lite salt

dash of oregano

freshly ground pepper

1/2 eggplant, sliced

1/2 cup (125ml) egg substitute

1/2 cup (125ml / 54g) breadcrumbs

4oz (112g) part-skim, shredded mozzarella cheese

nonfat cooking spray

1. In small saucepan, combine tomato sauce, tomato, water, dried onion, garlic powder, parsley flakes, salt, oregano and pepper. Heat to a simmer and set aside.
2. Dip eggplant slices in egg, then into bread crumbs.
3. Coat skillet with nonfat cooking spray and heat over medium flame. Lightly brown each side of eggplant.
4. Coat casserole dish with nonfat cooking spray. Arrange half of the eggplant slices in a single layer in casserole dish.
5. Top with half of the tomato sauce. Sprinkle with 2oz (56g) of the cheese.
6. Repeat process with remaining eggplant, sauce and cheese
7. Bake, uncovered, in a 400°F (200°C) oven for 10-15 minutes, or until cheese is melted.

Go Meatles

6 *servings*

SERVING SIZE:
4 MEATBALLS AND 1/4 CUP
(60ML) SAUCE

COUNTS AS:
1 PROTEIN
1 VEGETABLE

▸ *size according to plan*

family fare

Italian Style "Vegetarian Meatballs"

☀ Ingredients

12oz (336g) frozen vegetable
  protein crumbles, thawed

1/2 cup (125ml) egg substitute

1/4 cup (60ml / 27g) breadcrumbs
  (see recipe on
  page 154)

2 garlic cloves, minced

2 Tbsp (30ml) grated reduced-fat
  parmesan cheese

2 tsp (10ml) Italian herbs

1/2 tsp (2.5ml) fennel seed, crushed

1 1/2 cups (375ml) lite tomato
  sauce

1 tomato, chopped

2 Tbsp (30ml) onion, diced

1 tsp (5ml) basil

1/2 tsp (2.5ml) oregano

1 Combine vegetable crumbles, egg substitute,
   breadcrumbs, garlic, parmesan cheese, Italian herbs
   and fennel. Mash mixture lightly with fork. Form into
   24 balls.

2 Bake in baking pan at 350°F (180°C) until firm, about
   10 minutes.

3 To make sauce, combine tomato sauce, chopped
   tomato, onion, basil and oregano in small saucepan.
   Bring to a boil, then lower heat and simmer
   5 minutes.

4 Serve sauce over hot meatballs.

Mock-Sausage

 servings

SERVING SIZE: 1 PATTY

COUNTS AS:
1/2 PROTEIN

size according to plan

☀ Ingredients

3/4 cup (200ml) boiling water

2 Tbsp (30ml) low-sodium soy sauce

1 cup (250ml) textured vegetable
  protein (TVP) granules

1/2 cup (125ml) mashed firm tofu

2 tsp (10ml) marjoram

1/2 tsp (2.5ml) minced garlic

1/2 tsp (2.5ml) onion powder

1/2 tsp (2.5ml) thyme

1/2 tsp (2.5ml) red cayenne flakes

1/2 tsp (2.5ml) liquid smoke

1/2 cup (125ml / 63g) unbleached
  flour

nonfat cooking spray

1 In a bowl, pour the water and soy sauce over the TVP.

2 When soft, add the remaining ingredients, except flour
   and mix well.

3 When the mixture is cooled, add the flour.

4 Mix well with your hands and form into 12 thin patties

5 In a heavy skillet coated with nonfat cooking spray, fry
   until firm and browned, 7-10 minutes per side.

6 These can be refrigerated or frozen for later use.

207

**☘ Go
Meatless**

Vegetable Ziti Bake

2 *servings*

- **SERVING SIZE:**
  1 CUP (250ML)
- **COUNTS AS:**
  1 STARCH
  2 VEGETABLES
  1 DAIRY

▶ *size according to plan*

good source of calcium

☀ Ingredients

1/4 cup (60ml / 40g) diced onion

2 garlic cloves, minced

1/4 cup (60ml / 30g) thinly sliced carrots

1/4 cup (60ml / 18g) sliced mushrooms

1/4 cup (60ml / 28g) thinly sliced zucchini

1/2 tsp (2.5ml) garlic powder

1/2 cup (125ml / 28g) fresh spinach

2/3 cup (175ml / 106g) cooked ziti

1/4 cup (60ml) lite tomato sauce

1/2 cup (125ml) part-skim ricotta cheese

1/2 tomato, diced

2oz (56g) part-skim mozzarella cheese

nonfat cooking spray

1. Coat skillet with nonfat cooking spray; heat over medium flame.

2. Add onion, garlic and carrots to skillet and sauté 1-2 minutes, or until onions begin to soften.

3. Add mushrooms, zucchini and garlic powder, and sauté 2 minutes. Add spinach and cook until wilted. Remove vegetables from heat and set aside.

4. In large mixing bowl, combine ziti, ricotta cheese, tomato sauce and vegetable mixture.

5. Coat casserole dish with nonfat cooking spray. Pour ziti mixture into casserole and top with diced tomato.

6. Cover and bake in 350°F (180°C) oven for 20 minutes.

7. Remove from oven and top with mozzarella cheese. Bake, uncovered, 10 minutes, or until cheese is melted.

Edamame

3 *servings*

- **SERVING SIZE: 1 CUP (250ML) COOKED**
- **COUNTS AS:**
  1 PROTEIN

▶ *size according to plan*

good source of fiber

☀ Ingredients

1 pound (448g) frozen edamame

1 lemon

1 Tbsp (15ml) kosher salt

1. In medium sized pot, boil edamame for 5-8 minutes until tender, do not overcook.

2. Drain in colander and pat dry.

3. Place edamame in serving bowl.

4. Squeeze lemon juice on edamame and sprinkle with kosher salt.

✿ Go Meatle

Tofu Manicotti

good source of calcium

✳ Ingredients

2 manicotti shells

1/4 cup (60ml / 18g) fresh mushroom, chopped

1/4 cup green onion (60ml / 24g), chopped

1 tsp (5ml) snipped fresh parsley

1/4 tsp (1ml) dried Italian seasoning

dash of paprika and garlic powder

4oz (112g) tofu, drained

1 Tbsp (15ml) reduced-fat parmesan cheese

1/2 cup (125ml) skim milk

1/2 Tbsp (7.5ml) flour

1/8 tsp (.5ml) lite salt

1/8 tsp (.5ml) freshly ground pepper

1oz (28g) reduced-fat mozzarella cheese, shredded

nonfat cooking spray

1 Cook pasta shells according to package directions. Rinse in cold water; drain.

2 Coat medium skillet with nonfat cooking spray. Add mushroom and onion; cook until tender. Stir in parsley, Italian seasoning and paprika. Cool slightly.

3 Mash tofu in a bowl. Stir in parmesan cheese, mushroom and onion mixture.

4 Stuff each shell with 1/2 of the mixture. Arrange stuffed shells in baking pan.

5 For the sauce, combine milk, flour, garlic powder, salt and pepper in a medium saucepan. Cook, stirring, until slightly thickened. Pour sauce over shells.

6 Bake, covered, and in a 350°F (180°C) oven for 20-25 minutes, or until heated through.

7 Sprinkle with cheese and bake, uncovered, 2 minutes longer or until cheese is melted.

Baked Macaroni & Cheese

good source of calcium

✳ Ingredients

3 Tbsp (45ml) butter

3 Tbsp (45ml) all-purpose flour

2 1/2 cups (625ml) skim milk

freshly ground pepper

8oz (224g) shredded reduced-fat cheddar cheese

1 pound (448g) raw macaroni

nonfat cooking spray

1 Over medium heat, melt butter in medium saucepan. Add flour and stir until a paste forms.

2 Remove from heat and add the cold milk a little at a time, stirring well with each addition.

3 Return to heat once all the milk is added and the mixture is smooth. Stir over medium heat until sauce comes to a boil and slightly thickens. Pepper to taste.

4 Remove from heat and add the grated cheddar. Stir until cheese melts. Preheat broiler.

5 Meanwhile, cook macaroni in rolling boiling water according to package directions. Drain and toss with cheese sauce.

6 Transfer to a medium baking dish that has been coated with nonfat cooking spray.

7 Place under broiler until browned and bubbly, about 3-4 minutes.

♣ Go
Meatless

Vegetable Shepherd's Pie

4 *servings*

- **SERVING SIZE: 1/4 OF RECIPE**
- **COUNTS AS:**
  1/2 PROTEIN
  1 STARCH
  3 VEGETABLES

▶ *size according to plan*

☀ Ingredients

2 cups (500ml) water, divided

1/2 cup (120ml / 96g) uncooked lentils

1/4 cup (60ml / 46g) uncooked barley

1 medium carrot, diced

1 small onion, finely chopped

8oz (224g) low-sodium canned, diced tomatoes

1 garlic clove, crushed

1 tsp (5ml) flour

1 tsp (5ml) parsley

3 small potatoes, cooked and mashed

freshly ground pepper

1 Heat 1-1/4 cups (310ml) water; add lentils and barley simmer 30 minutes.

2 Heat remaining water in a separate saucepan, add carrot, onion and garlic; cook until tender, then add tomatoes, parsley and pepper, to taste.

3 Mix the flour with a little water and add to saucepan; cook, stirring, over low heat until thickened.

4 Combine vegetable mixture with cooked lentils and barley, place in ovenproof baking dish, cover with mashed potatoes.

5 Bake at 350°F (180°C) for 30 minutes.

Hot & Spicy Dahl

1 *serving*

- **SERVING SIZE: 1 RECIPE**
- **COUNTS AS:**
  1 PROTEIN
  3 VEGETABLES

▶ *size according to plan*

good source of fiber

☀ Ingredients

1-2 cups (250-500ml) cooked red lentils

1 Tbsp (15ml) minced ginger

2 Tbsp (30ml) cilantro

2 tomatoes, seeded and chopped

1/2 tsp (2.5ml) mustard seeds

5 green onions, chopped

2 jalapeños, seeded and chopped

2 tsp (10ml) ground coriander

2 tsp (10ml) ground cumin

3 garlic cloves, minced

2/3 cup (170ml) water

nonfat cooking spray

1 Coat skillet with nonfat cooking spray and heat over medium flame.

2 Add mustard seeds and cook 1-2 minutes.

3 Add onion, ginger, jalapeño and garlic.

4 Cook on medium heat until garlic browns.

5 Add cumin, coriander and tomatoes. Continue to sauté until tomatoes are cooked.

6 Add water, boil 5-6 minutes.

7 Add cooked lentils, stir well.

8 Add cilantro to mixture and remove from heat.

9 Serve immediately.

❖ Go
Meatles

1 *serving*

SERVING SIZE: 1 RECIPE
COUNTS AS:
  1 PROTEIN
  1 STARCH
  2 VEGETABLES

▶ *size according to plan*

meals in minutes

Tofu & Vegetable Stir-fry

☀ Ingredients

1/2 cup (125ml) water

1/4 cup (60ml) dry sherry

1 Tbsp (15ml) cornstarch

2 Tbsp (30ml) low-sodium soy sauce

1 packet artificial sweetener

1 tsp (5ml) very low-sodium bouillon granules

3/4 tsp (4ml) ground ginger

1/2 medium carrot, thinly sliced

1 garlic clove, minced

1 cup (250ml / 70g) broccoli florets

1/2 or 1 cup (124 or 248g) tofu, cubed

1/3 cup (85ml / 53g) cooked brown rice

1 Tbsp (15ml) sesame seeds, toasted

nonfat cooking spray

1 For sauce, stir together water, dry sherry, cornstarch, soy sauce, sugar substitute, bouillon and ginger. Set aside.

2 Coat wok or skillet with nonfat cooking spray. Preheat over medium-high flame. Add carrot and garlic and stir-fry for 2 minutes. Add broccoli; stir-fry for another 3-4 minutes, or until all vegetables are crisp-tender. Push vegetables from center of skillet to the side.

3 Stir sauce and add to center of skillet. Cook, stirring, until thickened. Add tofu.

4 Toss ingredients together to coat with sauce.

5 Serve with hot cooked brown rice. Sprinkle with sesame seeds.

Asparagus Soup

4 *servings*

SERVING SIZE: 1/4 RECIPE
COUNTS AS:
  1 STARCH
  1 VEGETABLE
  1 FAT

▶ *size according to plan*

☀ Ingredients

1 onion, chopped

2 Tbsp (30ml) butter

1 pound (448g) fresh asparagus, trimmed and coarsely chopped

1 cup (250ml) vegetable broth

1 dash garlic powder

1 dash white pepper

1 cup (250ml) 1% milk

1 Microwave onion and butter on high for 2 minutes

2 Add asparagus, vegetable broth, garlic powder and white pepper.

3 Microwave, covered, on high for 10-12 minutes.

4 Puree in blender.

5 Return mixture to microwave safe dish, stir in milk and microwave until heated through.

❖ Go
Meatless

Add
a little
✿Zest

The *L A Lite Cookbook* shows you just how to add a little spice to life. You'll find all the information you need for increasing flavor and decreasing fat with fresh herbs, spicy sauces and a variety of seasonings. These zesty recipes will keep your appetite satisfied and your taste buds tantalized!

Add a little Zest

Hot Spice Mix (Garam Masala)

Cajun Spice Seasoning

Teriyaki Sauce

Chocolate-Orange Sauce

Seasoned Margarine

Soy-Sesame Marinade

Spicy Curry Powder

Lemon Seasoning

Mushroom Sauce

Italian-Style Tomato Sauce

Margarita Marinade

Orange-Ginger Marinade

Chili Powder

Indian Spice Blend

Hot Citrus Rub

Vegetable Sauce

Plum Sauce

Basil Mayonnaise

Spicy Flavor Blend

Seasoned Salt

Herb Blend

Taco Seasoning Mix

Citrus Rub

Five Spice Powder

Fajita Seasoning Marinade

Teriyaki Marinade

Glossary of Sauce Terms

- **Roux** — A cooked mixture of equal parts fat and flour, such as butter and flour, which is cooked until desired color and flavor is reached; used as a base of many sauces and also to thicken soups, stews and other sauces.

- **Mayonnaise** — An emulsion of egg yolk, oil and lemon juice or vinegar.

- **Aioli** — A garlic mayonnaise, commonly served with fish or vegetables.

- **Pesto** — A puree of fresh herbs, such as basil, with olive oil, pine nuts and garlic; may also be available with sun-dried tomatoes or artichokes.

- **Hollandaise** — A rich sauce blend of egg yolks, butter and tarragon.

- **Bechamel** — A roux-thickened milk sauce.

- **Demi-glace** — A rich reduction of beef or veal broth into a velvety brown sauce.

- **Mornay** — A cheese and milk sauce made combining a roux with milk and adding parmesan or gruyere cheese.

- **Chutney** — Originated from India; a relish of fruits and spices, most common is a spicy mango chutney.

- **Tomato** — A common base sauce, in which garlic and vegetables are sautéed in olive oil and then tomatoes are added and simmer together .

- **Salsa** — Spanish for "sauce"; commonly thought of as a raw sauce of tomatoes and/or fruits or other vegetables, combined with garlic, herbs and olive oil.

Cut the fat...

- Choose vegetable or broth based sauces.

- Keep the sauce on the side to control how much you use with each bite.

- Use sauces and seasonings that are high in flavor—they are more satisfying to the stomach and taste buds.

- Use low fat milk or evaporated nonfat milk in place of cream.

Increase the flavor...

- Use fresh herbs at the end of the recipe or dried herbs at the beginning for optimum flavor.

- Select herbs and spices that will complement foods, such as rosemary or mint for lamb, nutmeg for spinach or dill for eggs.

- In place of salt, try fresh lemon juice to heighten flavors in a recipe.

- Roast vegetables with olive oil and garlic to bring out the natural sweetness.

Add
a little
❖ Zest

Hot Spice Mix (Garam Masala)

☼ Ingredients

4oz (112g) coriander seeds

1oz (28g) cumin seeds

1oz (28g) freshly ground pepper

1/2oz (14g) black cumin seeds

1/4oz (7g) black cardamom

1/4oz (7g) cloves

1/4oz (7g) cinnamon

1/4oz (7g) bay leaves

1/2oz (14g) dry ginger

1. Dry roast all ingredients, except ginger, by cooking the spices in a hot skillet, sliding the spices back and forth over the burner. Cook lightly until aromas are released.

2. Cool to room temperature. Add ginger to mixture; grind to fine powder in a spice/coffee grinder.

3. Store in an air tight container. (Unlimited use)

Cajun Spice Seasoning

☼ Ingredients

3/4 cup (200ml / 200g) lite salt

1/4 cup (60ml) ground cayenne pepper

2 Tbsp (30ml) ground white pepper

2 Tbsp (30ml) freshly ground pepper

2 Tbsp (30ml) paprika

2 Tbsp (30ml) onion powder

2 Tbsp (30ml) garlic powder

1. Combine all ingredients and mix well.

2. Place in an airtight jar.

Spice up the Roast Chicken with a Cajun twist.

Add a little ♣ Zest

Teriyaki Sauce

10 *servings*

- SERVING SIZE: 2 TBSP
- COUNTS AS:
  1 FAT

▶ *size according to plan*

☀ Ingredients

1 cup (250ml) low-sodium soy sauce

1/4 cup (60ml) canola or soybean oil

4 tsp (20ml) ground ginger

4 tsp (20ml) dry mustard

1 garlic clove, minced

1 packet artificial sweetener

1 Combine all ingredients and whisk vigorously to combine.

2 Use to flavor beef, chicken, pork or other meats.

Chocolate-Orange Sauce

6 *servings*

- SERVING SIZE: 3 TBSP
- COUNTS AS:
  1 FRUIT
  1 FAT

▶ *size according to plan*

☀ Ingredients

1/2 cup (125ml / 100g) artificial sweetener

1 cup (250ml) evaporated skim milk

1 Tbsp (15ml) lite corn syrup

2 squares (1oz / 28g) unsweetened or semi-sweet chocolate (for a sweeter sauce)

2 Tbsp (30ml) butter flavor vegetable shortening

1 Tbsp (15ml) orange zest

1/2 tsp (2.5ml) orange extract

1 Combine artificial sweetener, evaporated milk and corn syrup in a 2 quart (2L) saucepan.

2 Heat to a full boil over medium-high flame; cook for 1 minute, at a boil, stirring constantly.

3 Reduce heat to low; add chocolate and stir until smooth.

4 Remove from heat.

5 Stir in vegetable shortening, orange zest and extract.

6 Serve with fruit, or as desired.

Add
a little
❖ Zest

Seasoned Margarine

4 *servings*

- **SERVING SIZE: 1 TBSP**
- **COUNTS AS:**
  1 FAT

▶ *size according to plan*

☀ Ingredients
1/4 cup (60ml / 56g) lite margarine, melted

1. Mix with one of the following seasonings, then chill until solid.
   - ▶ Basil: 1/4 tsp (1ml) dried basil leaves.
   - ▶ Chive-Parsley: 1 Tbsp (15ml) snipped chives and 1 Tbsp (15ml) snipped parsley.
   - ▶ Curry: 1/4 tsp (1ml) curry powder.
   - ▶ Garlic: 1/4 tsp (1ml) garlic powder.
   - ▶ Lemon: 1 Tbsp (15ml) grated lemon peel, 2 Tbsp (30ml) lemon juice.
   - ▶ Cinnamon: 1 tsp (5ml) cinnamon and 1 packet of artificial sweetener.

Soy-Sesame Marinade

1 *serving*

- **SERVING SIZE: 1 RECIPE**
- **COUNTS AS:**
  1 FAT

▶ *size according to plan*

☀ Ingredients
2 Tbsp (30ml) low-sodium soy sauce

2 Tbsp (30ml) water

1 tsp (5ml) sesame oil

2 garlic cloves, crushed

1 tsp (5ml) artificial sweetener or brown sugar artificial sweetener

1. In medium bowl, combine all ingredients; whisk vigorously.
2. Add desired meat, poultry or seafood; toss to combine.
3. Cover and marinate in refrigerator 20 minutes before preparing as desired.

Marinate the Chicken Kabobs with this sassy seasoning.

Add a little ♣ Zest

Spicy Curry Powder

☀ Ingredients

20 green cardamom pods

2 cinnamon sticks, broken into pieces

5 bay leaves

1/2 tsp (2.5ml) whole cloves

1/4 tsp (1ml) grated nutmeg

2 Tbsp (30ml) anise seeds

1 tsp (5ml) black peppercorns

5 dried red chilies

10 dried curry leaves

6 Tbsp (90ml) coriander (cilantro) seeds

3 Tbsp (45ml) cumin seeds

3 Tbsp (45ml) ground turmeric

1 Tbsp (15ml) fenugreek seeds

2 Tbsp (30ml) black mustard seeds

1. Roast the spices in a small, heavy-bottomed pan over a medium heat for 4-5 minutes, stirring constantly until lightly darkened and fragrant.

2. Remove the spices from the pan and grind to a fine powder in a spice or coffee grinder.

3. Store in an airtight jar for up to 6 months. (Unlimited use)

Lemon Seasoning

☀ Ingredients

zest from 1/2 of a lemon

2 tsp (30ml) dried parsley

1/2 tsp (2.5ml) dried parsley

1/2 tsp (2.5ml) garlic powder

1/2 tsp (2.5ml) dried oregano

1/2 tsp (2.5ml) dried marjoram leaves, crushed

1/2 tsp (2.5ml) pepper

1. Combine all ingredients. Toss.

2. Refrigerate in covered, air-tight container. (Unlimited use).

Add a little lemon seasoning to the Herbed Chicken Recipe.

Add a little ✤ Zest

Mushroom Sauce

servings

- **SERVING SIZE:**
  1/4 CUP (60ML)
- **COUNTS AS:**
  1 VEGETABLE

▶ *size according to plan*

family fare

☀ Ingredients

1 Tbsp (15ml) lite margarine

1 1/2 Tbsp (22.5ml) flour

1/4 tsp (1ml) lite salt

1/8 tsp (.5ml) white pepper

1 cup (250ml) skim milk

1/2 cup (125ml / 78g) cooked
  mushrooms, sliced

1 In a medium saucepan, melt margarine over medium heat.

2 Stir in flour, salt and pepper.

3 Add milk slowly, stirring constantly. Cook, over medium-low flame, until thickened.

4 Add mushrooms. Continue to cook, until heated through.

Italian-Style Tomato Sauce

servings

- **SERVING SIZE:**
  1/2 CUP (125ML)
- **COUNTS AS:**
  2 VEGETABLES

▶ *size according to plan*

family fare

☀ Ingredients

1 Tbsp (15ml) olive oil

1/2 cup (125ml / 80g) white or
  yellow onion, diced

2 garlic cloves, minced

1 tsp (5ml) dried basil

1 tsp (5ml) dried oregano

1/4 tsp (1ml) lite salt

1 bay leaf

3oz (85ml) full-bodied red wine,
  such as Burgundy

1 (28oz / 784g) can crushed
  tomatoes, no salt added

1 In a large saucepan, heat olive oil over a medium flame. Add onion and garlic; sauté until begins to become translucent and soft.

2 Add basil, oregano, salt and bay leaf. Cook, stirring constantly, for approximately 1 minute.

3 Add wine, stirring to combine; cook to reduce volume of wine by half.

4 Reduce heat to medium-low flame. Add tomatoes; cook, stirring occasionally for approximately 20-30 minutes.

219

Add
a little
❖ Zest

Margarita Marinade

1 *serving*

SERVING SIZE: 1 RECIPE
COUNTS AS:
  1 FRUIT
  1 FAT

▸ *size according to plan*

✳ Ingredients
2 Tbsp (30ml) fresh lime juice

1 tsp (5ml) vegetable oil

2 Tbsp (30ml) water

1oz (30ml) tequila

1-2 garlic cloves, crushed

1. In a small bowl, combine all ingredients. Whisk vigorously to combine.

2. Add desired meat, poultry, seafood or vegetables. Toss to coat all pieces.

3. Cover and refrigerate for 20-30 minutes, turning occasionally, before cooking.

Orange-Ginger Marinade

1 *serving*

SERVING SIZE: 1 RECIPE
COUNTS AS:
  1 FRUIT

▸ *size according to plan*

✳ Ingredients
1/4 cup (60ml) orange juice

1/4 cup (60ml) low-sodium soy sauce

2 Tbsp (30ml) dry sherry

1-2 garlic cloves, minced

1/2 tsp (2.5ml) ground ginger

1. In a measuring cup, combine all ingredients. Whisk vigorously.

2. Pour marinade into a large zip-top bag; add desired meat, poultry or seafood. Shake to coat.

3. Refrigerate, turning over occasionally, for 20-30 minutes.

Try this marinade with the Ginger Chicken with Apricots.

Add
a little
❖ Zest

Chili Powder

❊ Ingredients
2 Tbsp (30ml) paprika

2 tsp (10ml) oregano

1 1/4 tsp (6ml) cumin

1 1/4 tsp (6ml) garlic powder

1 1/4 tsp (6ml) cayenne pepper

3/4 tsp (4ml) onion powder

1 Mix all ingredients. Place in an airtight spice jar. (Unlimited use)

Indian Spice Blend

❊ Ingredients
8 tsp (40ml) cumin

4 tsp (20ml) ground ginger

2 tsp (10ml) ground coriander

2 tsp (10ml) cayenne pepper

4 tsp (20ml) turmeric

2 tsp (10ml) freshly ground pepper

1 Combine all ingredients in an airtight spice jar. (Unlimited use)

Hot Citrus Rub

❊ Ingredients
1 Tbsp (15ml) lemon zest

1 Tbsp (15ml) orange zest

1 tsp (5ml) artificial sweetener

1 tsp (5ml) lite salt

2 tsp (10ml) garlic powder

1 tsp (5ml) cayenne pepper

1 Combine all ingredients in a small bowl.

2 Use to grill all your favorite foods. (Unlimited use)

Add
a little
❖ Zest

Vegetable Sauce

servings

- SERVING SIZE: 2 TBSP
- COUNTS AS:
  1 CONDIMENT

▶ *size according to plan*

☀ Ingredients

1/3 cup (85ml) fat-free sour cream

1/3 cup (85ml) parsley, chopped

2 1/2 Tbsp (37.5ml) red wine vinegar

1 tsp (5ml) Worcestershire sauce

1 tsp (5ml) dry mustard

1 garlic clove, minced

1 cup (250ml) fat-free mayonnaise

2 Tbsp (30ml) chives, chopped

1 Mix all ingredients well.

2 Refrigerate for at least 30-60 minutes before serving. Use on raw or cooked vegetables.

Plum Sauce

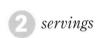

servings

- SERVING SIZE: 2 TBSP
- COUNTS AS:
  1 FRUIT
  1 FAT

▶ *size according to plan*

☀ Ingredients

2 Tbsp (30ml) plum jam

2 Tbsp (30ml) low-sodium soy sauce

1/2 tsp (2.5ml) hot chili oil

2 tsp (10ml) sesame oil

1/4 tsp (1ml) ginger, fresh, grated

1 Combine all ingredients and whisk vigorously to combine.

2 Use to flavor beef, chicken, pork or other meats.

Paint a little Plum Sauce on the Lamb Kabobs to add a little zing.

Add a little ❖ Zest

Basil Mayonnaise

16 *servings*

- **SERVING SIZE:**
  1 1/2 TBSP
- **COUNTS AS:**
  1 FAT

▶ *size according to plan*

☀ Ingredients
1 cup (250ml) lite mayonnaise

1/2 cup (125ml / 2g) fresh basil, roughly chopped

freshly ground pepper

1 Place all ingredients in a blender or food processor. Puree or blend until smooth.

2 Use immediately or refrigerate.

Spicy Flavor Blend

☀ Ingredients
1 Tbsp (15ml) dry mustard

2 1/2 tsp (12.5ml) onion powder

1 3/4 tsp (9ml) curry powder

1 1/4 tsp (6ml) white pepper

1 1/4 tsp (6ml) ground cumin

1 tsp (5ml) garlic powder

1 Mix all ingredients together in a small bowl.

2 Place into shaker and use as desired. (Unlimited)

Seasoned Salt

☀ Ingredients
1 tsp (5ml) lite salt

1 tsp (5ml) paprika

1 tsp (5ml) turmeric powder

1 tsp (5ml) onion powder

1 tsp (5ml) oregano

1 tsp (5ml) pepper

3/4 tsp (4ml) garlic powder

1/2 packet artificial sweetener

1 Mix all ingredients together in a small bowl.

2 Place into shaker and use as desired. (Unlimited)

Add
a little
✣ Zest

Herb Blend

☀ Ingredients
1 Tbsp (15ml) garlic powder

1 tsp (5ml) dried oregano

1 tsp (5ml) freshly ground pepper

1 Tbsp (15ml) parsley flakes

1 Tbsp (15ml) dried basil

1 Mix all ingredients together.

2 Place in shaker and use as desired. (Unlimited)

Taco Seasoning Mix

☀ Ingredients
2 Tbsp (30ml) chili powder

2 tsp (10ml) paprika

2 tsp (10ml) cumin

2 tsp (10ml) oregano

1/2 tsp (2.5ml) onion powder

1/2 tsp (2.5ml) garlic powder

1/2 tsp (2.5ml) cayenne pepper

1 Combine all ingredients in an airtight spice jar. (Unlimited use)

Citrus Rub

☀ Ingredients
1 Tbsp (15ml) lemon zest

1 Tbsp (15ml) orange zest

1 tsp (5ml) artificial sweetener

1 tsp (5ml) lite salt

1 Combine all ingredients in a small bowl.

2 Use to grill all your favorite foods. (Unlimited use)

Add
a little
❖ Zest

Five Spice Powder

☀ Ingredients

2 Tbsp (30ml) black peppercorns

3 star anise

2 tsp (10ml) fennel seeds

2 3-inch (8cm) cinnamon sticks, broken into small pieces

6 whole cloves

1 Dry-roast the peppercorns in a small skillet, sliding the skillet back and forth over the burner to prevent charring, until a pleasant aroma, 1-2 minutes.

2 Transfer to a bowl and set aside to cool.

3 Repeat this process, one ingredient at a time, with the remaining ingredients.

4 Put all the ingredients into a spice grinder and grind to a fine powder.

5 Transfer to a glass jar with a tight-fitting lid. Mixture will keep for up to 1 month. (Unlimited use)

Fajita Seasoning Marinade

SERVING SIZE: 2 TBSP
COUNTS AS:
  FREE FOOD

☀ Ingredients

1/4 cup (60ml) red wine vinegar

1 packet artificial sweetener

1/2 tsp (2.5ml) oregano

1/2 tsp (2.5ml) chili powder

1/4 tsp (1ml) garlic powder

1/8 tsp (.5ml) freshly ground pepper

1/4 tsp (1ml) lite salt

1 Combine all ingredients.

2 Use as a marinade for chicken or beef.

Teriyaki Marinade

① *serving*

SERVING SIZE: 1 RECIPE
COUNTS AS:
  1 FAT

▶ *size according to plan*

☀ Ingredients

1-2 tsp (5-10ml) brown sugar artificial sweetener

3 Tbsp (45ml) dry sherry

3 Tbsp (45ml) low-sodium teriyaki sauce

2 tsp (10ml) dark sesame oil

2 garlic cloves, crushed

1/2 tsp (2.5ml) ground ginger

1 In small bowl, combine all ingredients; whisk to combine.

2 Add desired meat, poultry, fish or vegetables to bowl, tossing to coat.

3 Cover and refrigerate 20 minutes before cooking.

225

Add
a little
❖ Zest

❧ Sweet Surrenders

Tasty treats can bring an instant smile to anyone, from smoothies and shakes to pudding, pies and crepes. Unfortunately, many of these treats are high in fat and/or sugar. But there are ways to cut the fat and calories while saving the flavor. For instance, fruit-based desserts that are high in fiber and low in fat are still a sweet treat!

Fruit and Yogurt Parfait recipe can be found on page 233

Sugar Substitutes

■ **Sweet 'N Low**® (Saccharin) — Earliest form of sugar substitute; 300-500 times sweeter than sugar; it is not stable at high temperatures and results in a bitter taste, best used at the end of recipes; 2 teaspoons Sweet 'N Low = 1/4 cup granulated sugar.

■ **Equal**® (Aspartame) — Made of 2 amino acids, the building blocks of protein; 180-200 times sweeter than sugar; breaks down and loses its sweet taste when heated, best for used in cold recipes; in recipes, you may use 1/4 cup Equal in place of 1/4 cup sugar; new Equal Sugar Lite is a product made especially for baking that is half sugar and half encapsulate Equal (making it heat stable).

■ **Splenda**® (Sucralose) — Made from sugar so its taste is closest to sugar; may be used teaspoon for teaspoon in place of sugar; heat stable and may be used in all types of recipes; also available in a sugar blend, called "Splenda for Baking," which is half sugar, half Splenda.

■ **Stevia** — A natural, non-caloric sweetener, derived from the plant, Stevia rebaudiana, which is an herb; native to Paraguay; only can be sold as a "dietary supplement" in the US and therefore is not labeled as a "sweetener"; in its natural state is 300 times sweeter than sugar, and even more so when processed; it is heat stable and may be used in cooking; 1/2 teaspoon stevia is equivalent to 2 teaspoons sugar.

TIP!

Keep brown sugar substitute soft when you buy it in a plastic bag. After you open the package store it in a plastic zippered bag to seal in the freshness.

Baking Substitutions

■ Use fruit puree, such as unsweetened applesauce or prune puree, in place of some of the fat.

■ Replace some of the whole eggs with egg whites or pasteurized egg substitute; it is best to keep some of the whole eggs in the recipe to maintain texture.

■ To cut back on sugar, use one-half or one-third sugar substitute — this will maintain flavor but cut back on calories.

■ Use evaporated milk in place of heavy cream.

■ If cutting out some of the sugar, add extra spices, such as cinnamon, nutmeg, cardamom and ginger, to enhance the flavor.

■ When making bread, increase the fiber by using whole wheat flour for all or half the flour.

TIPS!

• *When baking pies, cover the edges of the crust with foil to prevent the baked edges from browning. If the top of the pie is browning too much, place foil on top but pierce a hole in the center so the crust stays crisp.*

• *For the most delicious desserts, bake cakes, muffins and breads on the middle oven rack. Use the lower rack for yeast breads and pies.*

• *The best way to freeze baked goods is to wrap them in plastic wrap and then in freezer bags or sealed containers. When you want to thaw the dessert, keep it in the bag or container to let any moisture reabsorb if lost during freezing.*

Sweet Surrenders

Applesauce Oatmeal Cookies

3 *dozen cookies*

- SERVING SIZE: 2 COOKIES
- COUNTS AS:
  1 STARCH

▶ *size according to plan*

✴ Ingredients
1/4 cup (60ml) packed brown sugar

1/4 cup (60ml) artificial sweetener

1/2 cup (125ml) unsweetened applesauce

1/4 cup (60ml) egg substitute

1 cup (250ml / 125g) all-purpose flour

1 tsp (5ml) baking powder

1/2 tsp (2.5ml) salt

1 tsp (5ml) cinnamon

1 cup (250ml / 81g) oats

1/4 cup (60ml / 39g) raisins

1. In a large mixing bowl, mix together the brown sugar, sugar substitute, egg substitute and applesauce.

2. In a separate bowl, sift the flour, baking powder, salt and cinnamon; stir into the applesauce mixture.

3. Add the rolled oats and raisins. Stir until well combined.

4. Drop by spoonfuls onto the prepared cookie sheet.

5. Bake for 10 minutes in a preheated 350°F (180°C) oven.

6. Allow cookies to cool slightly before removing from the baking sheet.

Apricot Custard

1 *serving*

- SERVING SIZE: 1 RECIPE
- COUNTS AS:
  1/2 PROTEIN
  1 FRUIT
  1/2 DAIRY

▶ *size according to plan*

good source of fiber

✴ Ingredients
3 medium apricots chopped

1 egg beaten

1/2 cup (125ml) skim milk

1 packet artificial sweetener

1/4 tsp (1ml) vanilla

dash ground nutmeg

1. Divide chopped apricots into custard cups or soufflé dishes. Place cups in a shallow baking pan.

2. In a small mixing bowl, combine the egg, milk, artificial sweetener and vanilla. Pour egg mixture over apricots. Sprinkle with nutmeg.

3. Place the baking pan containing the cups on the oven rack. Pour boiling water around custard cups in baking pan to depth of 1-inch (2.5ml).

4. Bake in a 325°F (160°C) oven for 30-35 minutes, or until knife inserted in the center comes out clean.

✿ Sweet Surrender·

Sparkling Fruited Gelatin

4 *servings*

family fare

- SERVING SIZE: 1 CUP (250ML)
- COUNTS AS:
  - 1 FRUIT

▶ *size according to plan*

☀ Ingredients

2 apples

1/2 cup (125ml / 98g) canned, crushed pineapple, drained

1 tsp (5ml) lemon juice

10 grapes

1 package (3oz / 84g) sugar-free mixed fruit flavored gelatin mix

1 cup (250ml) hot water

6oz (200ml) diet ginger ale

1. Peel and core apples; cut in to thin slices.
2. Place apple slices in medium bowl. Add pineapple and lemon juice.
3. Slice grapes in half and add to fruit mixture.
4. In a separate bowl, mix gelatin and hot water. Stir until gelatin is dissolved.
5. Once dissolved, pour ginger ale into gelatin.
6. Refrigerate 30 minutes, or until gelatin mixture is the consistency of raw egg whites.
7. Add the fruit mixture to gelatin and fold in gently.
8. Refrigerate until firm.
9. Serve chilled.

Chocolate Banana Crunch Parfait

1 *serving*

- SERVING SIZE: 1 PARFAIT
- COUNTS AS:
  - 1 STARCH
  - 2 FRUITS
  - 1 FAT

▶ *size according to plan*

☀ Ingredients

1 packet L A Lite Chocolate Pudding mix

4oz (125ml) cold water

1/2 small banana, sliced

10 peanuts, crushed

1. Add pudding mix to water and stir thoroughly until smooth.
2. In a tall glass, layer one half of the pudding, then top with half of the banana slices and then half of the crushed peanuts.
3. Repeat layering steps.
4. Place in refrigerator until cold, and serve.

"These recipes are so much fun to create."

- Bella N.

❖ Sweet Surrenders

Chocolate Truffles

1 *serving*

- **SERVING SIZE: 6 TRUFFLES**
- **COUNTS AS:**
  1 DAIRY

▸ *size according to plan*

☀ Ingredients

3 Tbsp (45ml) fat-free cream cheese

2 packets artificial sweetener

1 tsp (5ml) rum extract

2 Tbsp (30ml) unsweetened cocoa powder, divided

1. Combine cream cheese, sweetener, rum extract, and 1 Tbsp (15ml) cocoa powder.

2. Mix well until all ingredients are blended.

3. Refrigerate 15 minutes.

4. Roll mixture into small balls (approximately 6).

5. Roll balls in remaining 1 Tbsp (15ml) of cocoa powder.

> "The desserts definitely satisfied my sweet tooth... and my husband's too."
> *- Sharon M.*

Baked Custard

2 *servings*

- **SERVING SIZE: 1/2 CUP (125ML)**
- **COUNTS AS:**
  1 DAIRY

▸ *size according to plan*

☀ Ingredients

1 egg

1 cup (250ml) skim milk

1 Tbsp (15ml) artificial sweetener

1 tsp (5ml) vanilla

1/4 tsp (1ml) salt

1-2 Tbsp (15-30ml) orange or lemon zest

nutmeg for garnish, optional

1. Break egg into small mixing bowl and beat slightly.

2. Add milk, artificial sweetener, vanilla, zest and salt; beat well.

3. Pour into damp custard cups and sprinkle with nutmeg.

4. Bake in 350°F (180°C) oven, in a shallow pan, of water for 40-50 minutes.

5. When custard is set, a knife inserted to the center will come out clean.

❖ Sweet Surrender

Fruit and Yogurt **Parfait**

1 *serving*

- SERVING SIZE: 1 PARFAIT
- COUNTS AS:
  1 STARCH
  1 FRUIT
  1 DAIRY

▸ *size according to plan*

good source of fiber

※ Ingredients
9 small strawberries, sliced

8oz (250ml) vanilla nonfat yogurt

1/4 cup (60ml / 36g) blueberries

1/3 cup (85ml / 20g) high fiber cereal

1 packet artificial sweetener

1 Dice 1 strawberry. Fold into yogurt.

2 In a bowl, toss remaining berries with artificial sweetener.

3 In parfait glass layer the yogurt, strawberries, blueberries and cereal.

4 Serve chilled.

Baked Apple **á la Mode**

1 *serving*

- SERVING SIZE: 1 APPLE
- COUNTS AS:
  1 STARCH
  1 FRUIT

▸ *size according to plan*

※ Ingredients
1 small apple

1/4 cup (60ml) diet black cherry soda

1 tsp (5ml) cinnamon

1/2 cup (125ml) fat-free sugar-free vanilla ice cream or frozen yogurt

1 Core apple and place in microwave-safe dish.

2 Pour soda in to middle of apple.

3 Sprinkle cinnamon over top.

4 Cook in microwave, on high, for 3-5 minutes, or until soft.

5 Top with ice cream.

"These recipes are just as good as any other cookbook I've used...even better."

- Lauren L.

❖ Sweet
Surrenders

Apple-Raspberry Crepe

 1 *serving*

- SERVING SIZE: 1 CREPE
- COUNTS AS:
  1 STARCH
  1 FRUIT

▶ *size according to plan*

❉ Ingredients

1/4 cup (60ml / 3g) raspberries

1 packet artificial sweetener

1/4 cup (60ml) unsweetened applesauce

1 crepe (see page 11 for recipe)

1. Place raspberries and sweetener in microwave safe dish.
2. Heat on high 2-3 minutes, or until hot.
3. Stir in applesauce.
4. Place filling over one half of crepe and fold over filling.

> "The cookbook desserts are so delicious, I feel guilty eating them."
>
> *- Lynn K.*

Frozen Fruit Pops

family fare

3 *servings*

- SERVING SIZE: 1 POP
- COUNTS AS:
  1 FRUIT

▶ *size according to plan*

❉ Ingredients

24 strawberries

1/2 cup (125ml) unsweetened applesauce

1/4 cup (60ml) apple juice

1 packet artificial sweetener

1/2 cup (125ml) boiling water

1/2 tsp (2.5ml) sugar free cherry gelatin mix

1. Place fruits, apple juice and sweetener in blender. Puree 1 minute. There may still be small chunks of fruit in the mixture.
2. In medium mixing bowl, dissolve gelatin in boiling water.
3. Once dissolved, add gelatin to fruit mixture and toss to combine.
4. Pour mixture into plastic ice pop molds.*
5. Place in freezer. Serve frozen.

* If ice pop molds are unavailable, pour mixture in to plastic cups and place in freezer. Once mixture begins to freeze, place ice pop sticks in to cups.

❖ Sweet Surrender

Peanut Butter Sundae **Parfait**

1 *serving*

SERVING SIZE: 1 PARFAIT
COUNTS AS:
1/2 PROTEIN
1 STARCH
1/2 DAIRY
1 FRUIT

➤ *size according to plan*

✳ Ingredients

1 packet L A Lite Chocolate Pudding mix

1/4 cup (60ml) cold water

1/4 cup (60ml) cold skim milk

2 Tbsp (30ml) fat-free whipped topping

1 Tbsp (15ml) peanut butter

1. Whisk pudding mix, milk and water together until smooth.

2. In a separate bowl, mix together peanut butter and fat-free whipped topping.

3. Layer pudding and peanut butter mixture in a glass.

4. Chill at least 1 hour before serving.

> "When it comes to desserts, these are guilt-free."
>
> *- Karen D.*

Rice **Pudding**

2 *servings*

SERVING SIZE: 1/2 OF RECIPE
COUNTS AS:
1 STARCH
1 FRUIT
1/2 DAIRY

➤ *size according to plan*

✳ Ingredients

1 Tbsp (15ml) lite margarine

1 Tbsp (15ml) flour

1/2 cup (125ml / 96g) raw rice

3/4 cup (200ml) skim milk

1 tsp (5ml) vanilla extract

4-6 packets of artificial sweetener

1/4 cup (60ml / 39g) raisins

dash of allspice

1/4 tsp (1ml) cinnamon

1. In medium saucepan melt margarine; add flour to melted butter, stirring constantly to make a roux.

2. Gradually stir in 1/2 cup (125ml) milk, mix well; heat over medium flame until warm.

3. Add rice, artificial sweetener, allspice and cinnamon.

4. Reduce heat and simmer.

5. Slowly add remaining milk during cooking until rice is tender.

6. Add vanilla and cook additional 1-2 minutes on low heat.

7. Remove from stove and add raisinis.

8. Pour in to bowls and refrigerate.

9. Serve chilled.

✿ Sweet Surrenders

Peach Melba Crepe

 serving

- **SERVING SIZE: 1 CREPE**
- **COUNTS AS:**
  1 STARCH
  1 FRUIT

▶ *size according to plan*

※ Ingredients

1/2 peach, diced

1 packet artificial sweetener

1/4 tsp (1ml) ginger

1 Tbsp (15ml) sugar free raspberry jelly or jam

1/4 cup (60ml / 31g) raspberries

1 Tbsp (15ml) fat-free whipped topping

1 crepe (see recipe on page 11)

1 Place diced peach, ginger and 1/2 packet of artificial sweetener in microwave safe dish.

2 Heat on high 2-3 minutes, or until hot.

3 Spread raspberry jelly over crepe.

4 Place peach mixture over half of the crepe and fold over filling.

5 Sprinkle remaining artificial sweetener over raspberries.

6 Top crepe with raspberries and whipped topping.

Watermelon Ice

1 *serving*

- **SERVING SIZE: 1 RECIPE**
- **COUNTS AS:**
  2 FRUITS

▶ *size according to plan*

※ Ingredients

1 1/2 cups (375ml / 228g) watermelon cubes

1 packet artificial sweetener

2 Tbsp (30ml) apple juice, chilled

2 ice cubes

1 Freeze watermelon overnight.

2 Once frozen, remove melon from freezer and place in blender.

3 Add remaining ingredients in to blender.

4 Blend on medium until smooth.

5 Serve immediately.

"You can eat desserts on the
L A Weight Loss program
and still lose weight. I did."

- Keri K.

❖ Sweet
Surrender

servings

SERVING SIZE: 1 SLICE
COUNTS AS:
1 STARCH
1 FRUIT

▶ *size according to plan*

family fare

Lemon Glazed **Cheesecake**

☀ Ingredients

Cheesecake

2 - 8oz (224g, each) packages fat-free cream cheese, softened

3/4 cup (200ml) artificial sweetener

1 Tbsp (15ml) flour

2 tsp (10ml) vanilla extract

1/2 tsp (2.5ml) fresh lemon peel, finely grated

1/2 cup (125ml) fat-free sour cream

3 egg whites

1/2 cup (125ml) graham cracker crumbs

2 cups (500ml) berries of choice

Lemon glaze

1/3 cup (85ml) artificial sweetener

1 1/2 Tbsp (22.5ml) arrowroot or cornstarch

1 1/2 Tbsp (22.5ml) fresh squeezed lemon juice

1/2 tsp (2.5ml) fresh lemon peel, finely grated

1/3 cup (85ml) water

1 Blend first 5 ingredients with electric mixer.

2 Blend in sour cream and egg whites.

3 Spray 9-inch (23cm) pie pan with nonfat cooking spray; sprinkle with graham cracker crumbs.

4 Pour in cheese mixture and bake at 325°F (160°C) for 40 minutes.

5 Cool to room temperature, then refrigerate for 3 hours.

6 For glaze, stir sugar substitute and arrowroot or cornstarch together in a small saucepan then add the lemon juice, lemon peel and water.

7 Whisk until smooth.

8 Heat, stirring constantly, until mixture is clear and thick.

9 Spread evenly over cheesecake; allow to set at room temperature, briefly.

10 Top with berries.

11 Slice pie into 8 slices.

---

serving

SERVING SIZE: 9 CHERRIES
COUNTS AS:
1 FRUIT
1 L A LITE

▶ *size according to plan*

Chocolate Covered **Cherries**

☀ Ingredients

1 packet L A Lite Chocolate Drink mix

9 medium cherries, pitted

1 Mix L A Lite Chocolate Drink Mix with 1/2 cup (125ml) water.

2 Dip cherries into chocolate mixture and place on wax paper.

3 Chill for 1 hour before serving.

❖ Sweet Surrenders

Mango-Passion Fruit Frozen Yogurt

9 *servings*

- SERVING SIZE: 3/4 CUP (200ML)
- COUNTS AS:
  1 FRUIT
  1/2 DAIRY

▶ *size according to plan*

☀ Ingredients
4 medium mangoes, peeled and cubed

1 cup (250ml) passion fruit pulp

1/3 cup (85ml) artificial sweetener

1/2 tsp (2.5ml) vanilla extract

2 cups (500ml) vanilla nonfat yogurt

1. In a food processor or blender, puree the mango; strain through a sieve.

2. Add the remaining ingredients; mix to combine.

3. Pour the mixture into a shallow 9-inch baking pan.

4. Cover with foil or plastic wrap.

5. Freeze until solid (1-2 hours).

6. Break the frozen mixture into pieces.

7. Puree in a food processor, until soft, but not completely melted.

8. Repeat the freezing and pureeing once more.

9. Serve or return to the freezer for later use.

Low-Fat Brownies

8 *servings*

- SERVING SIZE:
  1/8 OF RECIPE
- COUNTS AS:
  2 STARCH

▶ *size according to plan*

☀ Ingredients
3/4 cup (200ml) sugar

1/2 cup (125ml) flour

1/2 tsp (2.5ml) baking soda

2 egg whites, lightly beaten

1 tsp (5ml) vanilla

2/3 cup (165ml) unsweetened applesauce

1/4 cup (60ml) unsweetened cocoa powder

nonfat cooking spray

1. Preheat oven to 350°F (180°C).

2. Spray a square nonstick baking pan (8-inch x 8-inch / 20cm x 20cm) with cooking spray.

3. Combine the ingredients in a large mixing bowl, blend well.

4. Pour batter into pan and bake in preheated oven 20-30 minutes until baked.

5. To test if batter is done, insert a toothpick. If it comes out clean, brownies are done.

6. Remove from oven and let cool for 5 minutes in pan.

7. Gently remove from pan; place on wire rack and when cool.

8. Cut into 8 squares.

❀ Sweet Surrender

Lemon Sorbet

10 *servings*

- **SERVING SIZE:** 1/2 CUP (125ML)
- **COUNTS AS:**
  1 FRUIT

▶ *size according to plan*

☀ Ingredients

1 envelope unflavored gelatin

2 1/4 cups (560ml) water, divided

1/3 cup (80ml / 67g) granulated sugar, divided

1 Tbsp (15ml) artificial sweetener

2/3 cup (170ml) freshly squeezed lemon juice

2 large egg whites

2 tsp (10ml) grated lemon peel

1. In small saucepan, sprinkle gelatin over 1 cup (250ml) water; let stand 5 minutes to soften gelatin.
2. Add 1/3 cup (85ml) sugar and 1 1/4 tsp (6ml) artificial sweetener.
3. Cook over low heat, stirring until gelatin and sugar dissolve completely.
4. Pour into large bowl; add remaining water and lemon juice.
5. Chill syrup, about 2 1/2 hours.
6. In a bowl, beat egg whites with remaining artificial sweetener, until stiff, but not dry.
7. Fold into syrup mixture with lemon peel.
8. Pour into aluminum loaf pan or rectangular baking pan.
9. Cover with foil and freeze 2 hours or until frozen 1-inch (2.5cm) around edges.
10. Spoon into large bowl and beat until smooth.
11. Return to aluminum pan, cover and freeze 3 hours.
12. Transfer to bowl and beat again.
13. Return to pan, cover and freeze until firm, several hours or overnight.
14. To serve, let sorbet stand at room temperature about 15 minutes for easier scooping.

Bread Pudding

1 *serving*

good source of fiber

- **SERVING SIZE:** 1 RECIPE
- **COUNTS AS:**
  1/2 PROTEIN
  1 STARCH

▶ *size according to plan*

☀ Ingredients

1/4 cup (60ml) egg substitute

2 tsp (10ml) skim milk

1/2 tsp (2.5ml) cinnamon

1 tsp (5ml) vanilla extract

1-2 packets of artificial sweetener

1 slice lite bread

1. In a bowl, mix egg substitute, skim milk, cinnamon, sweetener and vanilla extract.
2. Tear bread into small pieces and add to mixture.
3. Place in custard cup. Set cup in baking dish containing 1-inch (2.5cm) water.
4. Bake at 350°F (180°C) for 30 minutes.

239

❖ Sweet
Surrenders

Stuffed Baked Apple

 serving

- **SERVING SIZE: 1 APPLE**
  2 FRUITS
  1 FAT

▶ *size according to plan*

good source of fiber

☀ Ingredients
1 apple

2 Tbsp (30ml) dried oatmeal

1 Tbsp (15ml) raisins

1 Tbsp (15ml) lite margarine

1 Tbsp (15ml) egg substitute

1 packet artificial sweetener

1 tsp (5ml) cinnamon

1 Core apple and peel a 1-inch (2.5cm) strip of skin around center of apple.

2 Place in a baking dish and set aside.

3 In a medium mixing bowl, combine oatmeal, raisins, egg substitute, artificial sweetener and margarine.

4 Stuff mixture into core of apple.

5 Sprinkle with cinnamon.

6 Pour water into baking dish, approximately 1/4-inch (1/2cm) depth.

7 Bake uncovered in 350°F (180°C) oven until tender, about 30 minutes.

8 While baking, spoon syrup that forms in pan over the apple.

Raspberry Chocolate Parfait

 serving

- **SERVING SIZE: 1 PARFAIT**
- **COUNTS AS:**
  1 STARCH
  2 FRUITS

▶ *size according to plan*

good source of fiber

☀ Ingredients
1 packet L A Lite Chocolate Pudding mix

4oz (125ml) cold water

1 cup (250ml / 123g) raspberries

2 Tbsp (30ml) fat-free whipped topping

1 Blend together pudding mix and water with a spoon.

2 Rinse raspberries and pat dry.

3 In a tall wine glass or narrow bowl, layer half of the pudding, followed by 1/2 cup (125ml) of the fruit, and then 1 Tbsp (15ml) fat-free whipped topping.

4 Repeat process/layers.

5 Garnish with mint, if desired.

6 Cool in refrigerate and serve.

 Sweet Surrender

Almond Cookies

dozen cookies

■ SERVING SIZE: 1 COOKIE
■ COUNTS AS:
  2 STARCHES
  1 FAT

▶ *size according to plan*

☀ Ingredients

1 egg yolk

1/3 (80ml / 67g) cup artificial sweetener

2 Tbsp (30ml) sugar

1/2 cup (125ml / 113g) butter

1 tsp (5ml) almond extract

1 1/2 cups (375ml / 188g) flour

1. Preheat oven to 350°F (180°C).

2. Beat the egg yolk, artificial sweetener, sugar, butter and almond extract in a large bowl.

3. Blend in flour a little at a time.

4. Shape a tablespoonful of dough into a ball.

5. Repeat with the remaining dough.

6. Place the cookies on an ungreased cookie sheet.

7. Bake for 20 minutes, or until lightly golden brown.

Chocolate Dipped Fruit Kabobs

serving

■ SERVING SIZE: 2-3 KABOBS
■ COUNTS AS:
  1 FRUIT
  1 L A LITE

▶ *size according to plan*

☀ Ingredients

1 envelope L A Lite Chocolate Shake mix

6oz (200ml) cold water

6 small strawberries

1/4 cup (60ml / 4g) pineapple, drained

1. Combine pudding mix with cold water, stir well until smooth, yet thin, and set aside.

2. Thread strawberries and pineapple onto 2-3 bamboo skewers.

3. Place on waxed paper.

4. Cover with pudding mixture.

5. Place in freezer until set.

❖ Sweet Surrenders

Grapefruit Watermelon Granita

4 *servings*

- **SERVING SIZE: 1/2 CUP (125ML)**
- **COUNTS AS:**
  1 FRUIT
  IF USING VODKA, COUNTS AS:
  1 FRUIT
  1 STARCH

▶ *size according to plan*

☀ Ingredients

1 cup (250ml) fresh squeezed grapefruit juice

1/3 cup (85ml) artificial sweetener

1 cup (250ml) watermelon pulp, seedless

1/4 cup (60ml) vodka (optional)

1. In a saucepan, bring grapefruit juice and artificial sweetener up to a simmer; stir until artificial sweetener is dissolved. Remove from heat and cool.

2. Puree grapefruit syrup with watermelon and strain.

3. Stir in vodka (optional) and place in freezer.

4. After an hour, stir granita. Stir 2 more times before frozen-solid.

5. To serve, scrape up granita granules with a fork and spoon into dessert glasses.

Tiramisu-Rice Dessert

family fare

8 *servings*

- **SERVING SIZE:**
  1 CUP (250ML)
- **COUNTS AS:**
  1/2 PROTEIN
  1 STARCH
  1/2 DAIRY

▶ *size according to plan*

☀ Ingredients

1 cup (250ml / 192g) long grain rice

2 1/2 cups (625ml) skim milk

1 Tbsp (15ml) instant coffee granules

2 cups (500ml) frozen fat-free whipped topping, thawed

3/4 cup (200ml) fat-free ricotta cheese

1/2 cup (125ml) artificial sweetener

2 Tbsp (30ml) coffee liqueur

unsweetened cocoa

1. In medium saucepan, combine rice, milk and coffee granules.

2. Stir occasionally until mixture comes to a boil.

3. Reduce heat to simmer; cover and cook 15 minutes or until rice is tender.

4. Cover and refrigerate until chilled.

5. In large bowl, combine rice mixture, whipped topping, ricotta cheese, artificial sweetener and liqueur; mix well.

6. Spoon into individual serving dishes or medium-size serving bowl.

7. Sift cocoa over rice mixture.

8. Cover and refrigerate for at least 1 hour before serving.

❧ Sweet Surrender

1 *serving*

good source of fiber

Apple **Crisp**

☀ **Ingredients**

2 small apples

2-3 packets artificial sweetener

1/4 cup (60ml / 20g) oatmeal

1/4 tsp (1ml) ground cinnamon

1/4 tsp (1ml) ground nutmeg

1 Heat oven to 350°F (180°C) Arrange apple slices in baking pan, coated with nonfat cooking spray. Mix remaining ingredients sprinkle over apples.

2 Bake until topping is golden brown and apples are tender.

"Oh, the cookbook was key. There was a recipe for every craving – it really helped me stay on target."

- M. Norton

■ **SERVING SIZE: 1 RECIPE**
■ **COUNTS AS:**
  1 STARCH
  2 FRUITS

▶ *size according to plan*

---

1 *serving*

Chocolate Covered **Strawberries**

☀ **Ingredients**

1 packet L A Lite Chocolate Pudding mix

4oz (125ml) cold skim milk

12 small strawberries

1 Mix chocolate pudding with milk.

2 Dip strawberries in pudding.

3 Place on waxed paper and freeze.

4 Berries are ready to be served once chocolate coating has solidified.

■ **SERVING SIZE: 12 BERRIES**
■ **COUNTS AS:**
  1 STARCH
  2 FRUITS
  1/2 DAIRY

▶ *size according to plan*

❖Sweet
Surrenders

Strawberry Daiquiri

1 *serving*

- **SERVING SIZE: 1 RECIPE**
- **COUNTS AS:**
  1 STARCH
  1 FRUIT
  1 L A LITE

▶ *size according to plan*

☀ Ingredients
1 packet L A Lite Vanilla Shake mix

1/2 cup (125ml) water

1 cup (250ml) ice cubes

12 small strawberries

1oz (28ml) rum (or rum extract)

1. Place all ingredients in a blender; puree until smooth.
2. Serve immediately, or freeze until ready to use.

Spiced Coffee

1 *serving*

- **SERVING SIZE: 1 RECIPE**
- **COUNTS AS:**
  1 UNLIMITED BEVERAGE

▶ *size according to plan*

☀ Ingredients
2 cups (500ml) brewed decaffeinated coffee

1 2-inch (5cm) stick cinnamon

1/4 tsp (1ml) whole allspice

2 strips of orange zest

1. In a saucepan combine coffee, cinnamon sticks, allspice and orange zest. Bring to boil, reduce heat.
2. Cover and simmer for 5 minutes.
3. Remove solids from coffee with a slotted spoon or by draining over a sieve. If desired, garnish with cinnamon sticks.

Hot Chai Tea

1 *serving*

- **SERVING SIZE:
  1 CUP (250ML) OF SPICED TEA**
- **COUNTS AS:**
  1/2 DAIRY

▶ *size according to plan*

☀ Ingredients
1/2 cup (125ml) hot strongly brewed orange spiced tea

1/2 cup (125ml) fat-free milk

1 Tbsp (15ml) artificial sweetener

1/4 tsp (1ml) vanilla

1/8 tsp (.5ml) ground cloves

1. Brew tea.
2. Place milk in glass measuring cup and heat on high for 30-40 seconds.
3. Combine all ingredients in beverage mug and mix until blended.

❖ Sweet
Surrender

Pineapple Slush

servings

- **SERVING SIZE: 1/3 OF RECIPE**
- **COUNTS AS:**
  2 FRUITS

▶ *size according to plan*

☀ Ingredients
20oz (560g) can crushed pineapple

1 cup (250ml) water

2 Tbsp (30ml) powdered sugar

1 packet artificial sweetener

1 Combine pineapple, water, sweetener and sugar in a freezer safe bowl; freeze for a few hours.

2 Remove from freezer and put in a blender.

3 Process at high speed; puree until smooth, about 3 minutes.

Vanilla Nut Milk

1 *serving*

- **SERVING SIZE: 1 DRINK**
- **COUNTS AS:**
  1 DAIRY

▶ *size according to plan*

good source of calcium

☀ Ingredients
8oz (250ml) skim milk

1 tsp (5ml) vanilla extract

1/8 tsp (.5ml) almond extract

1 packet artificial sweetener

dash of nutmeg

1 Combine all ingredients in small saucepan.

2 Cook over medium heat until warm stirring frequently; do not bring to a boil.

3 Serve hot.

Orange & Spice Tea

2 *servings*

- **SERVING SIZE:**
  1 CUP (250ML) OF SPICED TEA
- **COUNTS AS:**
  1 UNLIMITED BEVERAGE
  1 CONDIMENT

▶ *size according to plan*

☀ Ingredients
2 cups (500ml) water

1 cinnamon stick, broken into pieces

6 whole cloves

2 decaffeinated tea bags

juice from 1 orange

1 In a saucepan, combine water, cinnamon and cloves. Bring to a boil; remove from heat.

2 Add tea bags; steep for 5 minutes. Remove tea bags.

3 Stir in juice of 1 orange.

4 Sweeten to taste.

❖ Sweet Surrenders

Frozen Mocha **Drink**

1 *serving*

good source of calcium

- **SERVING SIZE: 1 DRINK**
- **COUNTS AS:**
  1 DAIRY
  1 L A LITE

▶ *size according to plan*

☀ Ingredients

1 packet L A Lite Chocolate
  Shake mix

1 tsp (5ml) instant coffee (decaf
  or regular)

1 Tbsp (15ml) hot water

8oz (250ml) plain nonfat yogurt

1/2 tsp (2.5ml) cinnamon

artificial sweetener to taste

1/2 cup (125ml) crushed ice or
  4 ice cubes

1 Dissolve coffee in hot water.

2 Add all ingredients to blender.

3 Blend on high until smooth.

4 Pour into container and place in freezer to chill.

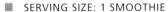

Classic Strawberry **Shake**

1 *serving*

good source of calcium

- **SERVING SIZE: 1 SMOOTHIE**
- **COUNTS AS:**
  1 STARCH
  2 FRUITS
  1/2 DAIRY

▶ *size according to plan*

☀ Ingredients

1 scoop L A Lite Strawberry-
  Banana Smoothie mix

12 small strawberries, sliced

4oz (125ml) skim milk

1/2 cup (125ml) sugar-free or
  fat-free vanilla frozen yogurt

3 ice cubes

1 Place smoothie mix, milk, ice and berries in blender.

2 Mix well.

3 Add yogurt and blend until smooth.

4 Serve immediately.

❖Sweet
Surrender

Orange Mango **Smoothie**

2 *servings*

- **SERVING SIZE:** 1/2 OF RECIPE
- **COUNTS AS:**
  1 FRUIT
  1/2 DAIRY

▶ *size according to plan*

☀ Ingredients
1 cup (250ml) crushed ice

1 cup (250ml / 165g) mango, cubed

1/2 cup (125ml) skim milk

1/2 cup (125ml) fresh squeezed orange juice

1 tsp (5ml) honey

1 In a blender, combine ice, mango, milk, orange juice and honey; blend until smooth.

2 Pour into 2 glasses and garnish with orange slice.

Peanut Butter **Shake**

1 *serving*

- **SERVING SIZE:** 1 SHAKE
- **COUNTS AS:**
  1/2 PROTEIN
  1 DAIRY
  1 L A LITE

▶ *size according to plan*

☀ Ingredients
1 Tbsp (15ml) peanut butter

8oz (250ml) skim milk

1 packet L A Lite Vanilla Shake mix

3 ice cubes

1 Blend all ingredients together; chill.

Cranberry **Blast**

1 *serving*

- **SERVING SIZE:** 1 SMOOTHIE
- **COUNTS AS:**
  2 FRUITS

▶ *size according to plan*

☀ Ingredients
1 scoop L A Lite Mixed Berry Smoothie mix

1/3 cup (85ml) cranberry juice

1/4 cup (60ml) diet cranberry ginger ale

3 ice cubes

1 Place all ingredients in blender, blend until frothy.

2 Serve immediately.

❖ Sweet Surrenders

Coffee Granita

2 *servings*

- **SERVING SIZE: 1/2 CUP (125ML)**
- **COUNTS AS:**
  1 CONDIMENT

▶ *size according to plan*

✳ Ingredients

1-2 packets artificial sweetener

2 Tbsp (30ml) instant espresso coffee powder

1/2 cup (125ml) cold water

2 Tbsp (30ml) fat-free whipped topping

1. In a bowl, combine artificial sweetener and coffee powder. Add boiling water; stir until dissolved. Stir in cold water.

2. Pour mixture into 9 x 5 x 3-inch (23 x 13 x 8cm) loaf pan. Freeze for about 2 hours or until firm.

3. Break frozen mixture into small chunks and place in a small chilled mixer bowl. Beat with electric mixer on low speed until fluffy.

4. Freeze mixture for 2 hours, or until firm.

5. To serve, scrape or scoop ice into small dessert dishes. Top with whipped topping.

Chocolate Raspberry Yogurt Shake

1 *serving*

- **SERVING SIZE: 1 SHAKE**
- **COUNTS AS:**
  1 FRUIT
  1/2 DAIRY
  1 L A LITE

▶ *size according to plan*

good source of fiber

✳ Ingredients

1/2 cup (125ml) skim milk

1/2 cup (125ml) plain fat-free yogurt

1 packet of L A Lite Chocolate Shake mix

1 cup (250ml / 123g) raspberries

1. Place skim milk, yogurt, shake mix and raspberries in blender; cover.

2. Blend until smooth.

3. Serve immediately.

"My kids always ask me for snacks from the L A Lite Cookbook."

- Karen T.

❀ Sweet Surrender

Apple Frappe

 1 *serving*

- **SERVING SIZE: 1 DRINK**
- **COUNTS AS:**
  - 1 STARCH
  - 1 FRUIT
  - 1 L A LITE

▸ *size according to plan*

☀ Ingredients

1/2 cup (125ml / 63g) chopped, cored and peeled apples

1/4 cup (60ml) cup water

ground cinnamon to taste

1/2 cup (125ml) frozen, fat-free and/or sugar-free vanilla yogurt

1 packet L A Lite Vanilla Shake mix

1. In a blender combine the apples, water, cinnamon and Vanilla Shake mix.
2. Process until smooth.
3. Add the frozen yogurt and mix until well-blended.
4. Pour into freezer-safe glass or mug and freeze until ready to use.
5. Serve cold.

Fresh Fruit Ice

1 *serving*

- **SERVING SIZE: 1 DRINK**
- **COUNTS AS:**
  - 1 FRUIT

▸ *size according to plan*

☀ Ingredients

3/4 cup (200ml) fresh fruit (suggestions: strawberries, raspberries, blueberries, blackberries, mango, watermelon, honeydew and cantaloupe)

1/2 cup (125ml) crushed ice

1 packet artificial sweetener

1. Peel, seed and/or core fruit. If necessary, chop roughly.
2. Add fruit, ice and artificial sweetener to blender.
3. Blend on high until smooth.
4. Serve in a champagne, cocktail or wine glass.

❖ Sweet
Surrenders

Home
for the
Holidays

Hosting a holiday party or going to one? Use these recipes for any special occasion and you'll always have something tasty to serve or bring...plus a clear conscience! All the recipes are healthy, light and nutritious. Your guests will be so pleased - it just might end up being a special recipe request for every holiday!

◄ Roasted Turkey with Mushroom Gravy recipe can be found on page 258

Healthy for the Holidays!

The key to successful weight loss and maintenance is moderation, and this includes the holidays. Many people feel that holidays are a time to let free or loose and forgo any diet or healthful eating habits. But with weight maintenance, comes self control and reliance to choose the right foods. Some foods will never be low in fat or calories, but there are many that can be altered to meet your needs. You'll find many of these types of recipes in this section. Remember though, these are still more caloric, sometimes higher fat, food choices, that should be limited to special occasions!

But what if you aren't the one cooking? What if you spend all your holidays visiting friends and family and are never home? There are a few tips to take with you:

■ Offer to bring a dish — this way you can have control over something that will be on the menu! You will know what you are eating and what went into the dish!

■ Make good choices, avoid the things you could have in an everyday setting, such as chips and dip — instead, go for something that is specific to the event or holiday.

■ Fill up on veggies or lower fat/calorie items — if you must try a bit of the richer, creamier items, have a little, but fill up on healthier choices, such as vegetables and dip, salads, lean proteins, such as turkey or lean beef and fruit.

■ Have a snack before you leave for the party, such as a piece of fruit and a glass of water. If you get to the party and you are famished, you are more likely to overindulge!

TIP!

Make good choices, such as vegetables and dip, salads, lean proteins, such as turkey or lean beef, and fruit.

Tips for the Perfect Holiday

Looking for a special gift for the holidays? Home made dishes are a warm, considerate, and much appreciated way to say "happy holidays." You'll find everything you'll need inside the *L A Lite Cookbook*. Here are great ways to wrap up a cake, a plate of cookies, an appetizer or any special dish:

- **Gift Basket** — A gift basket makes a beautiful presentation. Purchasing them can be costly so why not make your own? Colorful tins of Almond and Applesauce Oatmeal cookies and Chocolate Truffles placed in a white basket and wrapped in clear wrap with red and green ribbon is a very festive, fun gift.

- **Holiday Dish** — Why not make a Lemon Glazed Cheesecake and place it in a pretty holiday cake dish or plate…the dish will also be a part of the gift!

- **Holiday Canister** — A fun holiday canister filled with cookies and goodies from the *L A Lite Cookbook* is unique way to spread the holiday cheer!

What wine should I serve when entertaining for the holidays?

Planning a holiday celebration and wondering what wine goes with what? Here's a simple chart to help your remember when to Bordeaux and when you to Chardonnay!

- **Salmon** — A medium bodied wine, red or white like Pinot Noir or White Burgundy is perfect for salmon.

- **Pork** — For pork, try a medium full-bodied white with fruit aromas and a strong acidity like Riesling, Pinot Gris or Pinot Blanc.

- **Roast Beef** — A rich full-bodied red with substantial tannin like Cabernet Sauvignon or Rivera del Duero Red is ideal for Roast Beef.

- **Chicken** — Light chicken dishes go great with a Chardonnay or Pinot Grigio.

- **Turkey** — A medium bodied red like Pinot Noir is an excellent accompaniment to roasted turkey.

(When drinking wine, be sure to count one 3oz glass of wine as one fruit exchange!)

❖TIPS!

• Have smaller helpings at dinner so you can try a wider variety of foods and won't feel as bad at the end of the party. Eating only 1/2 as much as you normally would take can prevent overeating.

• Save yourself some time by setting the table for the holidays the night before. The holiday will become a little hectic and scrambling for extra place settings and silverware will be the last thing on your mind.

Home
❖ for the
Holidays

Challah

18 *servings*

- **SERVING SIZE:**
  1/18 OF BREAD (APPROX 1OZ)
- **COUNTS AS:**
  1 STARCH

▸ *size according to plan*

☀ Ingredients

1 packet or 1 Tbsp (15ml) active dry yeast

2 Tbsp (30ml) sugar

1/4 cup (60ml) warm water

2 cups (500ml / 248g) all-purpose flour

2 cups (500ml / 248g) whole wheat flour

1/2 tsp (2.5ml) lite salt

1 egg

2 Tbsp (30ml) vegetable oil

1 1/4 cup (310ml) cold water

1 egg, beaten

1 Tbsp (15ml) poppy seeds

nonfat cooking spray

1. Dissolve the yeast and sugar in 1/4 cup (60ml) of warm water. Let stand for 5 minutes.

2. Combine flour and salt in a large mixing bowl.

3. Make a well in the center of the flour mixture; add the egg, oil, yeast mixture and cold water. Mix well.

4. Knead the dough on a floured board, adding more whole wheat flour, as needed, until dough is smooth and elastic.

5. Place in an oiled bowl.

6. Cover with a damp towel and let rise until doubled, about 1 hour.

7. Divide the dough into three parts.

8. Roll, by hand, each third into a strip, about 15 inches long.

9. Braid the strips together and place on a baking sheet that has been lightly coated with nonfat cooking spray. Brush with the beaten egg. Sprinkle on the poppy seeds.

10. Cover and let rise until loaf has doubled in size.

11. Bake in a 375°F (190°C) oven for 40-45 minutes, or until golden brown.

Winter Salad

4 *servings*

- **SERVING SIZE:**
  1/4 OF RECIPE
- **COUNTS AS:**
  2 VEGETABLE
  1 FAT

▸ *size according to plan*

☀ Ingredients

2 heads bibb lettuce

1 bunch watercress

1 apple, chopped

2 Tbsp (30ml) chopped pecans, toasted

3 Tbsp (45ml) balsamic vinegar

1 Tbsp (15ml) Dijon mustard

1 Tbsp (15ml) olive oil

1 tsp (5ml) honey

1. Clean and chop lettuces. Toss together and divide among 4 salad plates.

2. Combine apples and pecans; sprinkle over lettuce.

3. Whisk together remaining ingredients; drizzle over salads.

Home
❖ for the
Holidays

Potato Latkes

- SERVING SIZE: 2 PANCAKES
- COUNTS AS:
  1 STARCH
  2 VEGETABLES

▶ *size according to plan*

☀ Ingredients

1 pound (448g) zucchini, peeled

1 pound (448g) potatoes, peeled

2 large onions, chopped

1 pound (448g) fresh spinach

1 large egg

2 egg whites

1/2 cup (125ml / 63g) flour

1/2 tsp (2.5ml) ground cumin

1/2 tsp (2.5ml) dried ground coriander

ground white pepper

1/4 tsp (1ml) lite salt

nonfat cooking spray

1. Grate potatoes, zucchini and onion in food processor (work quickly to avoid discoloration). Squeeze out any liquid. Place in a large mixing bowl.

2. Add spinach, egg, egg whites, flour, cumin, coriander, salt and pepper, to taste; mix well.

3. Coat large skillet with nonfat cooking spray.

4. Spoon batter into pan, being careful not to crowd.

5. Cook until crisp and brown on one side, then turn over and fry on other side.

6. Keep finished pancakes warm in oven until all pancakes are cooked.

7. Makes 24 pancakes.

Baked Stuffed Zucchini

8 *servings*

- SERVING SIZE: 1/4 ZUCCHINI
- COUNTS AS:
  1 VEGETABLE

▶ *size according to plan*

family fare

☀ Ingredients

2 zucchini, cut in half lengthwise

1 small onion, finely chopped

1/4 cup (60ml) lite tomato sauce

1/2 tsp (2.5ml) parsley

1 garlic clove, chopped

2 Tbsp (30ml) matzo meal

1. Scoop out pulp/flesh of the zucchini halves.

2. Heat pulp, onion, sauce, parsley and garlic in a pan for 5 minutes. Add matzo meal to mixture and mix well.

3. Stuff shelled zucchinis with mixture.

4. Place in a baking dish with a little water on bottom.

5. Bake in 450°F (230°C) oven for 30 minutes, until zucchini shells are soft.

Home
❧ for the
Holidays

Filet Mignon with Mushroom & Wine Sauce

4 servings

- **SERVING SIZE: 1 STEAK AND 1/2 CUP (125ML) SAUCE**
- **COUNTS AS:**
  1 PROTEIN
  2 VEGETABLES

▸ *size according to plan*

☀ Ingredients

1/3 cup (85ml / 32g) chopped green onion

1/2 pound (224g) fresh shiitake mushrooms, stems removed

1 1/2 cups (375ml) red wine, divided

1 small (10-12fl oz / 310-375ml) can low-sodium beef consommé, undiluted

freshly ground pepper

4 filet mignon steaks (4 or 6oz / 112 or 168g, each)

1 Tbsp (15ml) low-sodium soy sauce

2 tsp (10ml) cornstarch

1 tsp (5ml) dried thyme

nonfat cooking spray

1. Coat a skillet with nonfat cooking spray and heat over medium flame.

2. Add onions and mushrooms; sauté for 4 minutes.

3. Add 1 cup (250ml) wine and 3/4 cup (200ml) consommé; cook for 5 minutes, stirring frequently. Remove the mushrooms with a slotted spoon; place in a bowl.

4. Increase heat to high; cook wine mixture until reduced to 1/2 cup (125ml), about 5 minutes.

5. Add reduction to mushrooms; set aside. Wipe pan with paper towel. Sprinkle steaks with pepper.

6. Coat a nonstick skillet with nonfat cooking spray and heat over high flame. Add steaks; cook 3 minutes on each side.

7. Reduce heat to medium-low; continue to cook another 2-4 minutes, or until desired level of doneness.

8. Combine soy sauce with cornstarch.

9. Add 1/2 cup (125ml) wine and remaining consommé to skillet; scrape bottom of skillet to loosen browned bits. Bring to a boil; cook 1 minute.

10. Add mushroom mixture, cornstarch mixture, and dried thyme to skillet; bring to a boil, and cook 1 minute, stirring. Serve sauce over steaks.

Glazed Ham

8 servings

- **SERVING SIZE: 3 OR 5OZ (84 OR 140G) COOKED**
- **COUNTS AS:**
  1 PROTEIN

▸ *size according to plan*

☀ Ingredients

4-6 pound (1.8 - 2.7kg) ham

1 cup (250ml) apricot halves in lite syrup

3 Tbsp (45ml) no sugar added apricot preserves

1/2 tsp (2.5ml) whole ground cloves

1. Trim all visible fat from ham. Place ham in baking pan.

2. Pour apricot halves and juice over ham. Dot cloves throughout ham, gently pressing into flesh.

3. Heat ham in oven according to package directions.

4. To prepare glaze, place preserves in small dish. Place in microwave 10-20 seconds, until preserves begin to melt.

5. During last 30 minutes of cooking, brush ham with warm glaze. Continue to brush ham every 10 minutes until cooked through.

6. Preserves may need to be re-heated, as needed, before basting.

7. Allow to rest 5 minutes, before slicing.

Home
❖ for the
Holidays

Crown Roast of Pork

15 *servings*

- SERVING SIZE: 3 OR 5OZ (84 OR 140G) COOKED PORK ROAST AND 1/2 CUP (125ML) STUFFING
- COUNTS AS:
  1 PROTEIN
  1 STARCH
  1 FRUIT

▶ *size according to plan*

☀ Ingredients

27 pounds (3kg) crown pork roast (12 rib)

Stuffing

5 green onions, chopped

2 celery stalks, finely chopped

1 cup (250ml / 126g) red apple, peeled and chopped

1 cup (250ml /126g) green apple chopped, peeled and chopped

6 slices lite bread, cubed and toasted ·

2 Tbsp (30ml) dried sage leaves

1/2 tsp (2.5ml) dried rosemary

1/2 tsp (2.5ml) dried thyme

1/4 cup (60ml) beaten egg substitute

1/4 cup (60ml) skim milk

1/4 tsp (1ml) freshly ground pepper

nonfat cooking spray

Roast

1 Trim all visible fat from roast; season with pepper

2 Cut a piece of aluminum foil into an 8-inch square; place on rack in roasting pan.

3 Place roast; bone ends up, on foil-lined rack.

4 Bake in 325°F oven for one hour, before stuffing.

Stuffing

1 Coat skillet with nonfat cooking spray and heat over medium heat-high flame; add onion and celery. Cook, stirring, until tender.

2 Combine apples, bread cubes and seasonings in a large bowl; stir in vegetable mixture, egg and remaining ingredients.

3 Spoon stuffing into center of roast; cover with additional foil.

4 Insert oven-proof meat thermometer into roast, taking care not to touch fat or bone.

5 Bake at 325°F (160°C) for 1 1/2 hours, or until thermometer reaches 150°F (65°C).

Minted Leg of Lamb

12 *servings*

- SERVING SIZE: 3 OR 5OZ (84 OR 140G) COOKED LAMB
- COUNTS AS:
  1 PROTEIN

▶ *size according to plan*

☀ Ingredients

1 tsp (5ml) lite salt

1 1/2 tsp (7.5ml) dried mint flakes

1/2 tsp (2.5ml) cayenne pepper

9 pounds (4kg) bone-in leg of lamb

5 green onions, chopped

3 cups (750ml) dry white wine

1/2 cup (125ml) low-sodium chicken broth

1/3 cup (85ml) Dijon mustard

4 garlic cloves, chopped

2 Tbsp (30ml) low-sodium Worcestershire sauce

nonfat cooking spray

1 Combine first 3 ingredients; rub into lamb.

2 Place chopped onion in center of the roasting pan that has been coated with nonfat cooking spray; place lamb on top of onion.

3 Combine wine and remaining 4 ingredients; pour over lamb.

4 Insert oven-proof meat thermometer into thickest part of lamb, taking care not to touch bone or fat.

5 Bake at 325°F (160°C) for 1 hour 45 minutes to 2 hours 30 minutes, or until thermometer registers 150-160°F (65-70°C) Baste lamb every 30 minutes with wine mixture.

6 Let stand 10 minutes before slicing.

Home
❖ for the
Holidays

Roasted Turkey with Mushroom Gravy

10 *servings*

- SERVING SIZE: 4 OR 6OZ (112 OR 168G) COOKED TURKEY AND 1/4 CUP (60ML) GRAVY
- COUNTS AS:
  1 PROTEIN
  2 VEGETABLES

▶ *size according to plan*

☀ Ingredients

Turkey

3 Tbsp (45ml) chopped fresh rosemary

3 Tbsp (45ml) chopped fresh thyme

3 Tbsp (45ml) chopped fresh tarragon

1 Tbsp (15ml) freshly ground pepper

2 tsp (10ml) lite salt

20-22 pound (9-10kg) turkey

3 Tbsp (45ml) lite margarine, melted

4 cups (1L) low-sodium chicken broth

Gravy

1/2 cup (125ml / 48g) finely chopped green onions

1 cup (250ml / 70g) finely chopped fresh mushrooms

2 Tbsp (30ml) chopped fresh parsley

2 cups (500ml) low-sodium chicken broth

2 Tbsp (30ml) cornstarch

freshly ground pepper

Turkey

1　Mix first five ingredients in small bowl.

2　Rinse turkey, then pat dry with paper towels; place on rack set in large roasting pan.

3　Place herb mixture into main cavity. Tie legs together loosely to hold the shape of the turkey.

4　Position rack in lowest third of oven and preheat to 425°F (220°C).

5　Pour 2 cups (500ml) broth into the pan. Drizzle melted margarine over turkey.

6　Roast turkey for 45 minutes in 425°F (220°C) oven.

7　Remove turkey from oven and cover breast with foil. Reduce oven temperature to 350°F (180°C).

8　Return turkey to oven; roast turkey for 1 hour.

9　Remove foil from turkey; pour remaining 2 cups (500ml) broth into pan.

10　Continue roasting turkey until meat thermometer, inserted in thickest part of thigh, registers 180°F (85°C) (or until juices run clear when thickest part of thigh is pierced by skewer), basting occasionally with pan juices. Expected cooking time will be about 1-2 hours longer.

11　Transfer turkey to platter; tent with foil.

12　Let stand 30 minutes before slicing.

Gravy

1　In a saucepan, sauté onion, mushrooms, and parsley in 1/4 cup (60ml) broth until vegetables are tender.

2　Combine cornstarch, pepper, and 1/2 cup (125ml) broth; stir until smooth.

3　Add to cornstarch mixture to pan and mix well.

4　Bring to a boil, stirring occasionally. Boil for 2 minutes.

Home
❖ for the
Holidays

Grilled Chicken & Portabellas

4 *servings*

■ SERVING SIZE: 1 CHICKEN
  BREAST, 1 MUSHROOM CAP,
  AND 2 TBSP SAUCE
■ COUNTS AS:
  1 PROTEIN
  2 VEGETABLES

▶ *size according to plan*

☀ Ingredients

2 1/4 cups (560ml) Marsala
  wine, divided

2 Tbsp (30ml) reduced/low-
  sodium Worcestershire sauce

6-8oz (168-224g) skinless
  chicken breasts, size according
  to plan

1 pound (448g) portabella
  mushroom caps

1/4 cup (60ml / 24g) diced
  green onion

nonfat cooking spray

1. Combine 2 cups (500ml) wine, Worcestershire sauce, and chicken breast in a large zip-lock bag; seal and marinate in refrigerator 1 hour.
2. Remove chicken from bag, reserving marinade.
3. Prepare grill.
4. Lightly coat mushrooms with nonfat cooking spray.
5. Place mushrooms, top sides down, on grill rack coated with nonfat cooking spray; spoon 1 Tbsp (15ml) wine into each cap.
6. Add chicken and grill for 6 minutes on each side, or until chicken is done.
7. Cut mushrooms into 1/2-inch (1.5ml) thick slices.
8. While the chicken and mushrooms are grilling, place a medium skillet coated with cooking spray over medium-high heat until hot.
9. Add green onions; sauté for 1 minute.
10. Add the reserved marinade and bring to a boil.
11. Reduce heat, and simmer until reduced to 1/2 cup (125ml).
12. Serve chicken and mushrooms with sauce.

Balsamic Roasted New Potatoes

10 *servings*

■ SERVING SIZE: 2 POTATOES
■ COUNTS AS:
  1 STARCH

▶ *size according to plan*

☀ Ingredients

2 pounds (896g) new potatoes,
  quartered

1 Tbsp (15ml) minced garlic

1 tsp (5ml) chopped fresh thyme

1 tsp (5ml) chopped fresh
  rosemary

3 Tbsp (45ml) balsamic vinegar

1/4 tsp (1ml) freshly ground
  pepper

dash of lite salt

nonfat cooking spray

1. Heat large cast iron skillet, coated with nonfat cooking spray, over medium-high flame.
2. Add potatoes and seasonings and heat through.
3. Remove skillet from heat; place in oven, uncovered, at 425°F (220°C) for 30 minutes, or until potatoes are tender, stirring occasionally.
4. Add vinegar, and toss well.
5. Sprinkle with salt and pepper. Roast, uncovered, 6 more minutes.
6. Serve immediately.

Home
❖ for the
Holidays

Zucchini-Carrot Casserole

3 *servings*

- SERVING SIZE: 1/3 OF RECIPE
- COUNTS AS:
  3 VEGETABLES
  1 DAIRY

▶ *size according to plan*

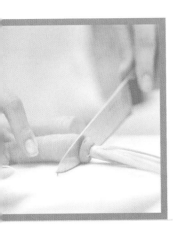

☀ Ingredients

1 onion, chopped

2 medium zucchinis, thinly sliced

1 medium carrot, thinly sliced

2 garlic cloves, chopped

1/4 cup (60ml) low-sodium chicken broth

1/4 cup (60ml) fat-free sour cream

4oz (112g) reduced-fat shredded cheddar cheese, divided

1/2 tsp (2.5ml) basil

1/4 tsp (1ml) oregano

1/4 tsp (1ml) onion powder

1/4 tsp (1ml) lite salt

1/4 tsp (1ml) freshly ground pepper

4 Melba toasts, crushed

nonfat cooking spray

1. Coat large skillet with nonfat cooking spray and heat over medium-high flame. Add onion to skillet, cook 1 minute.

2. Increase flame to high.

3. Add zucchini, garlic and carrots. Cook 1-2 minutes. Add broth and cook until vegetables are soft.

4. Once veggies are soft and all liquid has evaporated, remove from heat.

5. Stir in sour cream, 3oz (84g) cheese, salt and pepper.

6. Pour mixture into a large greased casserole dish.

7. In separate bowl, combine basil, oregano, onion powder and crushed Melba toast.

8. Top the zucchini mixture with Melba crumb mixture and remaining cheese.

9. Bake at 350°F (180°C) for 15 minutes, or until cheese is melted. Serve immediately.

Bread Dressing

12 *servings*

- SERVING SIZE: 1/2 CUP (125ML)
- COUNTS AS:
  1 STARCH
  1 VEGETABLE

▶ *size according to plan*

☀ Ingredients

1 cup (250ml / 120g) chopped celery

1 cup (250ml / 160g) chopped onion

1/3 cup (85ml) low-sodium chicken broth

1 tsp (5ml) ground sage or poultry seasoning

dash of lite salt

freshly ground pepper

12 slices bread cubes (use diet whole wheat bread and lightly toast to remove excess moisture)

1/2-3/4 cup (125-200ml) low-sodium chicken broth

nonfat cooking spray

1. In medium saucepan, cook celery and onion in 1/3 cup (85ml) broth, until tender. Remove from heat.

2. Stir poultry seasoning or sage, pepper and salt.

3. Place dry bread cubes in a large mixing bowl. Add onion mixture.

4. Drizzle with enough broth to moisten, and lightly toss.

5. Coat casserole dish with nonfat cooking spray. Place stuffing in dish and bake at 350°F (180°C) for 20 minutes, or until browned.

Home
❖ for the
Holidays

Wild Rice Pilaf

8 *servings*

- SERVING SIZE: 1/2 CUP (125ML)
- COUNTS AS:
  1 STARCH
  1 VEGETABLE

size according to plan

❉ Ingredients

1 1/4 cups (310ml) water

3 cups (750ml) low-sodium chicken broth

1 1/2 cups (375ml / 288g) uncooked wild rice

1 Tbsp (15ml) lite margarine

3 cups (750ml / 210g) sliced mushrooms

1 cup (250ml / 96g) chopped green onions

1/2 cup (125ml / 30g) finely chopped fresh parsley

1/3 cup (85ml / 36g) chopped pecans, toasted

3/4 tsp (4ml) poultry seasoning

1/2 tsp (2.5ml) lite salt

1/4 tsp (1ml) freshly ground pepper

nonfat cooking spray

1. Bring water and broth to a boil in a medium saucepan.
2. Add wild rice; cover, reduce heat, and simmer 1 hour or until tender. Drain any excess liquid.
3. Preheat oven to 325°F (160°C)
4. Melt margarine in a large, nonstick skillet over medium-high heat.
5. Add mushrooms and onion; sauté until tender.
6. Remove from heat; stir in parsley and next 4 ingredients.
7. Combine rice and mushroom mixture in a 2-quart casserole, coated with nonfat cooking spray.
8. Cover and bake at 325°F (160°C) for 25 minutes.

Southern Peach Shortcake

9 *servings*

- SERVING SIZE: 1/9 OF CAKE
- COUNTS AS:
  1 STARCH
  1 FRUIT

size according to plan

❉ Ingredients

3 peaches, sliced

10 packets of artificial sweetener

1/2 tsp (2.5ml) almond extract

1/2 tsp (2.5ml) cinnamon

1 cup (250ml / 126g) flour

1/3 cup (85ml / 67g) sugar

2 tsp (10ml) baking powder

2 Tbsp (30ml) oil

2 egg whites

1/4 cup (60ml) skim milk

nonfat cooking spray

1. Place peaches in bottom of well-greased 8-inch baking dish with nonfat cooking spray.
2. Sprinkle with 3 packets of artificial sweetener, almond extract and cinnamon.
3. Combine flour, remaining artificial sweetener, sugar and baking powder in mixing bowl. Add oil, egg and milk to flour mixture. Mix well.
4. Spread mixture evenly over peaches.
5. Bake at 400°F (200°C) for 30 minutes, or until lightly browned.
6. Cool for 15 minutes. To serve, place large serving plate over top of the cake and invert onto plate.

Home
❖ for the
Holidays

New York Cheesecake

8 *servings*

- SERVING SIZE: 1/8 OF CAKE
- COUNTS AS:
  1 STARCH
  1 FAT

▸ *size according to plan*

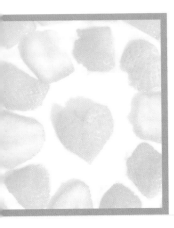

☀ Ingredients

50 reduced-fat vanilla wafers, crumbled

4 Tbsp (45ml) lite margarine, melted

8 Tbsp (120ml) artificial sweetener

2 packages (8oz or 224g each) reduced-fat cream cheese, softened

1 cup (250ml) reduced-fat sour cream

6 Tbsp (90ml) sugar

2 eggs

2 egg whites

2 Tbsp (30ml) cornstarch

1 tsp (5ml) vanilla

1 pint (500ml / 288g) strawberries, sliced (optional)

1. Mix 3/4 of vanilla wafer crumbles, margarine and artificial sweetener in the bottom of 9-inch (23cm) springform pan. Set aside 1 Tbsp of crumb mixture.

2. Pat the remaining mixture evenly on bottom and 1/2 inch (1.5cm) up side of pan.

3. Bake in preheated 350°F (180°C) oven until the crust is lightly browned, about 8 minutes or so. Cool on wire rack.

4. Beat cream cheese, sour cream, and sugar in a large bowl until fluffy; then beat in eggs, egg whites, vanilla and cornstarch. Pour mixture into pre-baked crust.

5. Place cheesecake in roasting pan on oven rack; and 1 inch (2.5cm) hot water to roasting pan.

6. Bake in preheated 300°F (150°C) oven just until set in the center, 45-60 minutes.

7. Remove cheesecake from roasting pan, sprinkle with reserved crumbs and return to oven. Turn oven off and let cheesecake cool in oven with door ajar for 3 hours.

8. Refrigerate 8 hours or overnight.

9. Remove sides of pan; place cheesecake on cake plate.

10. Serve with strawberries, if desired, to count as an additional fruit serving.

Egg Nog

2 *servings*

- SERVING SIZE: 3/4 CUP (200ML)
- COUNTS AS:
  1/2 PROTEIN
  1 DAIRY

▸ *size according to plan*

good source of calcium

☀ Ingredients

2 eggs, well beaten

3 packets artificial sweetener

dash of vanilla extract

2 cups (500ml) cold skim milk

dash of nutmeg, to taste

1. Combine egg and artificial sweetener.

2. Add vanilla extract and cold milk and beat well.

3. Pour into glasses or mugs and sprinkle with nutmeg.

Home
❖ for the
Holidays

Crustless Pumpkin Pie

8 *servings*

- **SERVING SIZE: 1/8 OF PIE**
- **COUNTS AS:**
  1 STARCH
  1/2 DAIRY

▶ *size according to plan*

❋ Ingredients

1 can (15oz / 420g) pumpkin, no salt added

1 can (12oz / 336g) evaporated skim milk

1/2 cup (125ml) egg substitute

2 egg whites

3/4 cup (200ml / 150g) artificial sweetener

1 tsp (5ml) ground cinnamon

1/4 tsp (1ml) ground allspice

1/4 tsp (1ml) ground ginger

1/8 tsp (.5ml) salt

1/2 cup (125ml / 59g) reduced-fat graham cracker crumbs

nonfat cooking spray

1. In a mixing bowl, combine the pumpkin, milk, egg substitute, egg whites and sweetener, beat until smooth.

2. Add the spices and salt, beat until well combined.

3. Stir in graham cracker crumbs.

4. Pour into a 9-inch (23cm) pie plate that has been coated with nonfat cooking spray.

5. Bake at 325°F (160°C) for 50-55 minutes, or until knife inserted near the center comes out clean. Cool before slicing.

Fruit & Nut Crisp

8 *servings*

- **SERVING SIZE: 1-INCH (2.5CM) SQUARE (1/8 OF PAN)**
- **COUNTS AS:**
  1 STARCH
  2 FRUITS

▶ *size according to plan*

❋ Ingredients

1/4 cup (60ml / 32g) flour

1/2 cup (125ml / 40g) uncooked instant oatmeal

1/2 tsp (2.5ml) allspice

3 Tbsp (45ml) lite margarine, softened

2 cups (500ml / 362g) canned pineapple chunks, drained

1 mango, peeled and sliced

1/2 banana, peeled and sliced

1 orange, peeled and sliced

3/4 cup (200ml / 115g) sliced papaya

1 kiwi, sliced

2 Tbsp (30ml) brown sugar

2 Tbsp (30ml) artificial sweetener

3 Tbsp (45ml) almonds, chopped

1 Tbsp (15ml) flour

1. In small bowl, combine flour, oatmeal, brown sugar, and allspice.

2. Add margarine; mix with fork, until a crumbly dough forms.

3. In large mixing bowl, combine all fruits, artificial sweetener, and almonds.

4. Sprinkle with flour and toss to coat.

5. Pour fruit mixture into greased 8-inch (20cm) square baking pan. Sprinkle oatmeal mixture on top.

6. Bake in preheated oven at 350°F (180°C) until crust is brown and fruit mixture begins to bubble, about 20-25 minutes.

Home
❖ for the
Holidays

The *L A Lite Cookbook* has been designed to spice up your L A Weight Loss program. Eating a variety of foods will not only keep you interested in your program, but it will also provide your body with the vitamins, minerals and other nutrients that are essential for balanced nutrition and good health. This cookbook will provide you with healthy and delicious recipes that can be used not only while you are losing weight, but for many years to come. Eating healthy is not only important for weight loss, but it's also important for maintaining your new weight for a lifetime.

Adopting a healthier lifestyle will not only help you lose weight, but can benefit the entire family. This cookbook includes many popular dishes that everyone will enjoy. Start off any meal with an appetizer, soup or salad. Next, with over a hundred entrée recipes, you will be sure to find a delicious entree to suit your mood. Finally, conclude your meal with a tantalizing dessert or delicious beverage.

Depending on the situation, it may make sense to adjust the diet and reduce or exclude the intake of some foods. Here are the most common cases for considering dietary modifications:

Dietary Substitutions

▶ **Lactose intolerant**
Use fat-free or skim Lactaid milk in place of skim milk in recipes. Soymilk may also be used.

▶ **Gluten and wheat free**
Use rice in recipes that call for pasta. Starches such as winter squash and potatoes are also delicious wheat and gluten-free alternatives.

▶ **Vegetarians**
Use your favorite vegetarian protein in place of any meat in a recipe. For example, instead of using beef in the beef teriyaki recipe you can use beans, seitan or textured vegetable protein instead. Tofu and tempeh can be used in place of chicken. Make substitutions accordingly.

▶ **Vegans**
Use soymilk in place of milk in recipes. Cheeses such as mozzarella and cheddar can be replaced with soy cheese. Ricotta and cottage cheese can be substituted with tofu. Animal proteins such as chicken and beef can be substituted with beans, veggie burgers or textured vegetable protein.

To make using this cookbook easier, we have included a number of icons; you will see these throughout the cookbook. Let these icons help guide you in choosing recipes that fit your lifestyle and nutritional needs. An explanation of each is listed below.

Symbol Key

▶ **Good Source of Fiber**

These recipes contain fiber (fiber is a component of foods that can not be fully digested.) Fiber has many health benefits, from improving digestion, relieving constipation, protecting against some types of cancers and lowering blood cholesterol levels. In addition, high fiber foods take longer to digest, keeping you satisfied longer.

▶ **Good Source of Calcium**

These recipes contain ingredients with calcium. Calcium is an essential mineral used to maintain strong bones and teeth. Adequate calcium intake can help prevent osteoporosis and is important for people of all ages.

▶ **Meals in Minutes**

Recipes that will take 20 minutes or less to prepare and reach the table. These recipes are great for people with active lifestyles. You will be able to prepare and cook a delectable meal in less time than waiting for take-out to be delivered!

▶ **Family Fare**

These are recipes that make more than one serving. These recipes were created so everyone can sit down and enjoy a healthy, well-balanced meal together. With this cookbook, you do not need to cook separate meals for your family and yourself to follow the program and achieve the success of your weight loss goals.

Some of the following terms are found in many of our recipes. For your convenience here are some definitions to help in the preparation of the recipes.

Julienne: Slicing foods into thin matchstick like strips.

Chopped: Cutting food into uniform bite sized pieces.

Grated: Thin shreds of a food. Large pieces of food are rubbed against a serrated surface such as a grater. A food processor can also grate many foods.

Zest: The colored portion of the skin/peel of a citrus fruit such as an orange, lemon or lime. Removing this outer layer of skin can add great flavor to foods.

Diced: Cutting food into small cubes.

Minced: Cutting food into very small pieces. Minced foods are smaller than chopped foods.

Working the recipes into your meal plan

You may notice that there are some ingredients in some of the recipes in this cookbook that are not on your weight loss plan. It is okay to use these recipes! These ingredients are portion controlled and the calories are factored into the exchanges.

In addition, some recipes do not appear to have the same exchanges and serving sizes as the menu plans. For example, a recipe may call for only half a cup of raw vegetables but may count as a whole vegetable serving. When working out the exchanges, the registered dietitians have looked at the recipe as a whole before determining what to count it as. As long as you measure out the portions of ingredients and count the recipes as indicated, these recipes can all be used on a regular basis.

Want to change the number of servings from a recipe? You can convert your favorite "Family Fare" recipe to a single serving or adjust any single serving recipe so it can make multiple servings. Here are a few examples:

A single serving recipe that calls for 2 tablespoons (30ml) of skim milk and 1/2cup (125ml) fresh broccoli can be adjusted to make 12 servings. There are 16 tablespoons (250ml) per cup, so the new 12 serving recipe would have 24 tablespoons or 1 1/2 cups (375ml) of skim milk. The new recipe would now call for 6 cups (1.5L) of broccoli.

A recipe that yields 12 servings that calls for 1/4 cup (60ml) of juice can also be modified to serve any number of people. 1/4 cup (60ml) is 4

tablespoons (60ml) or 12 teaspoons (180ml) , if changing this recipe to make 4 servings you would need teaspoons or 1 1/3 tablespoon (20ml) of juice. To make 1 serving you would use only a teaspoon (5ml) of juice.

Use the following conversion charts to help you adjust any of our delicious recipes.

Have you ever been confused by how many teaspoons equal a tablespoon, or how many grams equal an ounce? With the reference chart below, hopefully, we will answer all those questions about US and metric measurements.

Conversion Chart

1/4 tsp = 1.25 ml	
1/2 tsp = 2.5 ml	
3/4 tsp = 3.75 ml	
1 tsp = 5 ml	
1 Tablespoon (Tbsp) = 3 tsp = 15 ml	
1/4 cup = 60 milliliters (ml)	
1/2 cup = 125 ml	
3/4 cup = 200 ml	
1 cup = 250 l	
2 cups = 1 pint = 500 ml	
4 cups = 1 quart = 1 Liter (L)	
1 ounce (oz) = 28 gram (g)	
4 oz = 112 g	
8 oz = 224 g	
16 oz = 1 pound (lb) = 448 g	

Metric conversions

1 inch (in) = 2.5 centimeters (cm)

The following are flavorings, spices and herbs that can be used to make foods tastier without adding salt:

Beef: bay leaf, horseradish, marjoram, nutmeg, onion, pepper, sage, thyme.

Lamb: chili powder, curry powder, garlic, lemon juice, rosemary, mint, turmeric.

Pork: garlic, ginger, onion, sage, pepper, oregano.

Veal: bay leaf, curry powder, ginger, marjoram, oregano.

Chicken: cumin, garlic, ginger, lemon juice, marjoram, oregano, paprika, poultry seasoning, rosemary, sage, tarragon, thyme.

Fish: curry powder, dill, dry mustard, lemon juice, marjoram, parsley, paprika, pepper.

Carrots: cinnamon, cloves, chives, coriander, marjoram, nutmeg, parsley, rosemary, sage.

Corn: cumin, curry powder, onion, paprika, parsley.

Green Beans: dill, curry powder, lemon juice, marjoram, oregano, tarragon, thyme.

Peas: ginger, marjoram, mint, onion, pepper, sage.

Potatoes: dill, garlic, onion, paprika, parsley, sage.

Summer Squash: cloves, curry powder, marjoram, nutmeg, rosemary, sage.

Winter Squash: cinnamon, ginger, nutmeg, onion.

Tomatoes: basil, bay leaf, marjoram, onion, oregano, parsley, pepper.

Ingredient substitutions

If you cannot find…

Sugar Twin® Brown Sugar use Splenda® or other heat stable artificial sweetener instead.

Herbox® very low sodium broth and bouillon then choose a fat free broth with as little sodium as possible. Some very low sodium bouillons and broths contain potassium. Try to choose brands that do not have potassium as an ingredient.

Splenda® use another heat stable artificial sweetener.

- 1 Tbsp (15ml) flour can be substituted with 1 1/2 tsp (7.5ml) of arrowroot starch or 1 1/2 tsp (7.5ml) of cornstarch

- 1 clove of garlic can be substituted with 1/8 tsp (.5ml) of garlic powder

- 1 tsp lemon zest can be substituted with 1/2 tsp (2.5ml) lemon extract

- 1/4 cup (60ml) fresh chopped onion can be replaced with 1 Tbsp (15ml) of instant minced onions

- 1 tsp (5ml) of dry mustard can be replaced with 1 Tbsp (15ml) of prepared mustard

- 1 Tbsp (15ml) of finely chopped fresh herbs can be replaced with 1 tsp dried leaf herbs or 1/2 tsp (2.5ml) ground dried herbs

- Egg substitute can be replaced with egg whites. 2 egg whites will replace 1/4 cup (60ml) of egg substitute.

- Fresh vegetables can be substituted with frozen vegetables.

- Vegetarian Proteins found in any recipe, including those in the vegetarian section can be substituted with animal proteins. Poultry or beef could be used in place of Tofu in a recipe for BBQ Tofu.

- Meats can be substituted for one another.

Sugar Substitutes

Equal®	1 packet = 2 tsp (10ml) sugar
Equal Spoonful®	1 tsp (5ml) = 1 tsp (5ml) sugar
Equal Tablet®	1 tablet = 1 tsp (5ml) sugar
Splenda®*	1 tsp (5ml) granulated = 1 tsp (5ml) sugar
	1 packet = 2 tsp (10ml) sugar
Sweet 'N Low®	1 packet = 2 tsp (10ml) sugar
Sweet 'N Low® Brown	1 tsp (5ml) = 1/4 cup (60ml) brown sugar
Sugar Twin®*	1 tsp (5ml) granulated = 1 tsp (5ml) sugar
Sugar Twin Brown*	1 tsp (5ml) granulated = 1 tsp (5ml) sugar

1 packet = 2 tsp sugar
*Heat stable, can be used in baking
Artificial sweeteners are a great way to keep the sweet flavors in your favorite recipes and foods. Most of these are non-nutritive sweeteners, meaning that they have no nutritional value, so they do not contain significant calories.

Steps to reduce sugar in the diet

- Read the ingredient list on labels. If sugar is listed as one of the first five ingredients, the product contains a large amount of sugar as a sweetener.

- Use less white and brown sugar, honey, jam or jelly. Try sugar free jams and jellies.

- Purchase unsweetened cereals.

- Purchase fresh fruits, or choose canned or frozen fruits without added sugar.

- Try to avoid adding sugar to coffee, tea, cereal and fruit.

- Try reducing the amount of sugar in recipes. You can usually cut the sugar by 1/3 in most recipes without compromising flavor. Try introducing spices like cinnamon, cardamom, coriander, nutmeg, ginger and mace to enhance the sweet flavor of foods.

You'll be delighted with your L A Lite Cookbook. We have created the recipes that you want and your family will enjoy! In addition, we have included our clients favorites. This cookbook is great for clients on the program, as a gift for family or friends and can be used to prepare everyday meals or special occasion dishes for a party or get together! **Bon Appetite!**